POSTCOLONIAL VOICES
from DOWNUNDER

POSTCOLONIAL VOICES
from DOWNUNDER

Indigenous Matters, Confronting Readings

Edited by
JIONE HAVEA

PICKWICK *Publications* · Eugene, Oregon

POSTCOLONIAL VOICES FROM DOWNUNDER
Indigenous Matters, Confronting Readings

Pickwick Publications
An Imprint of Wipf and Stock Publishers
199 W. 8th Ave., Suite 3
Eugene, OR 97401

www.wipfandstock.com

PAPERBACK ISBN: 978-1-5326-0586-4
HARDCOVER ISBN: 978-1-5326-0588-8
EBOOK ISBN: 978-1-5326-0587-1

Cataloguing-in-Publication data:

Names: Havea, Jione, editor.

Title: Postcolonial voices from downunder : indigenous matters, confronting readings / edited by Jione Havea.

Description: Eugene, OR: Pickwick Publications, 2017 | Includes bibliographical references and index.

Identifiers: ISBN: 978-1-5326-0586-4 (paperback) | ISBN: 978-1-5326-0588-8 (hardcover) | ISBN: 978-1-5326-0587-1 (ebook).

Subjects: LCSH: Christianity and culture—Australia | Theology—Australia | Indigenous peoples—Australia | Indigenous peoples—New Zealand.

Classification: BR1480 P69 2017 (paperback) | BR1480 (ebook).

Manufactured in the U.S.A.   05/03/17

CONTENTS

PREFACE

SEVERAL OF THE ESSAYS in this monograph were presented at the "Postcolonial Engagement: Politics, Religions, Scriptures" conference held at United Theological College, North Parramatta (NSW, Australia on 1–2 August 2014), supported by a grant from the Public and Contextual Theology Research Centre (PaCT) of Charles Sturt University. PaCT extended its support with a Publication Grant. Not all of the presentations at that postcolonial conference are included here, and the essay by Mark G. Brett was not presented at the conference but later welcomed into the collection.

As a collection, the essays have decidedly *postcolonial voices from downunder* characteristics. Following my opening essay ("Postcolonize Now"), which offers postcolonizing ruminations around (rather than a survey *of* or recounting *about*) postcolonial biblical criticisms and postcolonial theologies, the essays are divided into two parts: (1) Indigenous matters contains four essays that present and address topics that are significant to First Peoples of, in and beyond Australia. These essays, echoing the #BlackLivesMatter movement among African-Americans in the United States of America, affirm that Indigenous black lives do matter. There are two moors of this affirmation: roots (indigeneity) and color (blackness). Both *matter* in the voices from downunder that recount and engage the different subjects addressed in this first cluster of essays. (2) Confronting readings contains eight essays that engage biblical texts, religious convictions, cultural biases, language struggles, as well as Second People's attitudes, perspectives and blind-spots. This cluster of readings meander from Zion/Jerusalem to the migrating languages of native Pasifika/Oceania, from the idealizing of Islam to the ideologies of Second Peoples, from the ideologies of settlers to the interests of migrants and refugees, from the blessings of biblical patriarchs and the hesitation of Balaam's ass to the spin doctors of Australian media, and side paths in between and around those.

In the cluster of *Indigenous matters* are four essays: **Gabrielle Russell-Mundine** and **Graeme Mundine** ("Inculturation, Assimilation, and the Catholic Church: An Indigenous Postcolonial Intervention") address the ways in which the Catholic Church in Australia, which has a relatively long and complex history of interaction with Indigenous Peoples, deal with the challenges of assimilation and inculturation. Christians came as purveyors of the Word of God, but the Word was wrapped in the culture of the countries from which they came. They brought with them a missionary fervor to evangelize, but over time they also implemented Government policies such as protectionism and assimilation. Despite this sometimes difficult relationship with the Church, for Indigenous People of faith, the melding of Christ and Culture is a comfortable progression from their own knowledge of God prior to colonization toward a more recent understanding about Jesus. However, the relationship between Indigenous culture and faith often remains contested and uncomfortable amongst the wider Church community.

The Catholic Church teaches that inculturation or the melding of culture and faith is both possible and desirable. However, for Indigenous Catholics there is still the question about whether they have been "joyfully received" by the Church, as was urged by Pope John Paul II, or to what extent the Catholic Church in Australia is a place of assimilation from an Indigenous perspective? Russell-Mundine and Mundine consider this question from the context of the history of the Catholic Church with Indigenous Peoples, drawing on their experiences to highlight aspects of Church practices and behaviors which are bound to the cultural practices of the dominant non-Indigenous cultures and which continue to impact on Aboriginal cultural expressions of faith.

Denise Champion and **Chris Budden** ("First Peoples, Ancient Spirit, and the Uniting Church Preamble: Opportunity and Challenge") offer a conversation over the 2014 Preamble to the Constitution of the Uniting Church in Australia (UCA), from the perspective of both First and Second Peoples. Their reflection juxtaposes the voices of a First Person (Champion) and a Second Person (Budden). Champion and Budden believe that the Preamble sits alongside the *Basis of Union* as one of the significant shaping documents of the UCA, and for the relationship between the Uniting Aboriginal and Islander Christian Congress (UAICC) and the rest of the Uniting Church. In their conversation, Champion and Budden show how the Preamble invites the stories and voices of Indigenous People, so that Champion could connect her stories to the gospel, but there are nonetheless colonial strands in the fabrics of the Preamble and of the Uniting Church in Australia (symptomatic of other Christian churches in the region).

Neville Naden ("Aboriginal Land and Australia's First Nations Peoples: Calling for Treaty, Recognition, and Engagement") presents a First People's assessment of the way that indigenous land has been viewed and controlled in colonial Australia. Since settlement, the First Peoples of Australia have fought for the recognition of their sovereignty and land custodianship. Federal and State Governments, as well as churches, have benefitted greatly as a result of dispossessing the First Nations Peoples of the land that God had apportioned them. In response, Naden outlines a theological framework for those who would argue that the colonization of Australia was God's will, and discusses some of the difficulties that consequently arise.

Indigenous People's experience of colonization is often grouped into a few collective descriptions, such as resistance or acquiescence. Postcolonial studies have recognized the heterogeneous nature of colonial contexts and encouraged more nuanced dialogue of various expressions within these descriptions. An increasing number and range of subaltern voices are emerging in contemporary discussions. These voices are not homogenous, and their concerns are not new. Archival sources of colonial churches, missions and government bodies indicate a variety of Indigenous responses to Christian faith throughout the colonial era. This variety of voices gives rise to multivalent perspectives and interpretations of the Bible and of Christian theology.

Grant Finlay ("Always Crackney in Heaven") examines oral and written responses by Christian Aboriginal people in *trouwunna* / Tasmania, the island south of mainland Australia, at a pivotal location during a crucial period of its colonial history, namely the Wybalenna Settlement on Flinders Island from 1832 to 1847. From largely unpublished sources Finlay discerns a variety of Aboriginal responses and interpretations of Christian faith. Finlay focuses on the topic of "heaven" in Aboriginal addresses at Wybalenna to highlight the variety of relationships and multiple layers of meaning that were occurring, and links that past experience with contemporary discussion of contexts for Indigenous theology.

In a context of enforced English-only Christian faith, Aboriginal people were not limited to this colonial language. They conversed primarily in first language, *creole* and, less often, in English. Their expressions of Christian faith were part of engaging in multiple contexts simultaneously as they negotiated relationships not only with colonial authorities, but also with each other. Their intra- and inter-clan relationships were more influential than Aboriginal-colonial relationships in the emergence of these initial expressions of Indigenous theology.

In the cluster of *Confronting readings* are eight essays: **Gregory C. Jenks** ("Pilgrims and Powerbrokers: The Russian Fascination with Jerusalem") examines the Russian "lust for Zion/Jerusalem." Palestine has experienced wave after wave of conquest and colonization, with the current occupation by Israel being both the latest and the most systematic. In the land where the Bible was formed we find a complex interaction of politics, scriptures and religions. Jenks focuses on Russian interests in Palestine as one significant historical expression of the desire to possess Jerusalem that has shaped Jewish identities, motivated the Crusaders, and remains at the heart of the conflict between Israel and Palestine. This "lust for Zion" has a complex relationship with the Bible, which has itself been repeatedly occupied by those seeking to colonize the land and drive out the Indigenous Peoples.

Garry W. Trompf ("Of Postcolonial Islam") highlights an internal Islamic tension between those who are generally more accepting of what has been left over from the colonial period, with a preparedness to work out future socio-political problems in terms of what has been immediately inherited from "modernizing processes," and those who want a fresh start with a revived Islamic basis, including those who prefer that the pristine Muslim arrangements should be restored. The postcolonial Islam addressed in this chapter, expectedly, is one that idealizes a recovery of Islam as a total way of life and thus allows back its full capacity as a traditional political and juridical force as much as a "separately religious" one, with a complete charge over human lives for their conforming to divine commands and *sharia* rulings.

Mark G. Brett ("A Suitably English Abraham: Emigration to Australia in the Nineteenth Century") discusses the use of the story of Abraham to justify the settlement of Australia. Following the legal abolition of slavery in the British Empire in 1833, the morality of colonization became a focus of attention in humanitarian circles. William Penn's peaceful example was celebrated in Quaker advocacy, and Abraham's journey to the Promised Land was promoted as an ideal in literature supporting the cause of emigration. The Colonial Office in London took a number of humanitarian initiatives, supporting the Treaty of Waitangi (1840), and in the Letters Patent of 1836 that established the new colony of South Australia, requiring evidence of treaties with "Aboriginal Natives." Initially heralded in the local press as the "New Penn," John Batman's attempt at a treaty in Port Phillip, on the other hand, was deemed unsuitable. In this essay Brett examines the complexities of biblical hermeneutics in the emigration literature of the time.

Grahame Rosolen ("Blessings and Curses in the Pentateuch and in the Contemporary Context") discusses the prevalence of the themes of blessings and curses in the Pentateuch. The Hebrew word *barak* (which appears 166 times in the Pentateuch) may be translated to mean "bless" and also to mean "curse." There is a reciprocal symmetry with the use of blessings and curses as they appear together in several key narratives within the Pentateuch. The ambiguity inherent in *barak* creates difficulties for translators but elegantly caters for those situations when what appears to be a blessing transforms into a curse and vice versa. Rosolen examines key narratives in the Pentateuch that illuminate aspects of the nature of blessings and curses—the blessing of Abraham, the blessing in the lives of Jacob and Joseph, the interplay between Balak and Balaam, and the speeches of Moses to Israel. The categorization of situations as blessings or curses may differ depending on the perspective adopted. Those who focus on the blessing rather than the giver of the blessing and who seek to manipulate the flow of the blessing should consider the algorithmic choices articulated by Moses, and to ponder the rhetorical question Joseph posed to his brothers, "Am I God?"

Anthony Rees ("[S]Pinning Balaam against the Wall") revisits the story in Numbers 22–24. Using the "spin doctor" feature of the practice of politics in Australia as a way of looking at a particular piece of scripture, Rees turns to the prophetic oracles of Balaam in Numbers 23–24 in which Balaam is an expendable but at the same time re-usable spin-doctor.

Karl Hand ("Serving Mammon on Stolen Land: Reading Luke 16 towards a Second Peoples' Hermeneutic") proposes a Second People's hermeneutic. If the Australian church has "internalized the values of an invading society and its racist and class-based explanations and justifications of invasion" (Budden 2009, 7), then these internalized values must also inform our reading and preaching of scripture. Hand sketches a Second Peoples' hermeneutic of scripture on the basis of his reading of the parables of Luke, which are texts thickly interwoven with both imperial/colonial power relations and missionary zeal. As tales of moral uplift, Lukan parables could be used as inspiring and useful theme-texts for the practice of invasion.

The life of the lost Son (Luke 15:11–32) who scattered his resources on profligate living resonates with the picturing of Aboriginal culture that justifies the bans on grog and porn in the Northern Territory, and the relentless police attacks on the aboriginal community in the streets of Redfern and Waterloo, which tend to cite drug use and child welfare as justification. With an awareness of such racist and classist presuppositions, the parables of Luke can be interpreted suspiciously of such ends. The discursive and narrative logic of Luke 16, for instance, reveals and denounces the hoarding of resources through bureaucratic means in a way that, far from upholding such practices as the Northern Territory Intervention and the over-policing of Indigenous People in urban suburbs, exposes them as unjust. This rich man's single life-time of hoarding pales in comparison to the hoarding of Australian national resources by Second Peoples privileged under British and then Federal Australian colonial rule. Hand questions whether the vital structural and formal equality Budden outlines will be enough if unaccompanied by a Lukan program of radical redistribution of material wealth.

Matt Wilson ("Immigrant and refugee: *paroikous, parepidēmous* and politics in 1 Peter") proposes that *Paroikous kai parepidēmous* (1 Peter 2:11) imply an aspect of socio-political status in the mind of the author to the community addressed in 1 Peter. The phrase is most commonly translated "alien and stranger" but Wilson adopts Jennifer Bird's proposed alternative of "immigrants and refugees" and explores what this may mean for an Australian audience.

Terry Pouono ("Indigenous Language Loss: The future of *gagana Sāmoa* [Samoan language] in diaspora") looks at the future of the Samoan language in the migrant communities in Aotearoa / New Zealand. Many Samoans and Pasifika Islanders, as well as those outside the Pacific who are concerned with indigenous language sovereignty, have become concerned with the threat of local languages being lost to global English. This problem is particularly acute for Samoans in New Zealand.

Pouono's contention is that the penetrating domination of the English language via western education, as well as global networks, symbols and patterns circulated through mass media and media culture, contributes to the language problem by infusing values and ideas into the already ingrained ethnic subaltern personality. Pouono consequently asserts that the Congregational Christian Church Samoa (CCCS), regarded as a core language nest, out of negligence and partly because of a conservative myopic position, fails to provide an effective and relevant ministry for New Zealand-born Samoans by avoiding bilingualism in worship and its Sunday School program. The church fails to acknowledge that many New Zealand-born Samoans have a limited command of the Samoan language and consequently, the gospel message is not received in its fullness by the younger, New Zealand-born recipients.

Pouono brings back the attention of this collection of essays to the church. The colonial church, which now comes in native bodies and speaks native tongues, fails the native and Indigenous Peoples (especially in diaspora, but also at home) who are more and more postcolonial (in both orientation and preference). In this regard, the *voices from downunder* contained in this monograph, as a collection, invites further engagement with *indigenous matters* and practices of *confronting readings*.

The two parts of this book move from the struggles of Indigenous/ First Peoples in and because of church and social policies and practices, toward rereading religious and scriptural positions in the interests of both First and Second Peoples. The book in the end problematizes what it means to be Second People, given for example that Samoans in New Zealand are themselves First Peoples, and the need to attend to *indigenous matters*.

On the front cover is a painting by **Graeme Mundine** titled "Jubal Cross." Mundine explained (in an email) that "The center spiral is where we are all drawn to the mystery of Christ. The white dots are those first believers. We (Aboriginal Peoples) are symbolized by the Jubal (witchetty grubs) and are also drawn into this mystery." Another reading of this Indigenous artwork would notice that the cross (symbolizing the gospel) is slanted and fragmented, with the grubs looking like caterpillars crawling toward a ceremonial site (at the spiral) where they break out of their cocoons and fly, fly, fly. In this alternative reading, "Jubal Cross" embodies something similar to when *confronting readings* give wings to *indigenous matters*.

CONTRIBUTORS

Mark G. Brett teaches Hebrew Bible and ethics at Whitley College, University of Divinity. His research has focused on the book of Genesis, ethnicity, and postcolonial studies in the Australian context. He is the author of *Decolonizing God: The Bible in the Tides of Empire* (2008), *Political Trauma and Healing: Biblical Ethics for a Postcolonial World* (2016), and co-editor with Jione Havea of *Colonial Contexts and Postcolonial Theologies: Storyweaving in the Asia-Pacific* (2014).

Chris Budden has a long history of building relationships with First Peoples, and supporting their struggles for justice. At present he is the Interim National Coordinator of the Uniting Aboriginal and Islander Christian Congress (UAICC). His academic interests are contextual theology, particularly the development of a Second People's theology, theological ethics, and how Jesus is good news in a post-colonial, multi-faith context. He is an Associate Researcher with the Public and Contextual Theology Research Centre at Charles Sturt University, and author of *Following Jesus in Invaded Space: Doing Theology on Aboriginal Land* (Pickwick, 2009).

Denise Champion is an Adnyamathanha woman from the Flinders Ranges in South Australia. She has a special gift to be able to tell the stories of her people, and to relate them to the Gospel story. An ordained minister of the Uniting Church in Australia (UCA), Denise is currently the Minister at Port Augusta Congress Congregation, and regional (South Australia) Chairperson of the UAICC. Denise initiated a crosscultural program called *About Time* when working for the UCA in Port Augusta in the 1990's. More recently she has been involved with programs such as About Face, A Destiny Together, the Journey to Recognition, and Adnyamathana Pilgrimages, working with ministry candidates on a program called "Walking on Country." Denise is the mother of three young adults—Joel, Candace and Shellander—and a proud grandmother of five—Jakeevia, Jaeanne, Seth, Samson and Michael Jnr. Denise is passionate about her family, her people (including her language and culture), reconciliation and recognition of Aboriginal people as the first peoples of Australia. She is author of *Yarta Wandatha: The Land is Speaking. The People are Speaking.*

Grant Finlay worked as UAICC Tasmania Minister from 1995 to 2015. He holds a PhD from the University of Tasmania awarded in 2015, with a dissertation titled "Always Crackne in Heaven."

Karl Hand is the pastor of Crave Metropolitan Community Church which meets in Paddington, Sydney. He is from a Pentecostal background, and has an interest in Evangelical and Liberationist theologies and hermeneutics. His main scholarly interest is in the history of the synoptic tradition, particularly with reference to the Gospel of Luke.

Jione Havea is a native Methodist minister from Tonga who thinks postcolonially in his islandic and liberation readings. Jione is a researcher with the Public and Contextual Theology Research Center of Charles Sturt University (Australia) and Visiting Scholar at Trinity Methodist Theological College in Auckland (Aotearoa / New Zealand). Jione recently edited *Indigenous Australia and the Unfinished Business of Theology: Crosscultural engagements* (Palgrave, 2014) and co-edited *Bible, Borders, Belonging(s): Engaging Readings from Oceania* (SBL, 2015) and *Reading Ruth in Asia* (SBL, 2015).

Gregory C. Jenks is Australian religion scholar and Anglican priest. He is Dean of St George's College in Jerusalem, an Adjunct Senior Lecturer in the School of Theology at Charles Sturt University, and co-director of the Bethsaida Archaeology Project in Israel. His recent books include *The Once and Future Bible* (Wipf & Stock, 2011), *The Once and Future Scriptures* (Polebridge, 2013), *Jesus Then and Jesus Now* (Morning Star, 2015), and *Wisdom and Imagination* (Morning Star, 2015).

Graeme Mundine is a Bunjalung man with over thirty-five years' experience of working with Churches. He was the Executive Officer of the Aboriginal Catholic Ministry (ACM) in Sydney. Prior to that, Graeme was Executive Secretary of the National Aboriginal and Torres Strait Islander Ecumenical Commission (NATSIEC) which is the Indigenous commission of the National Council of Churches. He was also the inaugural Chair and Executive Officer of the National Aboriginal and Torres Strait Islander Catholic Council (NATSICC). Graeme has also been a Marist Brother and worked in schools and youth ministry, and he is currently teaching and undertaking postgraduate studies. In all these roles Graeme strives to bring a greater understanding to the non-Indigenous community of the issues concerning Aboriginal and Torres Strait Islander People. Graeme is committed to advocating for the needs of Aboriginal People within Churches, with Government and with the wider community.

Neville Naden ministers in Broken Hill amongst Barkinji people. He is passionate about understanding the issues of land that was taken from Indigenous People, in light of the Old Testament.

Terry Pouono is a PhD student at the University of Auckland and his research looks at various influences of the multi-faceted world on the Samoan Christian identity. The context of his research is the Samoan church in New Zealand. Terry completed his Bachelor of Divinity at Malua Theological College (Samoa) and his Masters at Bossey Ecumenical Institute in affiliation with the University of Geneva. From there, he taught Practical Theology at Malua Theological College for six years. While studying, he also works as a Lecturer at Laidlaw College in Manukau, South Auckland. An important aspect of his life is family—his wife and his four young children.

Anthony Rees is a Lecturer in Hebrew Bible/Old Testament at United Theological College, within the School of Theology of Charles Sturt University. His first book, a revision of his CSU PhD thesis, was published with Bloomsbury in 2015. He also authored the Numbers volume of the Earth Bible Commentary (Phoenix, 2015), and he continues to retain interest in postcolonial criticism and the reception of biblical texts.

Grahame Rosolen is a graduate of Sydney University with degrees in Physics and Electrical Engineering. He completed his PhD at Cambridge University where he developed a microscope for nanotechnology applications. Grahame has worked in many areas of science and engineering including microelectronics, nanotechnology and electron microscopy and he is currently working in robotics. He is studying theology at Charles Sturt University and some of his other interests include astronomy, Renaissance art and restoring old Volkswagen Beetles.

Gabrielle Russell-Mundine is a Senior Lecturer at the National Centre for Culture Competence, within the University of Sydney. Her diverse experience has been gained working in non-government organizations, politics, business, church and higher education. She has extensive experience in social justice education and advocacy, with a particular focus on Indigenous social justice issues. Gabrielle is interested in how to develop cultural competence from a non-Indigenous perspective and in particular how to facilitate a deeper understanding of transformative ways to learn and work together.

Garry W. Trompf is Emeritus Professor in the History of Ideas in the School of Letters, Art and Media, and Adjunct Professor in Peace and Conflict Studies, School of Social and Political Sciences, University of Sydney. He is also currently lecturing as visiting Professor of Church History at St Andrew's Greek Orthodox Theological College, within the Sydney College of Divinity, and, because he has been appointed to the Charles Sturt University teaching programme at United Theological College (North Parramatta) without teaching role, he hopes to be engaged there in other ways.

Among Trompf's books are *The Idea of Historical Recurrence in Western Thought* (vol. 2 almost completed); *In Search of Origins; Payback: The Logic of Retribution in Melanesian Religions;* and *Early Christian Historiography.* Among monograph series he edits are Gnostica (Routledge) and Studies in Religion, Politics and Society (ISPCK). He is currently writing a textbook on Religion and Politics.

Matt Wilson holds a PhD from Charles Sturt University (Australia). His main interests are in New Testament—particularly the Synoptic Gospels and the Catholic Epistles—and inter-faith relations. He currently serves as a minister of the UCA at Nowra NSW.

1

POSTCOLONIZE NOW

Jione Havea

Now IS THE TIME to postcolonize.[1] The invitation is serious. Lands, lives, liabilities, limits, longings, lore, and a whole lot more, *remain* unaccounted, unrecognized, uncompensated, unremitted. The invitation is also urgent— Postcolonize now. The invitation requires revisiting and rethinking the dreams and practices in and of Postcolonial Criticisms and Postcolonial Theologies. Accordingly, i[2] set in this opening chapter a place at which the invitation to postcolonize could be embraced. Moreover, i will situate

1. This essay is not *about* postcolonial criticism but an exercise in *doing* postcolonial criticism, in postcolonizing. This does not necessarily make me a postcolonial critic. I do not see myself, a native born and raised in the only surviving Polynesian monarchy (Tonga) who continues to work for the church, which arrived in to our region on vessels that brought explorers and colonialists, as a postcolonial subject. I therefore draw a distinction between "being postcolonial" and "doing postcolonial" thinking/reading. I fall nicely into the latter, evident in my playing with the colonial English language and mainline traditions.

2. I use the lowercase because i use the lowercase with "you," "she," "they," "it," and "others." I do not see the point in capitalizing the first person when s/he *is* in relation to, and because of, everyone/everything else. My i is in a similar resistance with the Samoan character Alofa when her European teacher required students to write about individual experiences: "You were always with someone . . . Nothing was witnessed alone. Nothing was witnessed in the 'I' form—nothing but penises and ghosts. 'I' does not exist, Miss Cunningham. 'I' is 'we' . . . *always*" (Figiel, *Where We Once Belonged*, 136, 137).

around that place the *voices from downunder* that speak within and through the covers of this book.

I will highlight and reflect on relevant issues in the rise of postcolonial criticism within Commonwealth and Third World Literature Studies, and its entry into biblical and theological studies where it cross-fertilizes with modes of contextual and liberation engagements.[3] In the process i will address matters that, in my humble opinion, require the attention and involvement of biblical critics and theologians in the Asia-Pasifika (and beyond) who decide to wade into the currents of postcolonial criticism. These matters, spread out like reefs in the sea, include native color and agency (identity); foreign and local empires (power); oral and visual native texts (scriptures); and the overlaying nodes of the secular and the sacred (space).[4] I will also situate the contributing voices to this collection of essays upon those proverbial reefs. The upshot of this multi-plying process is that the *postcolonial voices from downunder* presented in this monograph will at once be harboured as well as exposed.

POSTCOLONIZE THIS/THUS

The stories of postcolonial biblical criticism have been told many times,[5] and i will not repeat or interweave those here. I wish instead to highlight some of the elements that are pertinent for, and welcoming toward, the *postcolonial voices from downunder* that this monograph contains (ambiguity is intentional).

First, i draw attention to the rise of postcolonial criticism in the first world, within the halls of Commonwealth and Third World Literature Studies. From under the shadows of the British Empire and its former colony the United States of America, postcolonial criticism reaches out toward the so-called third world. Similar to the missionary and colonial projects that spread throughout the Asia-Pasifika (see the discussion of Emmanuel Garibay's "The Arrival" below), postcolonial criticism is a Commonwealth project aimed to aid (save?) the third world. Or is this another exercise in colonial control?

---

3. Cross-fertilization is a procedure that tends to scatter and spill, and consequently messes things up. So will be my selective recount and reflection herein.

4. The tentacles of colonialism extend widely in the Asia-Pasifika (with the arrival of White Europeans, and the navigating Polynesians and occupying Indonesians), hence the gravity of the invitation to postcolonize.

5. See, e.g., Sugirtharajah, ed., *Postcolonial Bible*; Dube, *Postcolonial Feminist Interpretation*; Sugirtharajah, ed., *Postcolonial Criticism and Biblical Interpretation*; Segovia and Moore, ed., *Postcolonial Biblical Criticism*; Liew, ed., *Postcolonial Interventions*.

The major theorists behind postcolonial criticism, at least the ones whose views have been privileged by the opportunities of publication and citation (e.g., Edward W. Said, Gayatri C. Spivak, Homi K. Bhabha), trace their roots back to the former British colonies of India and Palestine (in the regions of Asia and the Middle East, part of the so-called, and problematized, Orient) and they have admirers, followers and disciples in other regions, from Africa to Europe, to America and the Caribbean, to Pasifika and in between. They have critics as well in those same locations[6] who ask: For which and whose third world do postcolonial theorists speak and advocate? From under the protection and comforts of British and American empires, do postcolonial theorists see the real struggles of the everyday third world(ed)? These questions would have been severe if postcolonial criticism was uni-form, rigid and static. This is not to push the questions under the mat, so to speak, but to register, engage and postcolonize them—the questions and the questioners deserve the attention of postcolonial critics who operate from colonial contexts.

Second, i note the entry of postcolonial criticism into the halls of biblical and theological studies. The aggravation of postcolonial biblical criticism and of postcolonial theologies is also in response to what happened, and continues to happen, in the third world, and this is clearly conveyed in the subtitle of the *Voices from the Margin* collection of essays: *Interpreting the Bible in the Third World.*[7] One of the feats of this collection is its ability to fuse the horizons of biblical criticism with those of theological reflection,[8] a move that purists on both sides—mainline biblical scholars and traditional systematic theologians—find problematic. The fact that Orbis is releasing a fourth edition of *Voices from the Margin* in 2016, twenty-five years later, is evidence of both the relevance of the postcolonial attention to the third world as well as the unfinished business of postcolonial criticism. There are lots and lots more to be done, postcolonially. *Postcolonial Voices from Downunder* echoes the *Voices from the Margin,* and this collection of voices from downunder also comes from a former colony of the British Empire—Australia, and some of its neighbors.

The endurance and transformation (conversion?) of *Voices from the Margin* over its first three editions locate postcolonial criticism in the company of two modes of cultural criticism: contextual and liberation criticisms. There are other companions, aggravated by other struggles, such as

6. See West, "What Difference Does Postcolonial Biblical Criticism Make?"

7. Sugirtharajah, ed., *Voices from the Margin.*

8. From here onward in this essay, in order to reduce the messiness of my selective recounting, i use "postcolonial criticism" as reference to both "postcolonial biblical criticism" and "postcolonial theologies."

the burdens of discrimination and minoritization because of gender, colour, class, caste, faith, sexual orientation and lots more. What's important with these various modes of criticism is the shared conviction that postcolonial criticism is not some airy fairy cerebral exercise in textual analysis but interventions (with scriptural texts) from rooted (in context) positions in the process of which interpreters seek some kind of relief (for subalterns). In this regard, postcolonial criticism is an undertaking that is intentional about *confronting*, hence the second attribute in the subtitle to this collection—*Confronting readings.*[9]

There are several ways in which postcolonial criticism is *con-fronting*. First, postcolonial criticism exhibits double conning moves: to contest and challenge (the powers that be), as well as to trick and deceive (in the interests of the minoritized).[10] The postcolonial critic is therefore, so to speak, a con-reader.[11] Second, following upon its conning (doublecrossing) efforts, postcolonial criticism is also a labour in "fronting" in the sense that it seeks to put forward, to make present, and to advocate (for and with the minoritized). The con-fronting components, together, show that postcolonial criticism is not replacement for contextual and liberation criticisms but rather, the crossing of the two. In deed, postcolonial criticism requires dynamic embroiling in contextual and liberating events. And third, postcolonial criticism will be confronting to the gatekeepers of oppressing traditions, cultures, scriptures and theologies. This much is expected. What frustrates me herewith is when some of the minoritized communities [are said to] justify and defend what Audre Lorde called "the master's tools."[12] How often do academic, public and church leaders explain that they can't introduce or support changes and alternative positions because ordinary people prefer the master's tools? The problem with this is clear, as Lorde puts it: "For the master's tools will never dismantle the master's house. They may allow us to temporarily beat him at his own game, but they will never enable us to bring about genuine change." Hence the need for postcolonial critics to be all the more confronting.

Third, drawing from the energies of the #BlackLivesMatter (BLM) campaign among African-Americans—BLM motivates communal and international solidarity and action in the exposure of, and in demanding justice for, brutal acts (especially by public officials, including police shooting

9. The essays are divided into two clusters—*Indigenous matters* and *Postcolonial readings*—hence the two parts of the book (which are related because there are postcolonial flavours in the first part and attention to indigenous interests in the second part).

10. See Havea and Melanchthon, "Culture Tricks in Biblical Narrative."

11. See Havea, "Cons of Contextuality."

12. Lorde, *Sister Outsider*, 110–14.

of innocent people) that disadvantage, assault the dignity of, and murder black people—the *confronting* components of postcolonial criticism affirms that the lives and dreams of minoritized black peoples and communities *matter.* Hence the first attribute in the subtitle to this collection—*Indigenous matters.* The starting point for this collection of *postcolonial voices from downunder* is the affirmation of the sovereignty, spirit, stories, land, lives, hopes and future of indigenous Australians (see the chapters by Gabrielle Russel-Mundine and Graeme Mundine, Denise Champion and Chris Budden, Neville Naden, Grant Finlay). While Australia is more than its indigenous land, people and heritage, Australia is *unfair* (thus contradicting the commitment of its national anthem, *Advance Australia Fair*) without accounting for Indigenous Australia.[13]

What *matter* in this monograph, are more than Indigenous Australia. The voices ripple toward, and spill over, the borders and politics of Australia (see chapters by Mark G. Brett, Grahame Rosolen, Anthony Rees) toward Jerusalem, Palestine, and the fascination of the Russians (see chapter by Gregory C. Jenks), to the worlds of Islam (see chapter by Garry W. Tromf), to second peoples' modes of interpretation (see chapter by Karl Hand), to strangers and refugees in biblical texts and in today's society (see chapter by Matthew Wilson), and to the future of the native language of [Samoan] immigrants in diaspora (see chapter by Terry Pouono).

Fourth, i return to the native and local critics of postcolonial criticism who are, correctly, suspicious because of the "English" outlook and tonality of postcolonial criticism. Doesn't postcolonial criticism look very much like another Western project seeking colonial expansion? and native endorsement? Doesn't postcolonial criticism look like, so to speak, another wolf in a grandmotherly sheepskin? another settler in a saviour's white garb? another emancipator coming to capture and prolong the missionary era? These questions are confronting, but they demand engagement. And to these questions i add the two most interesting charges that i have heard concerning postcolonial criticism: it is the "scholarly compensation for colonial exploitation" in the past and "flattery to conceal ongoing colonization" of minds, manners, customs, and hearts. These also demand engagement, and my contribution to this engagement is to return to the native and local matters of colour, agency, empire, scripture and space, which i will address not in turn but in fusion. My return, and therefore orientation, is to Pasifika (Oceania, Pacific islands, or Southern Sea islands).

13. See also Havea, ed., *Indigenous Australia and the Unfinished Business of Theology.*

WHERE TOO?

Colonizers take over more than lands and resources. Colonizers steal peoples and generations also, together with the minds, stories and souls of generations to come. And colonizers often arrive in the arms of missionaries, as portrayed in the Filipino artist Emmanuel Garibay's work titled "The Arrival" (2004).[14]

At the foreground of "The Arrival" are three characters: at the center is the colonizer, who wears a crown and who arrives holding an image of himself, in which he wears a crown of thorn and a stigmata on the back of his right hand; behind and to the left of the colonizer is the Pinocchio-like missionary, holding a cross with his left hand while his right hand comes around the shoulders (as if for support, and in approval) of the colonizer; and to the right of the colonizer is a half-naked, exposed and faceless, native woman who approaches with humility and bearing a gift of fruits. The message is clear and offensive: the colonizer arrives as resurrected Christ, in the arms of (authorized and empowered by) the Christian mission, and the native is expected to receive them with the fruits of the land (a figure for the land of the natives). The feet of all three characters are under water, inviting the viewer to feel the rise of sea-level, and the vessel that brought the crowned colonizer and the red-hooded missionary is at the background, as if to remind viewers of Noah's Ark, which floated away to leave many innocent creatures, including many faultless children, youth and adults, to drown in God's wrath (flood). Garibay *confronts* the colonial legacy of the theologies and readings that postcolonial critics in the Asia-Pasifika have inherited.

Yet, there are Pasifika islands and peoples whose colonization remain unaccounted, and undressed (for covering, for healing), hence my grammatically problematic question, "Where too?"[15] My question is not only about direction, but also about inclusion. In other words, "where too" in Pasifika could postcolonial critics con-front? The agitations for this question are two: the colonial legacy of some of the islands in the region, especially my home island of Tonga, and the ongoing colonization of Pasifika islands by foreign powers. In Pasifika, colonization is not a black versus white struggle. We have native Pasifika empires as well.

14. This artwork is on the cover of Jagessar and Burns, *Christian Worship*, where it is discussed in pp. xii–xvi.

15. The grammatically problematic questions that i use as heading for the sections of this essay break through the barriers of the written from the fluid and playful world of orality / talanoa (see explanations below).

First, i address the Pasifika native empires. Prior to "discovery" by western explorers and geographers, Polynesians were skilled navigators who visited, flirted, fooled, married and occupied the islands of their neighbors. The Samoans and Tongans for instance have a long tradition of cultural exchange, of intermarriage and land grabs, between themselves and with the neighbouring islands of Tokelau, Rotuma and Tuvalu. The lineages and ancestries (what the Maoris call *whakapapa*) in these three island groups show evidence of invasion by Samoans and Tongans. In Pasifika, the invasion of languages and of wombs was as, if not more, injurious as the invasion of (is)lands.

After "contact" with Europeans, and with the "confirmation" of the Christian mission years later, converted Tongan chiefs under the leadership of Maʻafu ventured into the waters of Fiji and grabbed some of the islands in the Lau group. At the ideological and linguistic levels, the Tongan campaign in Fiji was so successful that "Viti" (name of the group in the indigenous language) became "Fiji" (the Tongan name for the group). Illusion of superiority was the wind in the sails of the Tongan invaders: the fair skin Christianized Tongans thought that they were better than the darker skin Fijians. And the accusation that the blacker Fijian natives were savages and cannibals, most likely inspired (and this is not an excuse) by the European missionaries for whom being "white as snow" was metaphor for absolution and holiness, was on the tongues and hearts of the colonialist Tongans (who were my blood and relative uncles). Color was as much a factor in the maneuverings of native empires as it was in the European colonial endeavor.

To embroil in postcolonial criticism in Pasifika requires *confronting* native empires, with their Christian garbs. This is one way of accounting for the questions raised by native and local critics of postcolonial criticism.

Second, i turn to the continuing colonization of Pasifika island nations by foreign powers. Pasifika continues to be the playing ground for major world powers. The United States of America, France, Chile and Indonesia are the big players (occupiers) in Pasifika. The colonies of the USA include Hawaiʻi (but USA does not see this as colonial occupation), Guam, Northern Mariana Islands and Tutuila (which they call American Samoa), with the independent states of Marshall Islands, Micronesia and Palau held under the Compact of Free Association (meaning that the USA has authority over the aid and defense of those small nation states). France occupies Kanak (New Caledonia) and Maohi Nui (French Polynesia), Chile occupies Rapa Nui, and Indonesia occupies West Papua.

Our waters also suffer from other forms of foreign occupation, for example, the lingering toxic impact of nuclear testing, the floating islands of plastic rubbish dumped into the sea, the human induced climate change, the sea-bed mining projects, and the gobbling fishing (especially for tuna) vessels. In our largely oceanic region, the occupation of the waters is equally devastating as the occupation of the (is)lands. It is thus wearisome to consider postcolonial criticism, or to speak postcolonially about anything, in Pasifika, because of the continuing foreign occupation of a region that has more water than land space.

On the other hand, Pasifika's occupied islands are among the "where too" that await postcolonial biblical and theological *con-fronting*. Some occupied islands have received more attention than others, and the occupation of some have for years been considered unproblematic and necessary, if not normal also. This is the case especially when the occupying nation is one of the champions of peace, justice and democracy.

WHOM FORE?

In a crowd, it is easy to be lost and unaccounted. And for the lost and unaccounted ones, it is empowering when someone seeks and advocates for them. Hence my second grammatically problematic question, "Whom fore?" This is my way of asking, whom from the crowd to seek, recognize and advocate, in order to bring them to the fore? For whom to con-front? And in whose interests? To engage these questions, i turn back to one of the occupied (is)lands in Pasifika: West Papua.

West Papua and Hawai'i share the blind spot in the attention of postcolonial critics, but for different reasons—Hawai'i primarily out of respect (and fear) toward the USA, and West Papua because of distance. West Papua is so far out of the way of Euro-American postcolonial theorists. West Papua falls within the part of the Asia-Pasifika that scholars prefer to fly over.[16] It is in fact at the meeting point of Asia and Pasifika, in other words, West Papua is at the hyphen of the Asia-Pasifika. For this reason, i opt to (is)land on West Papua in this reflection.

Pasifika's largest island (in terms of its land space, its population, and its 700+ living languages) is divided between two nations—Papua New Guinea (PNG) to the east, and Indonesia occupies the western part (making it Indonesia's largest province). This Indonesian part is West Papua, a sovereign nation established and recognized in 1961 (see below). The indigenous population of West Papua share the same customs, heritages and colorfulness as the indigenous people of PNG and the Torres Strait Islands (north of Australia). West Papua and PNG are located on the same island, and they deserve to be recognized as one. But West Papua is bordered off

---

16. Cf. Spivak, *Other Asias*, 9–10, 248.

from PNG, and the land and native people are excluded from relatives east of the Indonesian border, and from the rest of native Pasifika.

West Papua has a long history of colonization. The Dutch claimed West Papua in 1898, and it remained a Dutch colony when Indonesia received its independence from the Netherlands in 1949. The Dutch gave independence to West Papua only in 1961. And instead of returning and therefore re-joining West Papua with PNG, as one, the expected rituals of independence and of nation building were performed—the morning star (announcing a new dawn) flag was raised, a national hymn was sung, and the natives celebrated in their indigenous ways. Indonesia shortly afterwards invaded West Papua, called it Irian Jaya (in honor of the Dutch occupation), and unrest grew. This accelerated into a war, in which an established nation attacked a newly formed one. Indonesia was the bully in this war. In 1962 the USA stepped in to bring West Papua under the protection of the United Nations. And in 1963, without consulting the native people of West Papua or their *wantoks* ("one talks," speakers of the same language, who share the same values and traditions) in PNG, the UN gave control over West Papua to Indonesia. Since 1963, Indonesia has occupied West Papua with the blessings of the USA and the UN, and Indonesia refuses to give independence because the black natives were seen to be "too primitive" to lead and decide national affairs. In the case of West Papua, Indonesia has been singing the same lyrics as the earlier teams of European colonizers and missionaries.

Since Indonesia's invasion and occupation of West Papua, members of the Indonesian forces, carrying out the wishes of the Indonesian government, have slaughtered over 500,000 natives. This number is staggering. The slaughter of the West Papua natives is clearly a genocide. In 2014, West Papua was Indonesia's largest province in terms of land size and mineral resources but the second least populous province (the least being the province of North Kalimantan which was formed in 2012).

Moreover, Indonesian forces have tortured, raped and imprisoned thousands more (see freewestpapua.org). It is easy to conclude, noting that West Papuans have a different ethnic heritage from Indonesia's indigenous and ethnic majority population, that Indonesia's agenda is the ethnic cleansing of West Papua. This is a crime against humanity. The critical *matter* here therefore is whether "we" count West Papuans among humanity.

West Papua is situated in Pasifika but it is politically, economically and ideologically controlled from Asia. West Papua is therefore a thorn on the side of the designation of our region as the Asia-Pasifika. Some of the islanders in Pasifika are dispossessed and oppressed by some of the islanders from Asia. The dignity and sovereignty of West Papuan natives are violated by their Indonesian neighbors, with the full recognition of the USA and the

UN. *Who will be neighbor* to the natives of West Papua? PNG and Australia, who are not far away in distance from West Papua but their indigenous populations are *wantoks* with the West Papuans, are not very neighborly. The question about neighbor brings to the *front* the struggles of Palestinians also, "a people not fighting to destroy its neighbor, but a people fighting for the right to be a neighbor."[17]

West Papua is a thorn also on the side of postcolonial critics in the Asia-Pasifika and beyond. Why is it easy to ignore the black skin and fuzzy hair natives of West Papua? Why is it convenient for scholars to fly over West Papua, but for mining companies from those scholars' homelands to extract the rich natural resources of West Papua? When might the natives of West Papua count among the numbers of humanity? When might West Papua be among the "whom fore" of postcolonial criticism?

WHAT L'S?

"Looser" is a pejorative pronouncement delivered silently with the thumb and forefinger forming the letter "L" on the accuser's forehead. The L-condemnation is directed towards someone who is perceived to be incompetent and ineffective, hopeless and useless, and fruitless—a slacker, a loafer, a waste of time. I dip this L-condemnation in the fluidity of orality, or what we in Pasifika call *talanoa* (story, telling, conversation),[18] in order to ask "What else?" are there in Pasifika for postcolonial consideration. I propose three "L's/something else" for consideration:

First, the opportunities in orality. Natives from oral preferring cultures appreciate some respect toward, and the scripturalizing[19] of, native and indigenous oral and visual *texts of belonging.*[20] The "Christ against Culture" crusade of the early missionaries privileged the Judeo-Christian scriptures over against the local wisdom (preserved in the talanoa forms of myths and legends, dances and songs, weavings and paintings, and so forth) of our ancestors. The ancestral wisdom and teachings were not written with Roman

---

17. Ateek, *Justice, and Only Justice,* 47.

18. Talanoa is a native Pasifika word that connotes three events—story, telling, conversation—at once (see Havea, "Diaspora contexted"). There is no *story* (talanoa) if there is no accompanying *telling* (talanoa) and *conversation* (talanoa); *telling* (talanoa) is empty without *story* (talanoa) and *conversation* (talanoa); and *conversation* is dry without *story* and *telling* (talanoa). In oral preferring cultures, talanoa (story, telling, conversation) has the capacity to make hopes and desires come alive. In other words, talanoa (three-in-one) makes hopes and desires, and more, "real," in oralizing ways.

19. See Wimbush, "Scripturalizing."

20. See also Havea, "Engaging Scriptures from Oceania."

scripts or according to proper English grammar, but with indigenous patterns, crafts and scripts. They are therefore scriptures in their own rights, but they have not received the privileges of canonization nor the affirmation of publication and citation.

The early Pasifika contextual thinkers appealed to the wisdom of our ancestors to adorn foreign scriptures and teachings with native garbs. Native and indigenous scriptures were cut and pasted, trimmed and edged, in order to cushion the Judeo-Christian scriptures and doctrines into *place*, the upshot of which was the secularizing of native and indigenous values and wisdom. But if the urgent call to postcolonize is heeded, then now is the time to embrace native and indigenous talanoa (both singular and plural forms) in their own rights (see chapter by Denise Champion and Chris Budden) as scriptures. The native and indigenous talanoa are not the stories of "L's," but *talanoa of belonging* that bear witness to ancient spirits and ways that were "something else."

Brenda Morton's artwork titled "Women's ceremony" is an example of a rich and deep indigenous scripture.[21] This visual scripture lines up three waterholes diagonally across the center, representing sites for an exclusive ceremony for women. The center of this scripture is tilted (so Graeme Mundine's "Jubal cross" on the cover of this book), inviting the viewer/reader to tilt what s/he usually sees as level or normal. The three waterholes are linked. At the surface-ground level, however, the streams that link the waterholes are dry—represented by the brownish and reddish dots that line between the three waterholes. But Morton connects the waterholes under the ground with bluish dots, for water, around the edges. To the left and right edges are four camps *only for women,* where women would meet to prepare before they approach the waterhole at the middle to hold the ceremony that this indigenous text scripturalizes. The waterhole in the middle is the focus of this scripture, but Morton invites the viewer to see/read interconnectedness between the three waterholes. This scripture embodies the connectedness of sacred sites, and the ways in which a ceremony connects people from different communities.

This indigenous scripture provides a healthy alternative to the patriarchal bible of the Judeo-Christian faiths. Moreover, it provides an indigenous answer to the problem of drought in Australia and in the contemporary climate changed world. That answer is straightforward: water is available underground. They who can't find water are looking at the wrong places. The answer to the lack of water does not come from above. Rather, the answer

---

21. See also Havea, "Bible on Postmodern Surfaces."

comes from below, from down under. This indigenous answer is relevant for the shortage of water, and for the future of postcolonial criticism as well.

Second, the opportunities in talanoa (story, telling, conversation). In talanoa circles, the subject cannot be a loner. Talanoa does not allow a subject to be an independent and unattached individual. Appealing to the resistance by Alofa, "'I' does not exist . . . 'I' is 'we' . . . *always.*"[22] Talanoa is possible because of relationships; talanoa makes and breaks relationships. The talanoa subject *is* in community, and in solidarity. Talanoa is about something more, something *else,* than just being vocal and choral. Talanoa is also about being relational and reciprocal. Exchange of talanoa and of gifts is expected in the course of talanoa.

The tendency to romanticize the practices of storytelling (talanoa as telling) prevents one from seeing the politics of talanoa (as story, telling and conversation). Talanoa has power to convince, hurt, dispossess and displace. The ways in which biblical stories justify the robbing and dispossession of the natives of Palestine from their land,[23] and at the same time authorize Israeli settlers, are painful examples of the power of stories (talanoa) and of telling (talanoa). But talanoa also has power to heal, return and reinstate. This capacity is still far off from the lives of the colorful natives of Palestine and West Papua, thus making the invitation to postcolonize all the more urgent.

Third, the sacred-secular discrimination. The invitation to embrace native and indigenous scriptures invites also the problematizing of the divide between the sacred and the secular. It was in the interest of early missionaries to imagine that their Christian cultures were sacred while those of the natives were secular, so that our ancestors could be out-casted. The foregoing reflection has shown, on the other hand, that native and indigenous scriptures were not the accidental findings by savages, but the creation of thoughtful and creative ancestors whose wisdom lives on, albeit in different forms and fashions, among contemporary talanoa folks. Our ancestors were not looser-s (Ls) but exceptional (something else) people. And so are the indigenous and native peoples of today.

WHY KNOT?

To postcolonize is not to just analyze colonial literature and discourses in order to explain and understand why settlers invade (is)lands and exploit

22. Figiel, *Where We Once Belonged,* 137.
23. See Isaac, "Towards a Shared Land Theology."

native peoples,[24] and it is more than simply interrogating the politics of knowledge that encourage, certify and sustain the creation, exercise and distribution of social and political control over occupied (is)lands, native peoples and their heritages. To postcolonize is also to respond to the invention (misrepresentation) of colonized lands and peoples by imperial regimes, and correspondingly to expose and "talk back" to the invention and representation by the imperial regimes of themselves. Ultimately, to postcolonize is to *place*. The *voices from downunder* in this collection do this in different ways.

As a collective, this book begins (see chapters by Gabrielle Russell-Mundine and Graeme Mundine, Denise Champion and Chris Budden, Grant Finlay) and ends (see chapter by Terry Pouono) with the impact of churches in the colonizing of the land, cultures, minds and languages of indigenous and native peoples, at home and in diaspora. The overlaying of colonization and the Christian mission is exposed, as well as the overlaying of politics and religions in Australia and beyond (see chapters by Neville Naden, Gregory C. Jenks, Garry W. Trompf, Mark G. Brett, Anthony Rees). The reaches of this book extends from Aboriginal land and First Peoples to Second Peoples, as refugees and migrants, and from ancient sovereignties and living stories to the need to interpret texts in "the now" (see chapters by Grahame Rosolen, Karl Hand, Matthew Wilson, Terry Pouono) that is flexible and ongoing.

The voices in this collection address a variety of struggles, politics, traditions, scriptures and imperial regimes, which they postcolonize in different ways. As a collective, these voices entangle, thus explaining "Why [the book is like a] knot?" These voices are gathered in this monograph in order to peddle the *postcolonial voices from downunder* and to tout the vitality of (the invitation toward) postcolonial criticism.

WORKS CITED

Ateek, Naim Stifan. *Justice, and Only Justice: A Palestinian Theology of Liberation.* Maryknoll: Orbis, 1989.

Budden, Chris. *Following Jesus in Invaded Space: Doing Theology on Aboriginal Land.* Eugene, OR: Pickwick Publications, 2009.

Dube, Musa R. *Postcolonial Feminist Interpretation of the Bible.* St Louis: Chalice, 2000.

Figiel, Sia. *Where We Once Belonged.* New York: Kaya, 1999.

Havea, Jione. "The Bible on Postmodern Surfaces." In *Ecumenical Directions in the United States Today: Churches on a Theological Journey,* edited by Antonios Kireopoulos with Juliana Mecera, 172–89. New York: Paulist, 2012.

24. See also Budden, *Following Jesus in Invaded Space.*

————. "Cons of Contextuality . . . Kontextuality." In *Contextual Theology for the Twenty-First Century*, edited by Stephen Bevans and Katalina Tahaafe-Williams, 38–52. Eugene, OR: Pickwick Publications, 2011.

————. "Diaspora Contexted: Talanoa, Reading, and Theologizing, as Migrants." *Black Theology* 11.2 (2013) 185–200.

————. "Engaging Scriptures from Oceania." In *Bible, Borders, Belonging(s): Engaging Readings from Oceania*, edited by Jione Havea, David Neville and Elaine Wainwright, 3–19. Semeia Studies. Atlanta: Society of Biblical Literature, 2014.

————, ed. *Indigenous Australia and the Unfinished Business of Theology: Cross-cultural engagements*. New York: Palgrave, 2014.

Havea, Jione, and Monica J. Melanchthon. "Culture Tricks in Biblical Narrative." In *Oxford Handbook to Biblical Narrative*, edited by Danna Nolan Fewell, 563–72. London: Oxford, 2015. DOI: 10.1093/oxfordhb/9780199967728.013.49.

Jagessar, Michael N., and Stephen Burns. *Christian Worship: Postcolonial Perspective*. London: Routledge, 2011.

Isaac, Münther. "Towards a Shared Land Theology: A Palestinian Christian Perspective." In *Hermeneutics from a Palestinian's Perspective*, edited by Ranjan Solomon and P. Mohan Larbeer, 1–34. Bangalore: BTESSC, 2015.

Liew, Tat-siong Benny, ed. *Postcolonial Interventions: Essays in Honor of R. S. Sugirtharajah*. Bible in the Modern World 23. Sheffield: Phoenix, 2009.

Lorde, Audre. *Sister Outsider*. New York: Crossing, 1984.

Segovia, Fernando F., and Stephen D. Moore, eds. *Postcolonial Biblical Criticism: Interdisciplinary Intersections*. New York: T. & T. Clark, 2007.

Spivak, Gayatri Chakravorty. *Other Asias*. Malden, MA: Blackwell, 2008.

Sugirtharajah, R. S., ed. *The Postcolonial Bible*. Bible and Postcolonialism 1. Sheffield: Sheffield Academic, 1998.

————. *Postcolonial Criticism and Biblical Interpretation*. New York: Oxford University Press, 2002.

————, ed. *Voices from the Margin: Interpreting the Bible in the Third World*. Maryknoll, NY: Orbis, 1991.

Part 1

INDIGENOUS MATTERS

2

INCULTURATION, ASSIMILATION, AND THE CATHOLIC CHURCH

An Indigenous Postcolonial Intervention

Gabrielle Russell-Mundine
and Graeme Mundine

THE CATHOLIC CHURCH IN Australia has a relatively long and complex history of interaction with Aboriginal peoples. Christians came as purveyors of the Word of God, but the Word was wrapped in the culture of the countries from which they came. They brought with them a missionary fervor to evangelize, but over time they also implemented Government policies such as protectionism and assimilation. Despite this sometimes difficult relationship with Church, for Aboriginal people of faith the melding of Christ and Culture is a comfortable progression from their own knowledge of God prior to colonization to a more recent understanding about Jesus.

Aboriginal understandings of inculturation are in keeping with Catholic Church teachings which indicate that the melding of culture and faith is both possible and desirable. This message is not well understood amongst the non-Indigenous Church community where the relationship between Indigenous culture and faith remains contested and uncomfortable.

Nowhere was this more clearly enunciated than in 1986 when Pope John Paul II gave a speech to the Aboriginal peoples of Australia. This speech has become a much loved and much quoted oration and inspired

Aboriginal Catholics to more fully embrace their place in the Church and develop structures to enable them to do so. It also inspired non-Indigenous Catholics to open up the dialogue about the place of Aboriginal people in the Church. As Pope John Paul II said:

> That Gospel now invites you to become, through and through, Aboriginal Christians. It meets your deepest desires. You do not have to be people divided into two parts, as though an Aboriginal had to borrow the faith and life of Christianity, like a hat or a pair of shoes, from someone else who owns them. Jesus calls you to accept his words and his values into your own culture. To develop in this way will make you more than ever truly Aboriginal.[1]

Despite this call to a truly inculturated Church, divisions do remain and often Aboriginal people still identify a disconnect between what the Church teaches and what they experience as Aboriginal Catholics. Questions remain about the extent to which the Catholic Church in Australia is a place of assimilation from an Aboriginal perspective. This chapter considers this question from the context of the history of the Catholic Church with Indigenous peoples and draws on the experiences of the authors to highlight aspects of Church practice and behaviors which are bound to the cultural practices of the dominant non-Indigenous cultures and which continue to impact on Aboriginal cultural expressions of faith. In this chapter, we commence from a consideration of the Doctrine of Christian Discovery and how the justification of colonization which developed over centuries continues to reveal itself in the Church of today. We also briefly highlight that the Church does understand inculturation at a theoretical level but despite clear enunciation of the concepts in practice there continue to be barriers in a context such as Australia where Aboriginal cultures are not the dominant culture of the Nation. Finally, the authors use recent experiences to highlight some of the ways in which Aboriginal people experience the Catholic Church as assimilationist.

THE DOCTRINE OF CHRISTIAN DISCOVERY

Long before the British hoisted their flag on Australian soil, Indigenous peoples around the world had already experienced the often devastating impact of Church doctrine. In fact, the Church was instrumental in developing the principles and rationale that European powers used to justify

---

1. Pope John Paul II, *Address to the Aborigines of Australia*.

their invasion of the lands of other peoples. Now referred to as the Doctrine of Discovery, or as some claim it is more correctly called the Doctrine of Christian Discovery,[2] the Church developed a coherent framework of colonization and dominance over Indigenous peoples, lands, and resources which led to centuries of destruction and ethnocide.[3] According to Miller, the Doctrine of Christian Discovery can be traced to the Crusades to recover the Holy Lands and in particular to Pope Innocent IV's comment in 1240 that it is legitimate for Christians to invade the lands of the infidels because the Crusades were Just Wars fought for the defense of Christianity. While Innocent IV did concede that "pagans" had Natural Rights, he also stated that they had to comply with European concepts of Natural Law and religion. The concept of Natural Law later developed to include the European right to travel and settle new land and while the colonizers allowed that Indigenous peoples retained some rights, the Europeans' Natural Law rights took precedence.

In 1455, Pope Nicholas V issued the Papal Bull *Romanus Pontifex*. This Papal Bull was a well thought out manifesto of colonization which lent legitimacy to Portugal's push to conquer lands in West Africa. In 1493, Pope Alexander VI extended the right to conquer newly found lands to Spain with the Papal Bull *Inter Caetera*. Miller[4] makes the point that by 1493 the Catholic Church had established that: it had the authority to grant Christian Kings and Queens title and ownership of the lands of the infidels; the European exploration was facilitated by the Pope's guardianship over the earthly flock; Spain and Portugal held exclusive rights over other European countries to colonize other lands; the mere discovery of the lands was sufficient to create the rights.

England and France also used the Doctrine of Christian Discovery to justify their colonizing activities. However, as they did not wish to offend the Spanish and the Portuguese, they confined themselves to lands unknown to Christians, in other words, to lands so far un-colonized. The term colonization is derived from the Latin *colere* which means "to till, cultivate, farm land,"[5] it is logical then from the British perspective that they applied the principle of *Terra Nullius* to the Australian Continent, which meant the land was "empty" according to European sensibilities about what occupied and farmed land meant. When the British arrived in Australia they were already attuned to seeing lands as empty and non-Christian peoples as

2. Special Rapporteur, *Preliminary Study of the Impact on Indigenous Peoples*, 56.

3. Ibid., 6.

4. Miller, "Christianity, American Indians, and the Doctrine of Discovery."

5. Newcomb, *Pagans in the Promised Land*.

pagans ready to be civilized. The British declaration of Australia as *Terra Nullius* was just another step in the process of implementing the Doctrine of Christian Discovery.

THE CATHOLIC CHURCH IN AUSTRALIA

The Catholic Church did not arrive in Australia with the specific intent to evangelize Aboriginal people. They were more concerned with the Catholics who were transported, or later emigrated here. In fact, the Catholic Church faced an overtly hostile environment as they tried to establish themselves in the new colonies. The British considered the Church of England the State Church which, for the Catholics, ensured a constant struggle with the Colonial authorities. Catholic chaplains were not given permission to settle and the Catholic Church was not recognized as an official religious body.[6] Pope Pius VII appointed a Prefect-Apostolic but the authorities would not permit him to remain in the colony. It was not until 1820 that two Priests were allowed to remain and minister in the colonies.[7] This tenuous status continued until 1836 when Governor Richard Bourke introduced the *Church Act* which placed all denominations on equal footing.[8] Given the hostile environment it is not surprising that Priests focused on the needs of the immigrant Catholics and that there was little pastoral concern for Aboriginal people from the early Australian Catholic Church.[9] Additionally, Girola[10] states that the institutional church saw ministry to the Aboriginal people as the responsibility of the religious orders and many missions failed, or did not even start, due to lack of institutional support.[11]

However, as the colonies expanded there were individuals that were attuned to the atrocities being foisted upon Aboriginal people and their needs. For example, Father Therry, one of the two priests who had arrived in 1820, did express concerns about Aboriginal people. He made an offer to Governor Darling to take care of 50 Aboriginal children on the proviso that the Government would provide food and other necessities of life, an offer which was ignored[12]. One of the most often cited Catholic champions of Aboriginal people is Archbishop Bede Polding. In 1845, Polding appeared

6. Thorpe, *First Catholic Mission to the Australian Aborigines*, 1–12.
7. Ibid., 5.
8. Ibid., 9.
9. Ibid., 11.
10. Girola, *Rhetoric and Action*.
11. Ibid., 35.
12. Thorpe, *First Catholic Mission*, 8.

before a Parliamentary Select Committee on Aborigines and commented on the "grossest barbarities" Aboriginal people were subjected to as they were dispossessed of their lands.[13] In 1863, Polding wrote to Salvaldo, then the Bishop of Port Victoria, and said

> Alas, the march of European civilisation is the march of desolation, and unless means are used which our Liberals repudiate, the black savage will be exterminated to make place for a white savage—far more ruthless. They are shot down in Queensland like wild dogs—and with as little remorse. Even poison has been used lately.[14]

In his 1869 Pastoral letter Polding explained further that

> the want of success (of efforts of missionaries) must be attributed to the bad feeling and want of confidence, naturally caused by the mode in which possession has been taken of their country—occupation by force, accompanied by murders, ill-treatment, ravishment of their women, in a word to the conviction of their minds that the white man has come for his own advantage, without any regard to their rights . . .[15]

It was also Polding who brought four Passionist Missionaries to establish the first Catholic Mission on Stradbroke Island in 1843, although that was not a great success and failed by 1846.[16]

Not long after Polding established the short lived mission on Stradbroke Island in Queensland, over in the West the Benedictines, under the guidance of Rosendo Salvado, established a mission at New Norcia in 1844. In a report for the Vatican Congregation of Propaganda Fide in 1883, Salvado criticized the lack of attention given to Aboriginal people compared to the European settlers.

> Observing the general and utter state of neglect, on the part of Catholics, in which the savages ('selvaggi') find themselves all over Australia, in whose immense extension nothing exists for them but the one and only Benedictine Mission of New Norcia, so harshly opposed by the one who should be its supporter and defender, several times it occurred to me that while the care of

13. http://www.goodsams.org.au/who-we-are/history/john-bede-polding/   (accessed 15 May 2013).

14. Polding, cited in Howes, *Aborigines and Christians*, 7.

15. Polding, "Archbishop Polding's (1842–1877) Pastoral Letter 1869."

16. http://www.sydneycatholic.org/about/key_dates_in_our_history.shtml   (accessed 15 May 2013).

the souls of those savages is entrusted to the same ones to whom the care of the souls of the Europeans is entrusted, it will almost be miraculous if the true conversion and civilization of only one savage is obtained. These will always remain neglected, because the care of the Europeans will absorb, as it has so far, the whole mind and resources of those [missionaries] and for the poor savages i.e. for the legitimate owners of those same lands on which houses and churches are being built for the Europeans, there will never be one penny, due to them in justice rather than in charity; and I am so convinced of this that if it were possible to separate the two jurisdictions I would not hesitate for one moment to humbly propose it.[17]

Salvado's documents are important to help us understand the history of the Church and Aboriginal peoples. It is interesting as well that his conclusion at that time was that the Aboriginal people would always remain "neglected" and that the two jurisdictions should be separated. That is an argument that still has currency from an Aboriginal perspective as we discuss further in this chapter.

In 1926, a report of the Australian missionary conference identified that out of a total of 29 missions operating around Australia, at that time, the Roman Catholic Church were administering only four missions in Western Australia and one in Bathurst Island. The language of the missionary conference report in 1926 clearly showed the prevailing thinking that linked Christianity to a "civilizing" process and failed to recognize Aboriginal religion, spirituality or self-determination. For example, it was stated that

most of the semi-civilised blacks and half-castes have some knowledge of Christianity, and many reckon themselves members of some denomination or a mission, but without a constant supervision they very soon lapse into a condition of non-religion.[18]

Further, that report highlighted how the various denominations working in Missions both reflected and created the views of the day. The dialogue was seemingly untroubled by thoughts of the needs, hopes or desires of Aboriginal peoples, but rather the discussion proceeds with no expectation that Aboriginal people themselves should have any input, or say in where or how they were to live. For example, after discussing the various aspects of different types of mission the conclusion is that:

17. Girola, *Bishop Rosendo Salvado's 1883 Italian Report to Propaganda Fide.*

18. Australian Missionary Conference, *Australia Facing the Non-Christian World,* 12.

The natives when segregated, respond wonderfully to the teaching of Christianity, and much real religion is shown by them. . . To save the aborigines, body, soul and spirit demands that every individual native should have a chance to develop under the best conditions, and it is almost unanimously believed that this can only be obtained where segregation is possible, and where a religious basis for their lives is obtainable, it becomes apparent that the task that remains is to have every aboriginal on some Mission Station or other. . . This could be done with wild blacks, but is much more difficult to manage with those who are more or less civilized.[19]

We can see from this evidence that the issue of colonization, culture and faith have always been inextricably linked and, as in other places, is a contentious issue in Australia. However, despite its complicity in the colonization of Indigenous peoples around the world the Catholic Church is cognizant of the interplay between the essence of its mission and culture:

[T]he Church, sent to all peoples of every time and place, is not bound exclusively and indissolubly to any race or nation, nor to any particular way of life or any customary pattern of living, ancient or recent. Faithful to her own tradition and at the same time conscious of her universal mission, she can enter into communion with various cultural modes, to her own enrichment and theirs too.[20]

Indeed, it is expected that integrating Church and culture is transformative for all. As Pope John Paul II explained, inculturation signifies "an intimate transformation of the authentic cultural values by their integration into Christianity and the implantation of Christianity into different human cultures."[21] Both culture and church are enriched and changed by their interaction:

. . . by inculturation, the church makes the Gospel incarnate in different cultures and at the same time introduces peoples, together with their cultures, into her own community. On the one hand the penetration of the Gospel into a given socio-cultural milieu "gives inner fruitfulness to the spiritual qualities and gifts proper to each people . . . strengthens these qualities, perfects them and restores them in Christ." On the other hand, the church assimilates these values, when they are compatible with

19. Ibid., 15.
20. *Gaudium et Spes*, 58.
21. John Paul II, *Redemptoris Mission*, 300.

the Gospel, to "deepened understanding of Christ's message and give it more effective expression in the liturgy and in many different aspects of the life of the community of believers."[22]

Given this clarity of thinking and instruction about inculturation why has the implementation with regards to Aboriginal people been problematic? In more recent times the institutional Church has certainly tried to engage more directly and meaningfully with Aboriginal people. In 1970, Pope Paul VI, for example, spoke to Aboriginal people while visiting Australia:

> We know that you have a life style proper to your own ethnic genius or culture—a culture which the Church respects and which she does not in any way ask you to renounce. . . Society itself is enriched by the presence of different cultural and ethnic elements.[23]

Following on from Pope Paul VI's visit the Australian Bishops did make statements on issues concerning Aboriginal people such as racism, land rights and poverty. In 1986, Pope John Paul II travelled to Alice Springs and made a speech which resonated with Aboriginal and Torres Strait Islander people then and continues to do so now.

Perhaps one of the most quoted passages from Pope John Paul II's speech is this section:

> You are part of Australia and Australia is part of you. And the Church herself in Australia will not be fully the Church that Jesus wants her to be until you have made your contribution to her life and until that contribution has been joyfully received by others.

It should not be ignored that the Pope saw a need to make such a statement and direct a clear message to both Aboriginal and non-Aboriginal people. Clearly, he felt the need to remind the Australian Church that Aboriginal people can remain strong in their culture and be members of the Catholic Church and that non-Aboriginal people are not the gatekeepers or arbiters of what is or is not Catholic. Through baptism we are all equal and unique before God and this should be joyfully received. But how do we interpret what "joyfully received" means?

The lived experience of either receiving or being received can be problematic in this context. We have no doubt that Pope John Paul II meant that Aboriginal people and their contributions should be experienced

22. "Instruction: Inculturation and the Roman Liturgy Congregation."

23. NATSICC, A selection of writings.

and welcomed by non-Indigenous people without censure or judgement. However, the use of this word can also reinforce the privilege and power of the mainstream non-Indigenous Church. It suggests that the receiver has the power to receive, which in turn highlights that the mainstream is in a position to make judgements about what it receives, or chooses not to, and also reinforces separateness between Aboriginal Catholics and other non-Indigenous Catholics. In other words, there is no sense that there are mutual meeting grounds between Catholics all equal in baptism, instead the phrase reinforces that the norm is established and essentially the mainstream Church is asked to "allow" in the Other and their Aboriginal cultures—albeit joyfully!

In addition to power and privilege what needs to be examined is the difference between culture and faith. There are some incontrovertible "truths" of the faith, but how they are expressed is largely cultural. Too often, what the mainstream church clings to as an incontrovertible truth is in fact a cultural expression that is changeable. A good example of this is the use of the metaphor of "Lamb of God." Clearly a lamb was a contextualized symbol that made sense to the people Jesus was talking to in his time. Sheep did not exist in Australia before they were introduced by the British, so there was no context for Aboriginal people to relate to that metaphor. However, other animals do have meaning, but as Matthew Gill found out from the ensuing controversy when he depicted Jesus as a Brush Turkey, non-Indigenous people fail to understand that these are culturally derived metaphors that do not detract from the central understanding of the Jesus story, but rather bring it alive and allow Aboriginal people to make meaning from the use of culturally and contextually appropriate signs and symbols.

Culture is not static and as has been clearly stated by numerous Popes and other teachings the Church expects that "This congregation of the faithful, endowed with the riches of its own nation's culture, should be deeply rooted in the people."[24]

Herein lies one of the current challenges for Aboriginal peoples and the Church more broadly—what is the Australian Nation's culture? For Aboriginal people their multiple cultures are not the same as the dominant White, Western, but increasingly multicultural, society. For authentic inculturation to occur the people doing the inculturation must be of the culture and the faith.[25] Yet, despite several Aboriginal Deacons and nuns, there are no Aboriginal Priests or Bishops; therefore there are no Aboriginal people in positions of real power within the Australian Church hierarchy.

24. *Ad Gentes*, 15.

25. Russell-Mundine and Mundine, "Aboriginal Inculturation."

Consequently, Aboriginal culture is not only dominated and subsumed by mainstream culture, even where there are efforts to engage with and incorporate Aboriginal culture the fact still remains that culture is always being interpreted and judged by non-Indigenous clergy. Even where clergy do have the capacity to engage with a deep understanding of Aboriginal cultures from the Aboriginal perspective there is always the barrier of a gatekeeper, of having to seek validation from another person about what is "allowable." Surely, it is an unjust system where a person of faith has to hope that their Priest will "get it" and allow them to express their faith in ways that make sense from their worldview? As Martin says "the definition of inculturation implies that the use of culturally specific material is designed for the purpose of helping believers find Christ."[26]

The issue is compounded by the fact that the clergy are representative of a colonizing system which has participated in the destruction of Aboriginal cultures, languages, and lands. A point often missed when non-Indigenous people comment that they too do not find their particular culture reflected in their experience of Church. This may well be true for those individuals, but the relationship of Aboriginal peoples and Church is bound up in over two hundred years of colonization which produces a specific context that is not transferable to other experiences.

The Australian Church does need to grapple with, and identify, the nation's culture. Most likely, as we come to terms with how we are a multicultural society, we need to allow for the possibility of multiple cultures reflected in the life of the Church, including the liturgy. For example, whilst we talk of the necessity of Aboriginal inculturation, there are limits to how appropriate this would be for non-Indigenous peoples. Whilst some aspects could be construed as having become "Australian" other cultural practices would be inappropriate for non-Indigenous Catholics to utilize and would effectively be cultural appropriation. Although cultural appropriation in the Church is often seen as a benign activity in fact it "presupposes the power and ability to do so, with Church representatives often making the determination."[27] Additionally, the multiplicity of Aboriginal cultures and languages means that inculturation is not as simple as creating one alternative liturgy, for example. These are complex issues and a one-size fits all approach will not work.

The required dialogue and critical reflection necessary to disentangle what we take as the central tenets of our faith and what is actually a cultural expression of a universal truth is not easy to do. Unless this dialogue is done

26. Martin, ""Jesus Was not an Indian," 141.
27. Ibid.

in a fulsome way, the Church will continue to only allow token and inconsistent Aboriginal signs and symbols and will continue to be experienced by Aboriginal people as assimilationist.

By assimilation we mean the forced absorption of Aboriginal peoples, languages and cultures into the dominant culture. In this context it means that Aboriginal people are prevented from living and expressing their faith in ways that are culturally relevant and are expected to conform to the dominant culture. In other words, they are expected to leave their cultural self at the door of the Church. Any analysis of assimilation in the Church therefore must go beyond a discussion about signs and symbols and include an honest dialogue and education about the ways in which its structures and practices continue to support the colonial agenda if they are to joyfully receive the contributions of Aboriginal peoples.

Often it is hard for non-Indigenous people to comprehend how Aboriginal people feel excluded and disempowered by their Church. Certainly, there are many signs that the place of Aboriginal people in the Church has moved in a positive direction in the past twenty years. We can point to the establishment of the National Aboriginal and Torres Strait Islander Catholic Council (NATSICC) and the development of Aboriginal Catholic Ministries (ACM) around the country. The Catholic education system too is a major provider of education to Aboriginal students. Various religious orders and church agencies are working effectively with Aboriginal people and providing vital services and ministries. However, despite such identifiable improvements significant barriers remain. Some examples from our experiences will illustrate our point.

In January 2014, the authors were sent a copy of comments made on social media. The discussion thread questioned whether there was a place for Aboriginal culture and symbols in the Mass. These are some of the comments (made by different people):

> I believe there is zero place for that sort of nonsense. This is the Catholic Church, not the Uniting Church. One of the reasons, among many, why I attend the traditional Latin mass for the most part. It's more or less impossible to muck it up with that sort of gunk. That sort of stuff you mentioned has a place in Australian society I believe, but not in Christianity.
>
> I think in this particular case (and in many) it is unfortunately a corruption of the efforts of evangelism. It's true that Catholic culture differs from country to country, and one of the marks of the Church is that it is universal. This being said, I think it's important to remember what was decreed in the Council of Trent, that the Church solemnly teaches that the

traditional ceremonies, vestments and external signs which the Church uses in the celebration of Mass are conductive to true piety.[28]

The use of art I understand, the transplanting of pagan ceremonies into the liturgy I cannot accept.

The 'smoking ceremonies' that sometimes appear are wrong, as are political 'welcome to Country' statements. Instruments and art are great, provided they enhance the liturgy for the church. That means that the congregation are traditional aborigines, not inner-city white trendies.

Long story short I believe if aboriginal Catholics wish to adopt some of their aesthetics into churches, then they can do so, but you may as well make the entire church along that particular aesthetic trend, not try and incorporate it into existing structures, because then it will just make it look tacky. Imagine having an aboriginal art altar-cloth in say, one of the major cathedrals. It would be an aesthetic nightmare.

There are many issues with these statements ranging from outright racism to lack of knowledge about the Church's teaching on inculturation. Whilst one might consider that these comments are not a representative sample, in fact these comments succinctly sum up the kind of encounters we have in our work on a very regular basis. They exemplify very well the barriers that Aboriginal people encounter as they try to take their rightful place in the Church and highlight that the concept (and experience) of being "joyfully received" is complex. These comments also highlight that inculturation is not as simple as incorporating Aboriginal signs and symbols into a liturgy because what becomes an inculturated Church for Aboriginal people then loses cultural relevance for others.

In these comments judgements are clearly made about what is Catholic and what is not—casting Aboriginal cultural expressions as "nonsense" or making claims that using Aboriginal symbols could not inspire piety. The commentators justify their position by drawing on their perception of one aspect of Church teaching but fail to engage in a fuller analysis of inculturation; they make value laden judgements about Aboriginal spirituality as "pagan"; they reduce Aboriginal culture to art or "gunk"; they make judgements about culture and "traditional" Aboriginal people; and they intimate that there is only one acceptable aesthetic. They are of course all non-Indigenous people reinforcing their own cultural worldviews as the norm.

28. Paragraphs 1746, 1757.

Another recent experience highlights how the cultural norm and positions of power and privilege are often reinforced even when attempting to engage with some of the issues. This example occurred at a Catholic conference and exemplified to us some of the big challenges that the Church still has to grapple with. While we consider it of utmost importance to critique these experiences we choose not to identify the conference. Our aim in discussing the conference is to make a point about systemic issues in the life of the Church rather than decry a particular individual or organizing committee. The fact remains however, that many elements of this conference were disempowering, problematic and good intentions are no defense against the misuse of power and privilege.

At this conference there was a stream which focused on Aboriginal culture and its place in a particular aspect of the Church. Over the four days of the conference there was a workshop each day in this stream. Two were facilitated by a White person who publically declared they had no special expertise in this particular area, but who had organized the Aboriginal stream. One workshop was facilitated by an Indigenous person from another country and the last workshop was run by Graeme.

The chosen workshop facilitators highlighted some of the issues which frame the dialogue about Aboriginal Catholics' place in the Church as being "about them" rather than "with them"; it was deemed acceptable for White people to uncritically set the agenda on Indigenous themes and facilitate sessions. To our knowledge, no attempt was made to engage any of the Aboriginal Catholics who do have significant expertise in this area to organize the Indigenous stream. To counteract this Graeme decided to attend and submitted a workshop proposal to ensure that there was some Australian Aboriginal input. Some of the issues raised by this experience include: White facilitators retaining positions of power and privilege in setting the agenda even while acknowledging a lack of experience in the Indigenous field; non-Indigenous people telling stories about their contact with Aboriginal people in an attempt to lend legitimacy to their position; behaviors which apparently seek to negate the lack of consultation with Aboriginal experts such as constantly requesting the very small number of Aboriginal people attending the workshops to contribute their knowledge from the floor, but not allowing them space to contribute their expertise and lived experience other than as an audience member; utilizing Aboriginal artefacts and perceived cultural practices ineptly and inappropriately.

Whilst this conference was promoted as engaging with Indigenous issues in the Church it effectively and systematically excluded Aboriginal voices and experiences from a discussion of immense importance to Aboriginal Catholics, on an issue where many conversations have already occurred and are ongoing amongst Aboriginal people (see for example the proceedings from a liturgy conference organized by the authors in 2013).[29] Although the language was arguably more subtle the tenor was not much different from the way the previously mentioned missionary conference in 1926 talked about Aboriginal people.

How do we create change and end this ongoing colonization and racism? There are structural issues to consider, which Aboriginal people have been considering for some time. The question of whether there should be an Aboriginal rite or an Aboriginal ordinariate repeatedly comes up.[30] As Salvaldo highlighted there are questions about whether it is possible for the needs of Aboriginal Catholics to be addressed within the mainstream Church or whether there does in fact need to be a separation. Aboriginal Catholics need to strengthen their networks, support their leadership and ensure that they are talking through these issues in their own time and ways. It should be recognized that Aboriginal Christians of all denominations are constantly engaged in this thinking because it is they who are living in the Aboriginal Christian borders. Essentially, it is only Aboriginal people that can find the path forward to inculturation. As Graham Paulson says:

> . . . the responsibility for the incarnation of the gospel into the many cultures and sub-cultures of our region lies with the Indigenous Churches. It is imperative that we enculturate that gospel with integrity and dignity. It is imperative that there be a dynamic demonstration of the outcomes of that gospel within the many cultural and sub-cultural contexts of our region.[31]

In our experience Aboriginal Catholics want to belong to the Catholic Church but in a way that speaks to them as Aboriginal people. Aboriginal Catholics are reclaiming their own spaces and inculturating the Church in ways that make sense to them, but unless non-Indigenous people are prepared to engage in the work of decolonizing themselves and Church structures and practices their efforts are futile and a schism may result. The work of decolonizing is a journey and not a one off event. Too often non-Indigenous people rush to learn about Aboriginal cultures and there it ends. Whilst a better understanding of Aboriginal peoples, cultures and our shared histories is absolutely vital, that is the beginning not the end point. A deconstructing and reconstructing of Faith and Church is necessary.

What does that mean in practice? The starting point is always the self. Critical reflection on one's self and one's culture is essential; examining, for

---

29. https://acmsydney.wordpress.com/2013/12/20/liturgy-conference-proceedings.

30. Russell-Mundine and Mundine, "Aboriginal Inculturation."

31. Paulson, "Towards an Aboriginal Theology," 318.

example, our worldview; our belief systems and how these create the behaviors and practices in which we engage. Our critical reflection and analysis must also turn to the organizations or Church bodies that we belong to and understand how power and privilege includes and excludes and look at the structures, behaviors and practices that are racist or that devalue Aboriginal peoples or contributions. In the example of the conference we referred to earlier a decolonizing approach could have been to invite expert Aboriginal and Torres Strait Islander people to develop the Indigenous stream; invite appropriate speakers to run the workshops; have an Aboriginal or Torres Strait Islander Catholic as a keynote speaker; invite local Elders to participate; include appropriate Aboriginal signs and symbols in the liturgies; ask an Aboriginal person to organize one of the liturgies; ensure that Aboriginal Catholic Ministries are invited and supported to attend. There are many seemingly small actions that could have been taken in this case which could have turned the experience from being disempowering to creating meaningful change in the Church.

CONCLUSION

This chapter has touched on deep issues of concern for Aboriginal Catholics. We have aimed to frame the context of the current situation for Aboriginal Catholics in the history of the Catholic Church's role in developing the narrative of colonization and ostensibly legitimizing the efforts of European countries to colonize the lands of non-Christian people including Aboriginal people. We have also outlined a history of the early Church in Australia which explains to some extent the lack of pastoral interest in Aboriginal people from the early days of colonization. We have drawn on personal experiences to highlight how these modes of thinking continue in the contemporary practices of the Church. Aboriginal Catholics are engaged in conversation about these issues across the country. They are discussing how best to proceed in a Church that continues to allow their cultures to be expressed on a limited and an ad hoc basis. If the Catholic Church in Australia is serious about "joyfully receiving" the contribution of Aboriginal people then they also need to work on a decolonizing agenda and to listen carefully to the voices and experiences of Aboriginal Catholics.

WORKS CITED

Aboriginal Catholic Ministry. *Liturgy Conference Proceedings*. https://acmsydney.wordpress.com/2013/12/20/liturgy-conference-proceedings.

Aboriginal Catholic Ministry. *Key Dates in Our History*. http://www.sydneycatholic. org/about/key_dates_in_our_history.shtml.

"*Ad Gentes*, Decree on the Church's Missionary Activity." In *The Documents of Vatican II*, edited by Walter M. Abbott. London: Chapman, 1966.

Australian Missionary Conference. *Australia Facing the Non-Christian World: Report of Australian Missionary Conference, Together with Addresses by Dr John R. Mott*. Melbourne: Alpha, 1926.

"*Gaudium et Spes*, Pastoral Constitution on the Church in the Modern World." In *The Documents of Vatican II*, edited by Walter M. Abbott. London: Chapman, 1966.

Girola, Stefano. *Bishop Rosendo Salvado's 1883 Italian Report to Propaganda Fide: A Significant Source for the History of the New Norcia Mission and Colonial Western Australia*. Number 21. Perth: New Norcia Studies, 2013.

———. *Rhetoric and Action: The Policies and Attitudes of the Catholic Church with Regard to Australia's Indigenous Peoples, 1885–1967*. Thesis. St. Lucia, Qld: University of Queensland, 2006.

Good Samaritans. http://www.goodsams.org.au/who-we-are/history/john-bede-polding.

Howes, Morgan B. *Aborigines and Christians: An Introduction to Some of the Issues Involved*. Queensland: Foundation for Aboriginal and Islander Research Action, 1977.

"Instruction: Inculturation and the Roman Liturgy Congregation for Divine Worship and the Discipline of the Sacraments." March 29, 1994.

John Paul II, Pope. *Address to the Aborigines of Australia*. Alice Springs, 1986. http:// w2.vatican.va/content/john-paul-ii/en/speeches/1986/november/documents/ hf_jp-ii_spe_19861129_aborigeni-alice-springs-australia.html.

———. *Redemptoris Mission*. Dec. 7, 1990, No 52. AAS 83 (1991).

Lewis & Clark Law School Legal Studies. Research Paper No. 2011–13. http://ssrn.com/ abstract=1803674.

Martin, Kathleen J. "Jesus Was not an Indian: Encountering Native Images in the Catholic Church." In *Indigenous Symbols and Practices in the Catholic Church: Visual Culture, Missionization and Appropriation*, edited by K. Martin, 137–62. New York: Ashgate, 2010.

Miller, Robert J. "Christianity, American Indians, and the Doctrine of Discovery." In *Remembering Jamestown: Hard Questions about Christian Mission*, edited by Amos Yong and Barbara Brown Zikmund, 51–68. Eugene, OR: Pickwick Publications, 2010.

Newcomb, S. *Pagans in the Promised Land: Decoding the Doctrine of Christian Discovery*. Golden, CO: Fulcrum, 2008.

Polding, Bede. "Archbishop Polding's (1842–1877) Pastoral Letter 1869." In *A Selection of Writings from Papal Documents and Bishops' Statements Concerning Church Social Teaching Relating to Aboriginal Australians, Handbook Supplement*. Brisbane: National Aboriginal and Torres Strait Islander Catholic Council Assembly, 2009.

Russell-Mundine, G. and G. Mundine. "Aboriginal Inculturation of the Australian Catholic Church." *Black Theology: An International Journal* 12.2 (2014) 96–116.

Special Rapporteur. *Preliminary Study of the Impact on Indigenous Peoples of the International Legal Construct Known as the Doctrine of Discovery*. Permanent Forum on Indigenous Issues, Ninth Session. New York, 2010.

Thorpe, Osmund. *First Catholic Mission to the Australian Aborigines*. Sydney: Pelligrini, 1950.

3

FIRST PEOPLES, ANCIENT SPIRIT, AND THE UNITING CHURCH PREAMBLE

Opportunity and Challenge

Denise Champion and Chris Budden

THIS IS A CHAPTER in two voices. We have not attempted to write a paper together, but to juxtapose the voices of a First Person (Denise Champion) and a Second Person (Chris Budden) in a conversation about the Preamble to the Constitution of the Uniting Church in Australia (UCA). Both of us believe that this Preamble sits alongside the *Basis of Union* as one of the significant shaping documents of the UCA, and for the relationship between the Uniting Aboriginal and Islander Christian Congress (UAICC) and the rest of the Uniting Church.

After an initial introduction of ourselves, Chris will introduce the Preamble, and then Denise will offer a detailed account of its contents. Denise will then tell how this document gives her space and permission to connect her stories to the gospel. Chris will finish the chapter by raising what he sees as the challenges to theology in the Preamble, and some questions about the colonial strands that still remain.

DENISE

Ngai Mityi Deniseanha, Ngatyu Yura Mityi Warrikanha. Ngaityu Ad-
nymathanha Yuarta, Ngatyu Yarta utyu Flinders Ranges yarta. Ngai utyu
Ararru artu.

I am Adnyamathanha person, from the Flinders Ranges in South
Australia. "Adnyamathanha" is made up of two syllables and means "rock
(adnya) group (mathanha)." So, we are the original "rock group." If you go
up to our country you will find it is very, very rocky up there. You will know
why they call us the rock group.

Denise is my Udnyu Mityi, my "white person" name. My *Yura* mityi
(Adnyamathanha name) is Warrikanha, which means I am second born and
female in my family. My name sets things into context, of who I am, where
I come in my family, and how I can relate to all people and other things
around me.

The other important thing you need to know about me is that I am
Ararru, which means I am the north wind. We have two groups, north wind
and south wind—Ararru and Mathari. We are a matriarchal society. We
take after our mother's ancestral lineage and so I am Ararru, my mother was
Ararru, my grandmothers were Ararru, and my children are Ararru. With
my grandchildren, though, only my daughter's children are Ararru, because
that is the lineage of the mother. When my son's children are born they are
from the opposite moiety.

I always say that Australia is one gigantic story book. The stories are
told in over 250 languages, and mine is just one of them.

CHRIS

I am a member of the Second Peoples. My family are uninvited guests, part
of an invading and occupying community. That I am welcomed as a col-
league of Denise's is a sign of grace. My interest is in the development of a
Second People's theology,[1] and how the Preamble challenges this theology
and the usual claims of Western Christian hegemony. I convened the working group that brought the Preamble to the Church, and yet I still think we
are entangled in colonial realities.

In 2009 the Uniting Church in Australia adopted a new Preamble to
its Constitution. Constitutions tell us who the group is, what its purpose is,
who belongs (and who does not), how people join and leave, who makes
decisions and by what authority, and how are people held accountable.

1. See Budden, *Following Jesus in Invaded Space.*

Preambles tell us something of the history of the community; how it got to be this sort of people. The Preamble to the post-apartheid South African Constitution is a classic example of this sort of Preamble.

The Uniting Church Preamble arose from the desire of leaders within the Uniting Aboriginal and Islander Christian Congress to have something in the law of the church that would name their place in the church in unavoidable ways.

The Preamble rehearses the history of Church Union, and then recognizes a number of matters that it believes are important to its life as a community of First and Second Peoples. The first three things it recognizes are affirmations of the place of God in this land prior to colonization. The next three are confessional—a recognition of the very ambiguous way the Church related to First Peoples. The final four honor the struggles of First Peoples, the establishment of the Uniting Aboriginal and Islander Christian Congress, and covenant-making.

DENISE

Much of my time is given to telling the stories of my people, and relating them to the Gospel story. I find a new freedom in the Preamble to do just that; to reclaim my community's ancient sense of God or the sacred in ways that enrich my life and understanding of Jesus.

At the beginning of Matthew 13 Jesus tells the parable of the sower. The disciples then come to ask Jesus about parables.

> Then the disciples came and asked him, "Why do you speak to them in parables?" He answered, "To you it has been given to know the secrets of the kingdom of heaven, but to them it has not been given. For to those who have, more will be given, and they will have an abundance; but from those who have nothing, even what they have will be taken away. The reason I speak to them in parables is that 'seeing they do not perceive, and hearing they do not listen nor do they understand'. With them indeed is fulfilled the prophecy of Isaiah, that says:
>
> 'You will indeed listen, but never understand,
>   and you will indeed look, but never perceive.
> For this people's heart has grown dull,
>   and their ears are hard of hearing,
> and they have shut their eyes;
>   so that they might not look with their eyes,
> and listen with their ears,

and understand with their heart and turn—
  and I would heal them.'
But blessed are your eyes, for they see, and your ears, for they
hear.

(Matt 13:10–16, NRSV)

What the Preamble has done for me as an Adnyamathanha person is that it has allowed me to tell my stories in my way. I have been able to recognize Christ in my stories, and I have been able to tell the good news through them.

That is so different to how I grew up as a young kid going along to Sunday School and growing up in church. A lot of what we were being taught was "your culture is evil and demonic and you shouldn't have anything to do with it." Now I have been challenged to look at our stories with the knowledge that this country is not a young country; it's a very, very old country. I started thinking about how we have stories that go right back to creation, and I started thinking about this memory, this long memory, that we as Aboriginal people have of God in this country. It goes back beyond 200 years and we have not been allowed or never really had the space to tell those stories and to see Christ in them.

THE CHALLENGE OF THE PREAMBLE
TO THE UNITING CHURCH CONSTITUTION

The Preamble represents a significant journey for the Uniting Church. It speaks of who the Uniting Church is as it takes seriously its place in the land alongside the First Peoples. For example, the fourth paragraph reads:

> As the Church believes God guided it into union so it believes
> that God is calling it to continually seek out renewal of its life as
> a community of First Peoples and of Second Peoples from many
> lands, and as part of that to RECOGNISE THAT.

Those last couple of words—to RECOGNISE THAT—are very important. We can have conferences, and we can sit down and talk about post-colonial stuff, but unless we start to recognize that God was here in this land it doesn't mean a lot. God did not come to this land on the *Endeavour.* God was not absent before 1788. God was already here, together with our stories and our songs and our ceremonies. I believe that the Preamble has given me the freedom and the space to be able to tell that story of that long memory of God that we have in this place.

The terms First Peoples and Second Peoples came from a lot of work that the Uniting Church and the UAICC did together. There was a lot of talk about how we should refer to ourselves, and First and Second Peoples were the two names that we settled on.

The Preamble suggests ten things that need to be recognized. The first three read:

> When churches that formed the Uniting Church [the Congregational, Presbyterian and Methodist churches] arrived in Australia as part of the process of colonisation they entered a land that had been created and sustained by the Triune God they knew in Jesus Christ.

> Through this land God had nurtured and sustained the First Peoples of this country, the Aboriginal and Islander peoples, who continue to understand themselves to be the traditional owners and custodians (meaning 'sovereign' in the languages of the First Peoples) of these lands and waters since time immemorial.

> The First Peoples had already encountered the Creator God before the arrival of the colonisers; the Spirit was already in the land revealing God to the people through law, custom and ceremony. The same love and grace that was finally and fully revealed in Jesus Christ sustained the First Peoples and gave them particular insights into God's ways.

WIDA ARDUPA[2]

Let me tell you a story about the Gum Tree Couple (Wida Ardupa).

> Wadu Matyidi, Wadu Mathana Yura ngawala wangkanga.
> Wangkangkadna nangka idla Wida Ardrupa Yuwatamangka.
> Wadu nguni yuwatamangkadna Vanbila utyu Wida Ardupa.
> Wida Ardupa nearringha madlapanha wida apinha akanaangka.
> Wandu Watya ngalawatanangkadna.
> Tha! Ubmarta vatyungha, miru mulda
> Yapa Yundangka wanhanga
> Vanbilar angkungha
> Naingka! Akaldangkadna Wida Ardupa arngku

2. A longer version of this story appears in Champion, *Yarta Wandatha*.

Yarta Vaniangkadna wanha vanbila yuwatamangka.
Naingka!

In ancient times our ancestors spoke these words. They told the story of the gum tree couple who stood side by side. Around about the gum tree couple, small gum tree saplings grew. There was new growth coming through strong. They grew well and tall and strong. Then one day some people came and cut a road through where the gum tree people stood. They dug a road. They dug the earth where the gum tree couple had stood. They broke the couple's connection with country and each other. This was a very deep sadness as they stood separate and alone.

What does that story teach us about the rule for living, about how to live with each other? Of course it tells about the relationship between this gum tree couple and how the young gum trees grew around them, and how there was growth, there was a family, and what happens when disconnection comes because of the road built between them. But it is more than that. It is also a very symbolic story about other relationships, and the boundaries of relationships. There is a moral teaching in this story, and an affirmation of the spiritual dimension of life.

It tells us about our relationship with each other, about our relationship with our environment. You will hear in the story about what kind of trees grew in this place. The telling of this story always has a fixed geographical location. When I tell the story, immediately my mind travels back to that place where our old people sat and told these stories. There is a place called Yankaninna, the site of the story of these gumtrees couples, and Yankaninna is a little station north of the Flinders Ranges where I come from. It is about our relationship to our environment because every story does relate to a specific place. It is also about our relationship with the spiritual world, particularly our creator.

One of the things that I often say is that it is a story of reconciliation between Aboriginal and non-Aboriginal people. The story tells in a non-threatening way the hurts or the interruption to the way Aboriginal and non-Aboriginal people have related to each other; symbolized by the cutting of the road through where the tree stood.

This disruption was forced on Aboriginal people by the churches, where Aboriginal people were told they had to leave their language and culture behind if they wanted to accept the support of the church. As a result many Aboriginal people still hold a lot of anger towards the church.

CONTINUING WITH THE PREAMBLE

The fourth clause under "RECOGNISE THAT" reads:

> Some members of the uniting churches approached the First Peoples with good intentions, standing with them in the name of justice; considering their wellbeing, culture and language as the churches proclaimed the reconciling purpose of the Triune God found in the good news about Jesus Christ.

You hear the good intentions in some of our missionary stories, and you hear of people standing with First Peoples. The intention, of course, was to proclaim the "good news." Good news is an interesting thing for me. What does that look like to us Aboriginal people?

The fifth and sixth clauses remind us that the church's record was not always good.

> Many in the Uniting Church, however, shared the values and re-lationships of the emerging colonial society including paternal-ism and racism towards the First Peoples. They were complicit in the injustice that resulted in many of the First Peoples being dispossessed from their land, their language, their culture and their spirituality, becoming strangers in their own land.

> The uniting churches were largely silent as the dominant culture of Australia constructed and propagated a distorted version of history that denied this land was occupied, utilised, cultivated and harvested by these First Peoples who also had complex sys-tems of trade and inter-relationships. As a result of this denial, relationships were broken and the very integrity of the Gospel proclaimed by the churches was diminished.

This is the part that really challenges me. How do I, as a disciple of Christ, follow Jesus in this land? How do we go to our people and say "Brother/ sister, God loves you," when already the integrity of that gospel proclaimed by the church has been diminished by what has happened in our history? I find that a lot of our people are stuck in that area where they can't see past the hurt and the loss. How do we convey to them the love of God?

There are a lot of people who have accepted the forgiveness of Christ in their lives and that has meant for them a sense of peace in their life, but has not freed them from poverty and the struggle to find freedom in their lives. One of the questions we explored at one time when we had all our elders together was: how were they feeling as Aboriginal people in the land? How did they view the gospel, and how does gospel and culture fit together, particularly as we share culture through stories and reflect on what they mean?

I see the wisdom of culture and the gospel as the same thing, because of this long memory that we have of God in this country. The Preamble has created the space for me to be able to tell my stories and then be able to see Christ in them. What I always say I also say now, that I am able to recognize the creator God in my stories.

We have one story called Nguthana Mai Ambtana—the Dreamtime spirit cooking the damper. It is the story about an older lady who took her two children on a journey. There was a famine in the land and so she journeyed in search of food. She came to this place and she said to her children, "You go now and find wood for the fire and we will make a camp here." And so she waited for her children to come home to this place where they would make their camp. The sun was going down and she started to get a bit worried. As parents, you would be worried when you haven't heard from them for a little while. You would be asking the question "Where are they?" So as the sun went down her children still hadn't returned home.

How would you as a parent feel if that were to happen? You would be frantic, you would be doing stuff; you wouldn't just be sitting and waiting for them to come home. You would be ringing the police, you would be going out looking for your children, and this is what this mother did.

As a mum she knew her children would be hungry, and she thought "well maybe if I make some food, the smell of the damper might bring my children home." So she did. She started to prepare and put the damper in the ground oven, as we did back then, and covered it over with the hot ashes. And if you go to that place it is called Nguthana Mai Ambtana. Just outside of Copley on the way to Nepabunna Mission, where my mob come from, you will see this little mound, yellow and grey and ashy in color. It looks as if a damper was in the oven and it had risen.

And, of course, the children hadn't returned. So when they hadn't returned she became very worried. She started to put some steps in the side of the hill. She thought, "if I get on top of the hill maybe I will be able to see all the way around. Maybe I will be able to see them from a higher vantage point." But she couldn't find them at all. And then she had exhausted all her human capacity to find her two children. And then, as she sat there in her grief, grieving for her two children, the song of the bellbird came to her:

Wayanha Yanarunga
Vaku. Vaku. Winmiri mandha
Wayanha Yanarunga.

Vaku. Vaku. Winmiri mandha.
Wayanha Yanarunga.
Vaku. Vaku. Winmiri mandha.
Wayanha Yanarunga.
Vaku. Vaku. Winmiri mandha.

The words of that song are "underneath the shadows of Mount Way-anha the bellbird is whistling." The bellbird led her to where her two children were. One was found up at Lake Lettie and the other at Mount Wayanha. She was able to bring her two children home.

I tell that story a lot of times because it is a story that I have told my children to keep them safe. To tell them of the safety of the home and why it's important to tell mum and dad where you are going and when you are coming home. It's a continuous living memory of a story that we can use today. It's also for me the story of the lost children, the stolen children, the children that were taken away.

It wasn't anyone's fault in the story that the children went off and be-came lost. There are many people who are lost; you can think of people in your own family who are lost, and just looking for the way to come home or looking for a place to call home. So it is a story of being lost and found. It is a story also about our parent, our creator God, one who has prepared for us a safe place where we can be together. In that story, interestingly enough, creator God is the mother; it is the woman. She prepares, and she provides. She is the one who longingly, lovingly, looks for her lost children. For us in that story too, the spirit comes in the song, to lead her to where her two children are. And to me it is a wonderful story of creator spirit working to find the lost. You hear the song in that story that talks about leading, guid-ing, pursuing us until we are found.

CHRIS

R. S. Sugirtharajah makes the point in *Postcolonial Reconfigurations* that postcolonialism is really about taking a critical stance on the side of those who have been oppressed in colonial and postcolonial situations.[3] The aim is to generate an alternative discourse that might challenge and undermine Western hegemony.

Denise has suggested ways in which the Preamble opens space for her to build new practices that further challenge that hegemony and its

3. Sugirtharajah, *Postcolonial Reconfigurations*, 13–14. There is a helpful short description of Postcolonialism in Heaney, "Prospects and Problems for Evangelical Postcolonialisms," 31–32.

expression in the theology of the church. I would like to build on that as a non-Indigenous person.

Theology and missiology are usually based on the idea of a universal human condition—image of God, sin, redemption and new life in Christ—in which culture or gender plays no meaningful part. That is, from a theological position people's deep differences make no difference to how they are seen in the purpose of God, and how we understand new life in Christ. The danger, of course, is that the stories and views of dominant communities simply become the implicit norm. Their world becomes the measure of what is human, and they claim that their culture best embodies and is an example of the redeemed and renewed life.

The Preamble forces us to rethink that framework, to take particular cultural identities seriously, and to talk of Jesus' work in different ways. It challenges the barely acknowledged assumption that Western theology is really universal, and is certainly the measure for how people speak about God, Jesus and salvation.

I think there are three challenges to the usual theology of the Church in the third clause under "to RECOGNISE THAT." I also think there is a need to ask whether the Preamble, in some ways, reinforces hegemony even as it challenges it.

First, "The First Peoples had already encountered the Creator God." Pre-contact Australia was not a godless place, and the First Peoples were not a pagan people. As Denise suggests, God did not come on the boat; God was already on the land before the Europeans arrived. This claim poses a significant challenge to the church. The church can no longer claim to hold the only story about God, or to be the only source of knowledge about God. The story of God in the land and among the First Peoples of Australia is thousands of years old. The following questions are therefore critical for the Uniting Church and for all Christian churches in Australia, and beyond: What can the church learn about God from First Peoples? How does the way in which God has been present in this place, bound by a different story and relationship with the earth challenge and deepen what the church is able to say about God? How do relationships between First and Second Peoples change if the church no longer simply dispenses knowledge about God but listens carefully and respectfully to what other people know?

There is also a question about the colonial nature of the Preamble at this point. Is this acknowledgement another form of control, a continuing colonial act because it names who God is for First Peoples—the "Creator God"? That is, is it saying the First Peoples knew the One that Christians have properly named, and is it suggesting that other names are not needed? Names are about relationships; they are particular to different people and how they name that which is sacred. Is the use of the word "God"—which is a universal claim about the sacred, not a particular, relational name—an act of violence? Is it a colonial act because the religious life of Aboriginal people is still being judged by Christian categories, rather than in its own right?

David Chidester suggests that invading societies change their view of the religious life of indigenous peoples depending on the stage of invasion and control. He suggests that frontiers are not lines or boundaries or border, but "a region of intercultural relations between intrusive and indigenous people."[4] At the frontier, at the point where relationships are most contested, the invading society denies that indigenous people have a religious life, for in that way they deny that they are human. This makes murder, massacre, rape, slavery and abuse easier to justify. When the frontier is closed, and control has been established, when people are segregated, enclosed and pushed to the edges of life, then religion becomes important again. It becomes an agent of control.

As Denise's section suggests, the Preamble is an important document. Yet before the church gets too smug, there is a need to at least allow the question to sit there: Is this allowing another form of control, a way to hold First Peoples within the church rather than engaging them as a religious "other"?

Second, "the Spirit was already in the land revealing God to the people through law, custom and ceremony." Here is an affirmation of revelation beyond Christ or the Scriptures, and runs into all the critiques that arise with the Reformed tradition about "natural religion" and the centrality / aloneness of Christ. There are important issues here for theology in Australia.[5]

Tink Tinker makes the point that the inclusion of the Hebrew Bible in the Christian canon "results in necessarily forcing all adherents to embrace a history that is not the natural or actual history of the persons or people who have become adherents."[6] Western Christians have embraced the Old Testament for so long that in some strange way it has become their his-

---

4. Chidester, *Savage Systems*, 20.

5. I began to explore some of these issues in *Following Jesus in Invaded Space*, 99–103. A lot more still needs to be done.

6. Tinker, *American Indian Liberation*, 131.

tory (which explains in part the failure of the Church to stand up for the Palestinians). In another way what it means is that the Old Testament is spiritualized, and turned into metaphors or models for our religious life that are divorced from any real social and historical community.

The important thing, though, is that when people appropriate a foreign history they, in some way, deny their own proper history and experience of God. This paragraph raises the issue of how people's real history is recognized, and whether that history becomes their Old Testament.

Third, "The same love and grace that was finally and fully revealed in Jesus Christ sustained the First Peoples, and gave them particular insights into God's ways." Here is not only revelation, but insights that challenge and broaden what Christians know. It is not just gospel completing the religious life of First Peoples, but also the other way—the Indigenous stories completing the religious life of Second Peoples.

The language of this section may imply that people knew things in the past that pointed them to Jesus, but now they do not need those past things. The intention, though, and one that needs to be strongly affirmed, is that the traditions and claims of Indigenous culture and spiritual life are still valid and still a source of life and liberation today.

This conversation has been about revelation. Very importantly it is about the presence of God; where God is known and met. Questions and challenges however remain: What is the relationship between revelation and salvation? Is the presence of God what salvation is all about; the wholeness that comes from *God among us*? Is this clause in the Preamble restrictive, or does it make space for Jesus to sit beside traditional faith as additional guidance for living rather than the sole claim to salvation? Does Jesus enlighten, deepen and enrich traditional life, and also provide new guidance for dealing with a settler-colonial society?

There is one further question. This paragraph flows from Indigenous Christians. It is an effort to honor their life and faith as First Peoples as they seek to be Christian. Is it, though—as I have asked above—still a colonial act, as it justifies and supports traditional beliefs in terms of Christian claims rather than on their own terms?

Like all documents in a colonial context this one is not simply about truth-telling, but negotiating what truth could be told (would be heard), and how those truths would be told. So, for example, it was not possible to simply affirm the previous beliefs of First Peoples, but that belief had to be related to Christian claims (which clearly became the measure of truth of those previous claims). Does this process mean that, while affirming the great value of the Preamble we must also be wary of the continuing colonial threads that hold it together?

Finally, Denise brings this conversation to another frontier:

Denise

A lot of my people are angry because of the way the missionaries made them leave culture at the door of the church. They had to choose between Jesus and what they knew about God in land and culture. Part of what the Preamble does is let us speak our language in the church, reclaim the ancient stories of God, and to name God in our way. It affirms who God has called us to be.

WORKS CITED

Budden, Chris. *Following Jesus in Invaded Space: Doing Theology on Aboriginal Land.* Princeton Theological Monograph Series 116. Eugene, OR: Pickwick Publications, 2009.

Champion, Denise with Rosemary Dewerse. *Yarta Wandatha.* Salisbury, SA: Denise Champion, 2014.

Chidester, David. *Savage Systems: Colonialism and Comparative Religion in Southern Africa.* Studies in Religion and Culture. Charlottesville: University Press of Virginia, 1996.

Heaney, Robert S. "Prospects and Problems for Evangelical Postcolonialisms." In *Evangelical Postcolonial Conversations: Global Awakenings in Theology and Praxis,* edited by Kay Higuera Smith, Jayachitra Lalitha, and L. Daniel Hawk. Downers Grove, IL: InterVarsity, 2014.

Sugirtharajah, R. S. *Postcolonial Reconfigurations: An Alternative Way of Reading the Bible and Doing Theology.* St. Louis: Chalice, 2003.

Tinker, George E. "Tink." *American Indian Liberation: A Theology of Sovereignty.* Maryknoll, NY: Orbis, 2008.

4

ABORIGINAL LAND AND AUSTRALIA'S FIRST NATIONS PEOPLES

Calling for Treaty, Recognition, and Engagement

Neville Naden

OVER THE PAST 228 years, since the colonization of Australia by White Settlers (First Fleet arrived in 1788), the First Nations Peoples of Australia have fought for the recognition of land custodianship. Federal and State Governments and the church have benefitted greatly as a result of dispossessing the First Nations Peoples of the land that God had apportioned them. In this chapter, I will outline a theological framework for those who would argue that the colonization of this country was God's will. I will also outline some of the difficulties in addressing these issues.

Growing up as an Aboriginal person, especially during my younger years, land was never an issue for me. My parents never spoke about the atrocities of the past and my family was not exposed to the truth. I failed to understand why such information was kept from us children. Even today, my parents don't speak about what took place 200+ years ago. Why? I can only surmise.

My dad was brought up in a Christian home. My grandparents were Native Workers with the Aborigines Inland Mission (today, the Australian

Indigenous Ministries). This organization did not encourage people to think about land in a way that was different to what they were taught. I suppose their attitude and the attitude of so many in their time was that, what happened back in 1788 was all a part of God's will and purpose for Australia, because nothing happens outside of God's will. This type of thinking prevailed for many years, and even up to this day.

COLONIZATION AND GOD'S WILL

Whilst attending an Aboriginal Evangelical Fellowship meeting in Sydney in April 2014, I struck up a conversation with a young Anglican minister. He was a fine young man who was well educated—he had a number of degrees in the area of theology. He was very supportive of Indigenous issues and worked tirelessly to help address the social disadvantage of our people. In speaking with him we began to talk about issues relating to the colonization of Australia. I spoke about the colonization as an unjust act. He immediately responded with a quote from Gen 50:20, where Joseph on his death bed comforts his family and says to them, "what you meant for evil God meant for good." The difficulty with trying to justify God as willing colonization from this verse, is that it is an account of one man who was sold into slavery. Joseph's situation had nothing to do with land dispossession. It is difficult to apply this principle to what happened in Australia. Why not? Because so many atrocities accompanied the act of colonization.

Joseph's story is often used to justify the colonization of this country by the British. The murder and rape of our women, the herding of our people into camps, originally known as "missions" and later became "reserves," the cultural genocide that took place where languages weren't permitted to be spoken (see chapter by Grant Finlay)—are all on the public records. The sites of significance for our people where they would worship and learn about the creator were desecrated and demolished. Sites where people would learn about their relationship with the land and the importance of their role in looking after it—the land that God had entrusted to them, where they would learn about Kinship and cultural practices—were not recognized.

When we read the story of Joseph we find that this is God revealing his plan of how the Messiah would eventually come. The central issue of the story of Joseph is not that Joseph endured suffering and injustice but that God's plan of redemption was being rolled out. There is no such big picture of God's plan in the colonization of Australia. Any attempt to apply such theology to justify the injustices that took place, namely that God intended the evil so that good might result, is heresy. So if this verse is used to justify the dispossession then one needs to be consistent in using the verse for every occasion that has happened in the history of humanity. The genocide of the Jews by Hitler. The Mugabe oppression in Zimbabwe. The sins of the world. The murders, the rapes and pedophilia. If we use such arguments, then we say that God approves of sin. This then beckons the question, when is sin, sin? The purpose for which the story of Joseph was written, was to show how God was unfolding his plan for the redemption of humanity. It was not to justify the unjust things that happened to Joseph.

I used to think that the slaughter, rape and the attempted genocide of the Indigenous peoples of the earth was a part of God's plan and purpose as he unfolded his plan of redemption. I too thought that God allowed this land to be colonized by the British and that God not only allowed it to happen but willed it. This thinking prevailed in my life right up until 2010 when I was asked to speak at a TEAR conference at Stanwell Tops in NSW. It was at this conference that I met Ron Sider, a Canadian born American theologian and social activist. Ron and I began a conversation around the issues of Colonization and I asked Ron, "why did God allow our country to be taken from us and the murder and atrocities to take place?" I outlined to him my view that I had come to understand about colonization. I told him that what took place in 1788 was part of God's unfolding plan for the redemption of my people. Ron was horrified that I could think that this was God's doing and he said to me that I was asking the wrong question. He went on to say that if I used this thinking to justify the atrocities of the past, when speaking of my people, then we must also apply the same principles to every other abuse on humanity. He went on to say that God allows mankind to have a free will and with that free will they abused it and used it to do evil things.

GOOD NEWS OR WAS IT?

There will be those who would say that it was God's way of bringing the message of the gospel to this land of ours, that people would hear the word of God, the message of salvation, and have an opportunity to respond to its message. Those of us sitting in postcolonial Australia are grateful for the coming of the gospel which gave us a clearer view of the source of salvation as seen in Jesus who is God's gift to us. The only problem with this is, when the gospel came to this country, the goalposts changed. Prior to the arrival of Europeans our people were judged according to their limited understanding of God. Ignorance's were overlooked before the gospel came. Paul in Athens in outlining to the Athenians who Jesus was, says in Acts 17:30, "In the past God overlooked such ignorance, but now he commands all people everywhere to repent." God accepted the ignorance of people but now they must respond to the call of God upon their lives.

Ignorance we are told, God overlooked. So for people to use the argument that the gospel came on the First Fleet and was God's plan of reaching the heathen is flawed. Prior to the coming of the gospel, God had long ago revealed himself to our people, and they were judged according to that limited understanding of who he was and their relationship with him.

WHO'S LAND IS IT?

Aboriginal people have always understood that the land was owned by the creator. The custodianship of the land, however, has been given to the indigenous peoples of the earth. Psalm 24:1 tells us that "The earth is the Lord's and the fullness thereof." Leviticus 25:23 also expresses this truth, "the land is mine and you are but aliens and my tenants." Aboriginal people have always understood that they were given custodianship of this land we now call Australia.

In Acts 17:26 Paul on his second missionary journey visits Athens. He comes across some images with the inscription to the unknown God. He says to the people of Athens that he wanted to tell them who this God was, that they had deemed unknown. As he begins his address he says,

> Men of Athens! I see that in every way you are very religious. For as I walked around and looked carefully at your objects of worship, I even found an altar with this inscription: TO AN UNKNOWN GOD. Now what you worship as unknown I am going to proclaim to you. The God who made the world and everything in it is the Lord of heaven and earth and does not live in temples built by human hands. And he is not served by human hands, as if he needed anything, because he himself gives all men life and breadth and everything else. From one man he made every nation of men, that they should inhabit the whole earth; and he determined the time set for them and the exact places where they should live.

The God who made the heavens and the earth apportioned his creation to his created humanity. Consequently, this land called Australia was given to my people by the Almighty. It was God who determined the time set for them and the places where they should live. It was given to our people by God. It stands to reason then, that if God had apportioned the land of Australia for Aboriginal people, then the principles for land management, as outlined in scripture should be applied.

What are the principles that governed land management and owner-ship in the Old Testament?

1. The land is owned by God and it is God who determined the boundar-ies where people would live.

2. Because land was owned by God, humankind do not have a right to give it away or sell it to someone else.

These first two principles are evident in the story of Naboth's vineyard in 1 Kings 21. We know the story well. Ahab the king had a palace in Jezreel which was right beside a vineyard owned by Naboth. Ahab thought that Naboth's vineyard would make a good place for his herb garden. Initially Ahab does the honorable thing and approaches Naboth and tries to negoti-ate a transfer of ownership of the property into his hands. He offered to swap Naboth's land for a better property, which Naboth refused to accept. He then offers to buy it from him, which he again refuses. Note Naboth's words in verse 3, "The Lord forbid that I should give you the inheritance of my fathers." So what was the problem? The land was not Naboth's to give away since it had been bestowed by God as an inheritance for Naboth's pre-decessors and subsequent generations.

He could not alter the intended purpose of God. This would be like taking someone's property that you are renting and giving it to someone else, or swapping it with someone else. It would be illegal. You just can't do it. It doesn't belong to you.

All land belongs to God and all land must be subject to the principles of land management as outlined in Leviticus 25. Land could not be sold but could be leased for no more than a 50-year period.

3. All land leased had to be returned to the original custodians on the day of atonement in the year of Jubilee. Ahab may have been able to acquire Naboth's vineyard if he negotiated a lease arrangement but greed got the better of him and his wife.

4. It is wrong to change the borders or boundaries of a property that God has given someone. This principle is clearly stated in Deuteronomy 19:14—"Do not move your neighbor's boundary stone set up by your predecessors in the inheritance you receive in the land the Lord your God is giving you to possess." It is a sin to unlawfully extend the bor-ders of a property for gain. That is the same as stealing the land. A classic example of this was the compulsory acquisition of the Murray Islands by the Queensland Government in 1879 when it extended its

sovereignty over the lands of the Meriam people. According to Deuteronomy 19, this was wrong and illegal.

In light of these principles, the question that needs to be asked is, when does governmental law override the laws outlined in the scriptures?

INTERNATIONAL LAW[1]

According to International law, there are three ways that land could be acquired:

1. By conquest: If a country was conquered, the rights of the indigenous inhabitants were retained under international law until and unless the new sovereign power decided to modify them.

2. By cession: If a country was ceded, in that an arrangement of occupancy was agreed on with the indigenous people, land would be surrendered in return for some benefit such as compensation or a treaty (as in the Treaty of Waitangi in Aotearoa / New Zealand).

3. By occupation or settlement: Where land was deemed to be *Terra Nullius* (empty land)—land belonging to no one or unoccupied land, such land could be deemed unsettled.[2]

What happened in Australia? When the First Fleet's passengers arrived and set foot on these shores, they didn't see anything that resembled ownership according to their culture and customs, such as thatched roofs or manicured gardens. Emeriti de Vattel, in his 1758 Law of Nations, and before him John Locke, held that failure to cultivate the soil meant there was no pre-existing title to land. De Vattel considered that, "Every nation is then obliged by the law of nature to cultivate the land that has fallen to its share; and it has no right to enlarge its boundaries, or have recourse to the assistance of other nations, but in proportion as the land in its possession is incapable of furnishing it with necessaries."[3] In effect he was saying that this land was too big for the few numbers that occupied it. Locke wrote,

1. "International law" was simply a convenient construct of colonial powers. In 1452, Pope Nicholas V issued the Bull Romanus Ponifex declaring war on all non-Christians throughout the world. In 1493, Pope Alexander IV made similar proclamations. Such edicts gave the Kings of Portugal and Spain the green light for conquest. By the early 1500s, such notions had developed into the Doctrine of Discovery legitimising dispossession of native tribes' lands. First Nations Peoples of the world were obviously not consulted when the Doctrine was formulated.

2. Mayne, *Mabo, Native Title*, 3.

3. De Vattel, *Law of Nations*, 1:7.

"He that in obedience to this command of God subdued, tilled and sowed any part of it, thereby annexed to it something that was his property, which another had no title to, nor could without injury take from him."[4] Herein lies the problem.

When Cook arrived in 1788 he did not see any evidence of tilled or sown land so he deemed it *Terra Nullius,* meaning unoccupied land. The fact that he had engaged natives when he first arrived on these shores should have indicated to him that this land belonged by someone else. Furthermore, it is believed that Sir Joseph Banks who accompanied Cook on the voyage was in possession of copies of diaries of earlier navigators who visited The Great South Land and who had commented on the presence of Aboriginal people.[5] Justice William Blackstone (1723–1780), whose publications on the common law legal system dominated English thinking for more than a century,[6] recognized that it was not the absence of the tilling and sowing of the soil that deemed something unowned, but the absence of any form of humanity. Hence the colonization of Australia was illegal, even according to International law.[7]

Cook carried with him instructions from the Admiralty which advised him as follows: "You are with consent of the natives to take possession of convenient situations. . . If you find the country uninhabited take possession for His Majesty."[8]

What happened in this country was that Aboriginal people were not given the respect of a sovereign nation. There were no negotiations for a treaty or any agreement by Cession.[9] At least Ahab negotiated initially with Naboth regarding his land. They couldn't come to any agreement and this resulted in Naboth's death. The interesting thing about the acquisition of this parcel of land was that it was not Ahab that had Naboth and his broth-

4. Locke, *Of Property,* Chapter V: The Second Treatise of Civil Government.

5. See Estensen, *Discovery.*

6. "A Biography of William Blacktone," http://www.let.rug.nl/usa/biographies/william-blackstone/

7. Blackstone, however, was not consistent in his judgments. In the case of the conquest of the British in taking land from the American Indians he declared in 1780 that it was an "Act of State" and therefore legitimate. In other words he considered it legal, albeit unjust. When Justice Blackburn rejected the Native Title claims of the Gove Peninsula Aborigines in the Northern Territory in 1971, he relied on the decisions of Justice Blackstone. See *Millirrpum v. Nabalco.*

8. Mayne, *Mabo, Native Title,* 3.

9. In June 1835 John Batman, an Australian grazier, businessman and explorer, arranged a treaty with a group of Wurundjeri elders, for the purchase of land around Port Phillip near Melbourne in exchange for clothing and implements such as tomahawks and knives. However, Governor Burke declared the treaty invalid.

ers killed. It was Ahab's deceitful wife, Jezebel. But Ahab was held accountable for her sin, because he was the recipient of stolen property.

Many whitefellas (white/European people) would say today that they are not responsible for the dispossession that happened two hundred years ago. Ahab could have cried innocent as well. But God deemed him to be guilty as charged because he engaged in Jezebel's sin in taking the land for himself.

Many have written to try and address the issue of land that was stolen from our people. It would seem that many whitefellas don't take notice of Aboriginal people when they press their claims for land ownership. In 2009, Peter Adams, Principal of Ridley College Melbourne, began to address the issue. He considered the illegal acquisition of land. The land was stolen from Aboriginal people. Hence the title of his paper, "Australia—Who's land?"

Adams outlines clearly what Aboriginal people have always known and have always claimed, namely, that all lands belong to God and this land was given by God to Aboriginal people as their possession to take care of. Adams says that because the land is God's, we as God's people should respect and honor God. It is God that made Australia and gave it to the first inhabitants. All creation should respect God's sovereign right to give land to whom he chooses and we should respect the people to whom it was and is given. Adams goes on to say that *Terra Nullius* treated people as if they had no significance. He says, "this was an insult to them and against God their maker."[10] Adams asks the question surrounding the attempted invasion by the Japanese. "If someone stole property, we would try to recover it. Similarly if the Japanese had successfully invaded Australia, and taken possession of it, we would have fought to regain possession of it."[11]

The custodianship of land is of primary importance to Aboriginal people. The irony of the land issue is this: those that stop boat people coming to this country of ours, are migrants themselves. Tony Abbot the former Australian Prime Minister, was born in England. Others have their lineage traced back to other parts of the world. They were recipients of land that was taken from a sovereign people and now they stop others from coming to this land. This is hypocrisy.

Adams points out that, "it is impossible to know the nation to whom God first gave some land, and they may not exist at the present time. That is not the case in Australia. We know those to whom God gave the land, and we know when it was stolen from them."[12] He goes on to say it is time to

10. Adams, "Australia—Whose Land?," 3.
11. Ibid.
12. Ibid., 4.

right the wrong. It is time to do that which is right. It is time for Christian churches to play their role. They have been recipients of land grants by governors and governments. Effectively, we have our churches on stolen land. We, the churches, are in receipt of stolen goods. What should our response be? It's time to right the wrong. But what can be done? Paul in writing to the church at Rome says "Owe no one nothing, except to love one another; for the one who loves another has fulfilled the law. The commandments, you shall not commit adultery; you shall not murder; you shall not steal; you shall not covert; and any other commandment, are summed up in this word, Love your neighbor as yourself" (Rom 8:8–10).

But how can the situation of the churches being in receipt of stolen goods be rectified. How can any situation regarding land in this country be rectified? Out of all the countries that were colonized by the British, Australia is the only country that has never entered into a treaty with the first nations people. Aboriginal people have never ceded sovereignty over their lands. A treaty is needed in order for the churches to move forward. This would at least fix the problem for the churches. Until this happens, the churches will always be seen as accomplices of the theft of this country.

Some have suggested constitutional recognition will fix the problem. The constitution in this country is illegal. A treaty would fix this problem as well.

WHAT MIGHT THE CHURCH DO?

In light of the above, we must ask the question, where to from here? There have been a number of suggestions as to the best way forward. In coming up with an appropriate outcome, we need to consider the facts at hand.

Firstly, some have suggested that people should just pack up and leave the country. Whilst this has happened in other parts of the world, this will not happen in Australia. The act of relocating oneself to another country has happened in countries where the colonizing people were a minority. In this country the colonizers are the majority. So this will not happen. Secondly, the majority of Aboriginal people in this country don't expect that this will ever happen. So how do we work towards a future that is acceptable to the original inhabitants of this country?

Colonization has done much to bring about the demise of our people. While our Aboriginal and Torres Strait Islander people make up 2.5% of the population of Australia, the adult incarceration rate is 27% across the country and 84 % in the Northern Territory. In the National Juvenile Justice

Centres, 50% of the population identify as being of Indigenous decent.[13] Something needs to be done to address these issues. Many who are incarcerated, especially women, have psychiatric disorders while others are imprisoned for menial crimes especially in Western Australia where mandatory sentencing legislation takes discretion away from the Judiciary. The estimated cost of incarcerating an adult male in the correctional system is $100,000 per year.[14] Many of the crimes committed are due to boredom and the lack of things to do. Maybe one way of addressing this issue is providing people with training and jobs. Put the money that would be spent on their incarceration and create employment and salaried positions.

Aboriginal people are more likely to die younger than non-Aboriginals. Indigenous males born 2010–2012 can expect to live to 69.1 years, compared with 79.9 years for non-Indigenous males. Indigenous females born during the same period can expect to live to 73.7 years, compared with 84.3 for non-indigenous females. Whilst there is a closing of the gap, much work still needs to be done in these areas.[15]

Is there any good news? While the amount of land determined to be Native Title in most states and territories is very small, there are two outstanding exceptions. Probably 40% or more of Western Australia and 40% of South Australia are now under some form of Native Title and it is instructive to note that in WA nearly all of the land has been determined to be Native Title *without litigation,* all stakeholders agreeing with the decision.[16] This is distinct from the Northern Territory 1976 Land Rights legislation which determined that about 50% of the land is Aboriginal freehold.[17]

There is still a need for the average Christian in mainstream Churches to be made aware of the marginalization and social disadvantage of many of their Aboriginal brothers and sisters in Christ. For example, none of the Indigenous pastors working for AIM or any of the Aboriginal ordained ministers working in the six Anglican parishes in the Northern Territory are paid a salary. They are supposed to fend for themselves. As Rob Haynes

13. *Australians together,* 22–25.

14. Civil Liberties Australia website. http://www.cla.asn.au/News/prison-costs-up-numbers-up.

15. *Australians together,* 22–25.

16. National Native Title Tribunal website: Determinations. http://www.nntt.gov.au/Mediation-and-agreement-making-services/Documents/Quarterly%20Maps/Determinations_map.pdf.

17. *Northern Territory Land Tenure.* http://www.regional.gov.au/regional/ona/land-tenure/pdfs/land-tenure-20130717.pdf. These maps should be used with caution since they show Aboriginal (and other) freehold title even though it may be assumed that most of this land is in fact Aboriginal land.

(former CMS missionary Groote Eylandt, Northern Territory) in "It's time to listen to Aboriginal Christians and time to respond" states, "the typical Aboriginal Christian leader is . . . someone who won't expect to live a long or fulfilling life, or have a rectory or car or even a proper wage."[18]

Respectful relationships are needed if we are going to forge a future of equality for our people in Australia. There are many ways this can be done, three of which are outlined below:

1. Recognition of the need for First Nations People to be invited to sit at the table when issues regarding land and property are discussed.

2. That when distributing the resources and assets of the church, priority be given to First Nations People of this country. After all, this is still their land.

3. That in church seminars, conferences, Synods and General Assemblies, Indigenous Christian leaders be given roles as keynote speakers so that non-Indigenous audiences might be better informed.

WORKS CITED

"A Biography of William Blackstone." http://www.let.rug.nl/usa/biographies/william-blackstone.

Adams, Peter. "Australia—Whose Land?" A John Saunders Lecture, Ridley College, Melbourne (10 August 2009).

Australians Together: Leaders Guide. http://www.australianstogether.org.au/group-leaders.

Carroll, Peter, and Steve Etherington, eds. *One Land, One Saviour.* Sydney: CMS Australia, 2008.

Civil Liberties Australia website. http://www.cla.asn.au/News/prison-costs-up-numbers-up.

de Vattel, Emmerich. *The Law of Nations or the Principles of Natural law: Of the Cultivation of the Soil,* 1758. http://www.lonang.com/exlibris/vattel/vatt-107.htm.

Estensen, Miriam. *Discovery: The Quest for the Great South Land.* St Leonard's, NSW: Allen & Unwin, 1998.

Locke, John. *Of Property.* 1690. http://ebooks.adelaide.edu.au/l/locke/john/l81s/chapter5.html

Mayne, Tom. *Mabo, Native Title, Wik and the Ten Point Plan.* Melbourne: World Vision Australia, 2003.

Millirrpum v. Nabalco Pty Ltd and the Commonwealth of Australia, Supreme Court of the Northern Territory, 2002.

National Native Title Tribunal website: *Determinations.* http://www.nntt.gov.au/Mediation-and-agreement-making-services/Documents/Quarterly%20Maps/Determinations_map.pdf.

18. Cited in Carroll and Etherington, *One Land,* 241.

Northern Territory Land Tenure. http://www.regional.gov.au/regional/ona/land-tenure/
pdfs/land-tenure-20130717.pdf.

5

ALWAYS CRACKNEY IN HEAVEN

Grant Finlay

ABORIGINAL PEOPLE'S EXPERIENCE OF colonization is often grouped into a few collective descriptions, such as resistance or acquiescence. Postcolonial studies have recognized the heterogeneous nature of colonial contexts and encouraged more nuanced dialogue of various expressions within these descriptions. An increasing number and range of subaltern voices are emerging in contemporary discussions. These voices are not identical. Furthermore, these discussions are not new. Archival sources of colonial era churches, missions and government bodies indicate a variety of Aboriginal responses to Christian faith throughout the colonial era. This variety of voices give rise to multivalent perspectives and interpretations of the Bible and Christian theology.

This chapter examines oral and literate responses by Christian Aboriginal people in *lutruwitta* / Tasmania, the island state south of mainland Australia at a pivotal location during a crucial period of its colonial history, namely the Wybalenna Settlement on Flinders Island from 1832–1847. From these largely unpublished sources a variety of Aboriginal responses and interpretations of Christian faith is discerned.

In a context of enforced "English-only" Christian faith, Aboriginal people were not limited to this colonial language, but conversed primarily in first language, *creole* and, less often, in English. Their expressions of Christian faith were part of engaging in multiple contexts simultaneously as they negotiated relationships not only with colonial authorities, but also with each other. Their intra-clan and inter-clan relationships were more influential than Aboriginal-colonial relationships in the emergence of these initial expressions of Indigenous theology.

This chapter will examine the topic of "heaven" in Aboriginal addresses at Wybalenna to highlight the variety of relationships and multiple layers of meaning that were occurring. It will conclude by identifying some of the links between that past experience and contemporary discussion of contexts for Indigenous theology.

WYBALENNA

The British Government established a colony in Van Diemen's Land, the island off the south coast of Australia that is now known as Tasmania, in September 1803. The Aboriginal name of Van Diemen's Land is *lutruwitta* in the *palawa kani* language program of the Tasmanian Aboriginal Centre.

When the British colony was established, there were approximately nine language or nation groups around the island. Within these larger political units were smaller clan groups, usually between four and six in each area.[1] In the 1820's the colonial government granted large areas of Aboriginal land to colonists. This led to conflict, which escalated into war, in what was known as the Black War, which culminated in government efforts to drive Aboriginal people into the southeast corner of the island in the campaign known as the Black Line in 1830.

At the same time Governor George Arthur appointed George Robinson to represent the Governor to "conciliate" with the Aboriginal people. An agreement was reached in October 1830, around the time of the conclusion of the Black Line, that the Aboriginal people would leave their lands and live for a time on an island in Bass Strait. This site was eventually located on the west coast of Flinders Island and became known as Wybalenna.

The Wybalenna settlement was established in 1832 and closed in 1847. Over that time between one hundred and fifty and two hundred (150-200) Aboriginal people lived there and when it was closed the surviving forty-seven people moved to an abandoned convict station south of Hobart called Oyster Cove.

Wybalenna is an important site in Tasmania's Aboriginal and colonial history. It is also significant in Aboriginal Christian history for it is the site of the first attempts at Bible translation, catechism classes and Christian addresses both oral and written. It is also the site of a petition to Queen

---

1. Ryan, *Tasmanian Aborigines*, 11.

Victoria requesting her to honor the agreement, or treaty, which the Aboriginal people had negotiated with Governor Arthur.[2]

This essay focuses on surviving written reports of Aboriginal people addressing each other about Christian faith in their own first languages at Wybalenna through the later part of 1837 and early months of 1838. These addresses were part of broader programs of Sunday church services and weekday catechism classes operating from 1835 to 1839 under the oversight of the catechist, Robert Clark, who was under the oversight of the Commandant George Robinson.

The first and only attempt at Bible translation occurred from June to December in 1833 when the first catechist at Wybalenna, Thomas Wilkinson, engaged in extensive conversations with members of the so-called "Ben Lomond" clan who were from the northeast area of Van Diemen's Land. Wilkinson began with the first chapters of Genesis and began creating a scripted form of the people's language. The translation was interrupted by ongoing conflict between Wilkinson and Commandant Darling that led to Wilkinson's removal in April 1834.

At the initiative of the "Ben Lomond" people a school began with the new catechist, Robert Clark. This evolved into an extensive school program in 1836 after George Robinson arrived as Commandant. Robinson adapted the "Bell and Lancaster" system from England whereby children were appointed to teach other children. Most of the Aboriginal teachers at Wybalenna were the children of clan leaders. One such teacher was Walter Arthur, son of Druleerpar from the "Ben Lomond" clan. Walter was involved in the hand written newspaper *The Flinders Island Chronicle*, which was regularly published, usually on a Saturday, from September 1837 to February 1838.

In response to the declining number of attendees at the catechism classes, Commandant Robinson tried something new at the end of April 1837. While the Catechist, Robert Clark, was away for a few days Robinson invited Aboriginal people to "exhort and admonish each other from the desk."[3] The invitation was initially taken up by a west coast man, Noemy, who proceeded to address his own people in their language and then to the whole group in the "language of the Settlement," the *creole* that was evolving among the clans.

> [Noemy] spoke with great confidence and vehemence and delivered a most instructive and interesting discourse partly in his own and partly in English. Spoke against the practice of thieving and desired them to live honestly. Told them of Jesus Christ and

2. Reynolds, *Fate of a Free People*.

3. Plomley, *Weep In Silence*, 439.

God our Father, of heaven, of glory, of going up to heaven, of hell. Said bad people went to hell, that good people went up to heaven; Devil is in Hell. King William, King George, Philip and Alfred spoke as well. It was a most interesting meeting.[4]

While Robinson invited the speakers, the initiative for the use of first language seems to have come from Noemy himself. At Wybalenna, Robinson was very firm in only speaking about Christian faith in the English language, even though he himself had spoken about Christian faith in an attempted Nuenonne / Bruny Island language earlier in 1829.[5] Throughout reports in 1837 and 1838 Robinson was scathing of Clark's attempts to preach or teach in the *creole* "language of the settlement."

From this initial address there developed a regular Saturday evening school at which several Aboriginal people from most clans spoke to their own clan and then to other Aboriginal people in *creole,* before addressing the whole audience in English.

All of these addresses were given only by men. The initial four men were all a generation older than the Aboriginal youths, Walter Arthur and Thomas Brune, to whom Robinson paid such close attention in writing the *Flinders Island Chronicle* in English. Robinson identified a further six men giving first language or *creole* addresses in September and October 1837, and Clark reported another six men giving first language addresses in early 1838, so there were at least ten to fifteen different men involved.

These men are identified with at least eight different clans: Tongerlongerter / William of Oyster Bay; Druleerpar / George of Ben Lomond; Noemy from West Coast; Tunnerminnerwait / Pevay / Napoleon from Cape Grim; Drinene / Neptune from North; Dowwringgi / Leonidas and Druemerterpunner / Alexander from Big River; Wooraddy / Alpha from Brune Island; Robert (North East); and Philip whose clan is unknown. Three of them are named as "King" or "Count" by Robinson, which seems to be Robinson's way of naming clan leaders.

Druleerpar / King George was leader of the Ben Lomond clan and father of Walter Arthur. He was probably involved in the beginnings of the Bible translation work with the first catechist, Thomas Wilkinson, in 1833 and seems to have fulfilled a leadership role on the Settlement particularly in nominating constables,[6] arranging and celebrating clan marriages[7] and

4. Ibid.
5. Plomley, *Friendly Mission,* 61.
6. Plomley, *Weep In Silence,* 441.
7. Ibid., 470, 518–19.

acting in a protective role for some others.[8] Together with two other iden-tifiable clan leaders Druleerpar welcomed Governor Franklin to the Settle-ment.[9] Druleerpar and Robinson gave gifts to one another, including a coat, which other identifiable clan leaders also received.

Druleepar was also involved in some prohibited trade with a soldier[10] and for a time kept a hunting party away from the Settlement because of the sickness there.[11] With these various leadership roles at Wybalenna, it is likely that Druleepar's address in the school was another expression of this role. He was familiar with Christian traditions and continued to speak his first language. While he cultivated a relationship with Robinson, he clearly, and perhaps more importantly, involved himself in arranging relationships within and between Aboriginal people.

It is possible that these initial four men used the opportunity of giving these first language addresses to (re-)assert their personal seniority among their own clan's people, and the other clans, through their use of their first language, and the newly added and potentially authoritative speaking posi-tion of the school "desk," which had previously been Robinson's own desk. Druleerpar is also interesting in that he may have actually put forward his own son, Walter Arthur, to become one of the teachers in the school to strengthen his, his family, and/or his clan's relationships with others. The "Ben Lomond" clan, at least initially, comprised the largest portion of the Wybalenna population.

Discussions around post-colonial theology often focus attention on the Indigenous-colonist relationship, however, it is essential that due regard be given to the inter-Indigenous relationships in each context as these shape who speaks to whom, about what, and in what detail. It is essential to be cognizant of inter-aboriginal political relationships as well as the more obvi-ous Aboriginal-colonial relationships. The addresses also indicate the mul-tilingual skills of these orators and the growing interpretation of Christian faith into first language and religious worldview.

Each of the addresses by these older men was translated usually by a woman from the same clan as the speaker. Sometimes the translator is an adult and sometimes a child of twelve or thirteen years of age. Through this role the women were able to provide some of their own "interpretation" in the translation, so while it seems they were not permitted to speak to the whole group, they did have a role in communicating to Clark what the men

8. Ibid., 452.
9. Ibid., 524.
10. Ibid., 461.
11. Ibid., 482.

said, so the catechist got to hear what the women said the men had said. There is no documentation of the women addressing each other in their first languages but there were several women-only catechism classes so it seems unlikely that they would not have had some conversations with each other at some time. There are however no surviving documents of these.

HEAVEN / CRACKNEY

Only a little is known of the religious life of Aboriginal people in *lutruwitta* before the British established their colony. It is a sobering point to acknowledge that there is a total absence of primary source material in terms of oral or written material produced by Aboriginal people themselves about their cosmology and religious practices prior to, and during, the early years of colonization. All extant records about *lutruwitta* Aboriginal cosmologies emerged in the context of colonial interactions and impositions and are, to some extent, an engagement with, or expression of, those contexts and intercultural or interreligious exchanges. They are also written almost entirely by colonists.

Aboriginal mythic life existed, though it is difficult to be precise about the details because of scant records. Robinson's writings are from a limited number of people and only one gender of Aboriginal people with whom he conversed. His writings were also for a colonial audience whose favor he was seeking. Nevertheless, sufficient information is available to demonstrate a substantial mythic context within which Aboriginal people interacted with Christian faith and religious practice. Rather than fallow ground seeking an external sower, they were skillful practitioner-storytellers with multiple interpretive paradigms and conversation points with those Christians with whom they engaged during the significant political, cultural and mythic upheaval that was occurring.

One such skillful storyteller was Woorraddy from the Nuenone (Bruny Island) clan. Woorraddy was the primary source for Robinson's writing of creation stories. In one reference Robinson wrote that Woorraddy

> said that MOI.NEE and DROME.MER.DEEN.NE fight in the heavens and that MOI.NEE tumbled down at Louisa Bay and dwelt on the land, that his wife came after him and dwelt in the sea, and that by and by the MOI.NEE children came down in the rain and went into the wife's womb and that afterwards they had plenty of children.[12]

---

12. Plomley, *Friendly Mission*, 373–76.

This is the earliest reference to "heaven" by an Aboriginal person. The Creator Beings "came down from heaven" from the star path known in English as the Milky Way. This was Aboriginal people's primary interpretive paradigm for "heaven."

At Wybalenna Robert Clark sought to incorporate these spatial references into his sermons. He spoke of Jesus Christ "tumbling down"[13] from heaven thereby associating Jesus Christ with the creator beings Moinee and Dromerdeene. Various Aboriginal people spoke similarly about heaven as part of creation:

> My dear friends you know that God made the heavens and the earth and sea and the trees and the stones and everything that moveth and he made you and me that we might serve him he made man and put him into the garden of eden a garden of pleasant and the all animals were not savage and transgression falled upon Adam and sin came upon all men black and white and then Jesus Christ came into the world to die for our sins according to the scriptures.[14]

Like other evangelical themes, a person's place in eternity received significant attention among the Aboriginal speakers and writers. There appear to be more contrasts among them on this theme of "heaven."

Some references to heaven were in the context of where a person "goes" after they die. Robinson was surprised to be told the deceased went to "England" after death. "I scarcely credited what I heard. I asked the question again, when they all replied that they went to England, that there was plenty of PARLEVAR in England."[15] Walter Arthur expressed something of this when he wrote, "[W]e skin black people died then arose from the dead became white men we begin to make friends of them call them father or Brother."[16]

While it is a common belief well documented on mainland Australia, this is the only reference I have found of this view in *lutruwitta*. The idea may have come from contact with Aboriginal people from New South Wales, who travelled with John Batman before joining Robinson.[17]

If white people were regarded as deceased Aboriginal people returning to their country, then future deceased Aboriginal people would go to that same place. If these deceased "Aboriginal" people call that place "England,"

13. Plomley, *Weep In Silence*, 440.
14. Robinson, *Robinson Papers*, 105, 109.
15. Plomley, *Friendly Mission*, 62, 230.
16. Robinson, *Robinson Papers*.
17. Plomley, *Friendly Mission*, 427, 428.

then it is not surprising that not-yet-deceased Aboriginal people would use the same word. It also suggests that the stories these returning white deceased Aboriginal people were telling about the Bible, the person Jesus, heaven, and singing songs of that country, were all occurring in a different mythic context than one of colonization. As noted previously, this mythic world was the interpretive context for what the Christian stories meant to Aboriginal people. It shaped how they related to each other, negotiated the end to hostilities with colonists, and their curiosity about and receptivity to the Christian faith.

The younger man, Walter Arthur, also wrote about "a world above the sky where you and I must go by and by when we die" where the final judgement and separation of "good" from "bad" will occur.[18] Walter also wrote of heaven as like a house. The "good" will "go to the houses of God" and to the bad "the Devil will take you to his own country there you be tormented forever."[19] Walter mentioned biblical metaphors in only one address, that of a "trumpet call" and "singing to the Lamb that was slayne[sic] for us."[20]

The other young man, the orphan, Thomas Brune, wrote more varied descriptions "about the way that we should get to heaven"[21] with more written about heaven than of hell. He once used the metaphor of "house" as Walter did, but never used "country" like Walter and the older men did. His dislocated experience having no family or clan at Wybalenna may be an explanation. Thomas most often used biblical phrases and metaphors such as the parable of the sheep and goats.[22] He was the only one to use the word "resurrection."[23]

The "returning" motif of conversion narratives is present in Thomas' writings where heaven is a place of returning to an innocence lost. Thomas described looking forward to heaven where "I am returning unto God and to Jesus Christ.[24]" This theme of heaven as a form of "returning" is expanded to describe people's age in heaven: "there will be no end of you you will be young men in heaven."[25] Several of the older men also used this metaphor.[26]

18. Robinson, *Robinson Papers*, 103.

19. Ibid., 105, 109.

20. Ibid., 105.

21. Ibid., 67.

22. Ibid., 73.

23. Ibid., 115.

24. Ibid., 127.

25. Ibid., 134.

26. Ibid., 151–52.

Among the older Aboriginal men the most common metaphor for heaven is "God's country," "a good country," "a happy place," in contrast to hell which is the Devil's house/country, a bad place.[27] The older men used fewer biblical references, probably because they had fewer skills in English literacy. Like the younger speakers, the older men described heaven as a place where they would return to a younger version of themselves. Noemy described it as: "if you go to heaven you will not die any more—you will be there little boys Angels little girls to you old women there always young forever there."[28]

"God's country" was not at all associated with being at Wybalenna, or being displaced from their own country through colonization. The ageing, sickness and death they experience at Wybalenna are not heaven. Colonial life is not heaven. They will only be in "God's country" after they die. Like their earlier, pre-contact, stories of life after death, once they die they will be located in a place away from where they are living now. The reference to being younger versions of themselves seems to harken back to pre-contact time in their lives. The scarcity of sources makes it impossible to make more detailed comparisons between the earlier stories and the Christian addresses, but there are glimpses of similarities and new thoughts.

Equally crucial are their first language, and *creole*, interpretations. Clark's notes include occasional *creole* words used by men such as Drue-merterpunner, "we die we go to heaven good people always *crackney* in heaven Mr Clark tell me + you Jesus Christ die was crucified—He die a little one not a long one then he jump up and went to Heaven by + by he bring you and me to Heaven if you are good people."[29]

Crackney is translated "to sit"[30] and was an important aspect of a creation story told by Wooraddy, when the first person "sat down" for the first time and "said it was NYERRAE good, very good."[31]

Another of the new thoughts was an expanding sense of the human population. Noemy, like Thomas, spoke of the universal population in heaven, "white men and black men there they are always singing about God."[32] The colonizing experience seems to have contributed to an expanding sense of becoming Aboriginal beyond the clan differentiations. Christian theology seems to have encouraged a growing experience of identifying with other

27. Ibid., 39–42, 47–48.

28. Ibid., 44–45.

29. Ibid., 50–51.

30. Plomley, *A Word-List*, 391.

31. Ibid., 373.

32. Robinson, *Robinson Papers*, 51–52.

"black" people, and a universal experience of "black and white" together in heaven or hell. This idea of equality of all blacks, and of black and white before God is used by Thomas to affirm that the Aboriginal people have all they need to know: "yes my friends . . . there is black men in other countries they knows [sic] about God and Jesus Christ they don't have more instructions than what you have they can read the Bible and understand it."[33]

Likewise, Drinene links their experience of listening to the Catechist and reading the Bible themselves with that of other "black men" elsewhere. "The parson/Catechist reads it in the Bible and he tells us there are a great many black men in another country who read Gods book about Jesus Christ the son of God."[34]

These are signs of self-confidence and self-reliance at Wybalenna. They anticipate a time when Aboriginal people know they will not need colonist teachers but will continue their current emphasis on teaching each other.

There is a clear difference between the sermons by the older men, including among the clan leaders, and those of the younger 15–16 years old Walter Arthur (son of a clan leader) and Thomas Brune (an orphan with no family or clans people). Thomas has more references to biblical texts about heaven, Genesis creation, etc. Walter has very few biblical allusions, but a lot more references to creation, land, waters, stars, etc. The older men were continuing their leadership roles within their own clans by arranging marriages, funerals and other life rituals, and they were also using the opportunity to negotiate the still developing inter-clan relationships and contribute to the developing sense of a "collective" identity as "Aboriginal people," which they did not have before colonization.

The addresses express a variety of individual theological and cultural emphases, biblical and cultural knowledge, as well as linguistic, literacy and oratory skills. They also express evolving interpretations of their collective experience of dispossession and removal. The responses were provisional and improvisational. The writings and addresses contain references to remembering their lives before arriving at Wybalenna. In this regard they contain elements of collective memory.

So while the writings of Walter Arthur and Thomas Brune in the heavily supervised written English sermons in the *Flinders Island Chronicle* lend themselves to be more like "ventriloquised versions" of what Robinson wanted them to write and say, these references to first language and *creole* sermons demonstrate Aboriginal agency, interpretation and continuing worldview within the context of several years at the Settlement, and at least

33. Ibid., 77.
34. Ibid., 44–45.

a year under the regimented catechetical teaching and strong emphasis on English reading and writing.

They also demonstrate the agency of as many women, including young girls, translating and to some extent interpreting the addresses of the men to present to the catechist Robert Clark, who then also interpreted them into a form he thought acceptable to the Commandant Robinson. Each of the men, as noticed by Robinson in his journal, were involved in behaviors that strengthened pre-existing political and cultural roles within their clans and they were strengthening these roles as they adapted to the Settlement context. And it's perhaps fair to say that the women probably did likewise.

These practices indicate their continuing worldviews and indeed that they were possibly expanding, rather than surrendering, their worldviews through interaction with the Christian teachings with which they were presented. They may have been exploring the power of the new colonial religiosity as part of confirming and strengthening their existing power and roles.

A further point relevant to contemporary post-colonial discussions is the more significant nature of oral addresses by older men compared with addresses written only in English by two younger men, one of whom was the son of a clan leader and the other an orphan with no clan affiliations at Wybalenna. The addresses from Wybalenna remind us that English is but one language and that writing is but one form of communication. Most Australian Indigenous theology continues to occur locally and orally rather than in printed forms. The use of multi-media technology, particularly video, could alter the centuries old apparent captivity to paper-text, and the primacy often given to authors over orators in academic discourses. Different media will alter the dialogue and open opportunities in ways that paper and text do not, particularly in a context of multi-lingual conversations.

INDIGENOUS THEOLOGY

The Tasmanian context offers something unique, particularly when many assume Indigenous theology can only be properly done in the central desert or other remote areas, among so-called "traditional" people. The interacting cultural renaissance, language reclamation, Christian traditions, political activism, and trans-generational experiences provide multiple voices and layered narratives that can make valuable contributions to those wider dialogues.

From a multi-layered religious world, diverse Aboriginal people actively expanded their complex dialogical identities in the heterogeneous contexts of colonial life through interactions with colonist Christians and each other. Their multiple voices shaped themselves and each other and continue to be heard in the dialogues between contemporary Aboriginal Christian people and others.

WORKS CITED

Plomley, N. J. B. *Friendly Mission.* Kingsgrove: Halstead. 1966.

———. *Weep In Silence.* Hobart: Blubber Head, 1987.

———. *A Word-List of the Tasmanian Aboriginal Languages.* Launceston: Privately Published, 1976.

Reynolds, Henry. *Fate of a Free People.* Ringwood: Penguin, 1995.

Robinson, G. A. *Robinson Papers,* A7044 CY548 and A7074 CY825. Mitchell Library, 1837.

Ryan, L. *Tasmanian Aborigines: A History since 1803.* Sydney: Allen & Unwin, 2012.

Part 2

CONFRONTING READINGS

6

PILGRIMS AND POWERBROKERS

The Russian Fascination with Jerusalem

Gregory C. Jenks

FEW PLACES ON THE earth fit the criterion of "lands that bear the marks of colonization" more strongly than Palestine.[1] This phrase certainly fits with the present experience of Palestinians, as well as that "lust for Zion" which has been a hallmark of Christian claims to the land in the Byzantine period, during the Crusades, and by various European powers in the nineteenth and early twentieth centuries. As a recent collection of essays indicates,[2] there is no lack of intersection with politics, scriptures and religions in modern Palestine and Israel.

Geography destined Palestine to serve as the great global interchange; the point where traffic from Africa, Asia, and Europe converges as humanity surges back and forth like waves on the beach. Adventurers, armies, merchants, and refugees have crossed the ancient land of Palestine since time before memory. In the process they have conquered and colonized. They have killed and they have settled among the natives. They have lived in

---

1. I dedicate this chapter to the people of Gaza who were under attack from air, land, and sea when an early version was presented to a seminar in Sydney on 1 August 2014. May peace surprise us all with its early arrival, and may justice and reconciliation be the unexpected fruit of these bitter days.

2. Ateek, Duaybis, and Whitehead, eds., *Bible and the Palestine-Israel Conflict*.

houses they did not build, drawn water from cisterns they did not dig, and gathered harvests from crops they did not plant (cf. Deut 6:10–11).

They have told stories about their gods, and claimed this land was given to them—and them exclusively—by their gods, who alone are true gods. In this land some of those stories became the Bible, and from this land Torah and Gospel have been shared with other parts of the world.

For some Christians in antiquity—and specifically Byzantine Christians after the merger of Christianity with imperial Rome—Jerusalem had become the center of the world; or, at least, the center of their world. The beautiful mosaic map from Byzantine Madaba in modern Jordan reflects the position of Jerusalem in the religious imagination of the believer.

The city had not always been at the center of the world, even the religious world. When it first appears in our historical records around 1,350 years before the Common Era, Jerusalem was a small settlement in the orbit of Egypt. In Amarna Letter 287 its local ruler (Abdi-Heba) wrote to Akhenaton asking for a handful of archers to help with some local disturbances involving the 'Apiru.[3]

The fortunes of Jerusalem were to change following the capture of the city by David and its eventual transformation into Zion, "the city of the LORD of hosts, . . . the city of our God, which God establishes forever (Ps 48:8 NRSV). It is possible to sketch a series of historical periods that have especially impacted on the fortunes of the city and its inhabitants since Jerusalem became the leading city of the Israelite—and later Jewish—communities:

Judean Jerusalem	950–750 BCE
Zion, protected by YHWH	750–600 BCE
Destruction and exile	586–539 BCE
Jerusalem in the Persian period	539–330 BCE
Jerusalem in the Ptolemaic period	300–200 BCE
Jerusalem in the Seleucid period	200–140 BCE
Hasmonean Jerusalem	140–40 BCE
Herodian Jerusalem (Early Roman period)	40 BCE–66 CE
Rebellions against Roman rule	66–73, 115–17, 132–35 CE
Byzantine Jerusalem	335–638 CE
Arab Jerusalem	638–1099 & 1187–1250 CE

3. Moran, *Amarna Letters,* 327–28.

Crusader Jerusalem	1099–1187 CE
Mamluk Jerusalem	1250–1517 CE
Ottoman Jerusalem	1517–1918 CE
Colonial Jerusalem	1700s & 1800s CE
British Jerusalem	1918–1948 CE
Israeli Jerusalem	since 1948

Each of these phases needs to be studied if we are to explore the significance of Jerusalem as both a location and a metaphor in world history. That will require a much longer study than is possible in this chapter. For our purposes, I will focus on the Russian interests in Jerusalem.

THE NEW ROME

The Russian fascination with Jerusalem may not be so well known as some other parts of the story just outlined, but—as we shall see—it explains much of contemporary history, both in Russia and in Palestine. To the extent that the story is new and surprising, we must acknowledge that our own perspectives on Palestine have been shaped by Western interests. To some extent, the particular religious communities with which we have an association—even if we are not currently adherents—will also have shaped our perspectives on Jerusalem and Palestine.

As a child, my own views on Israel and Palestine were shaped by British colonial interests and the dispensationalist theology of my original faith community. I was taught to see the issues through that pair of lenses, and it was never suggested to me that Catholics might have another point of view, or the Greeks, let alone the Russians. The Russians did feature in the "premillennial" scenario of my *Scofield Reference Bible*, but only as the atheistic hordes of Gog and Magog who were expected to attack Israel from the north in a futile attempt to destroy the people of God.

Viewed from the East, rather than from London, things look different. They have looked "different" for many centuries, but the cultural gatekeepers of Western Europe and its overseas colonial derivatives have often seemed unaware of this. That myopia has real world consequences when foreign policy dealing with the "Middle East" is shaped without reference to longstanding cultural traditions, including historic Russian connections to Palestine.

On 29 May 1453, Constantinople fell to the Islamic armies led by Sultan Mehmed II, who would continue his campaign to unite Anatolia under

Ottoman rule and expand their influence into Bosnia. The city had long been isolated from its once vast territories. After centuries of conflict with Persian and then Arab enemies, the city founded by Constantine as a New Rome in 330 CE was little more than a collection of small villages encircled by a defensive wall by the time of its capture. The flight of Eastern intellectuals to Italy and other parts of Europe before and during the final siege was to be one of the factors that sparked the Renaissance in Western Europe.

The impact of the city's capture would also trigger events in the distant north. The princes of Muscovy beyond the Black Sea saw themselves in a new light. They adopted the mantle of "New Rome," seeing themselves as a third and final iteration of Rome. As Constantinople had preserved the imperial flame when Rome fell to the barbarians, so Muscovy would preserve the flame of Byzantine culture—and it would especially protect the Orthodox faithful living under Muslim rule; in the Balkans and all the way to Jerusalem.

The Russian princes not only adopted the double-headed eagle of the final Byzantine dynasty, but also gave themselves a new imperial title: Caesar, Tsar. The Russian empire positioned itself as the leader of an Orthodox crusade to protect the holy places and local Christian (Orthodox) communities. Orthodoxy was to be protected not just from the Muslims, but also from the Catholics and the Protestants who were increasingly influential in the Middle East during the eighteenth and nineteenth centuries.

Before we consider the question of Russian pilgrimage to Jerusalem, we need to turn our attention to the seventeenth century. Pilgrimage to the Holy City was always a significant financial and logistical challenge before railways and steamships ushered in the era of mass transportation. Since the pilgrims could not easily get to the holy places, what if the chief holy place was re-created inside Holy Russia herself?

Novoiyerusalimsky—the "New Jerusalem" Monastery near Moscow—was founded in 1656. It is a careful replica of Church of the Resurrection (known as the Church of the Holy Sepulcher in the Western tradition) in Jerusalem, complete with a copy of the tomb (*aedicule*) of Christ from the church in Jerusalem at that time. Since that structure was destroyed in a fire that erupted inside the Jerusalem church in 1808, this element alone makes the Russian building of great historical interest.

The building has a few Russian architectural features (most notably the domes), but represents a serious attempt to bring Jerusalem to the Russian landscape. Non-Russian monks were recruited to live alongside Russian monks, in order to reflect the universal character of the Orthodox faithful.

This description of the project from a news report of a recent conservation project nicely captures the significance of the monastery:

The monastery consists of a walled-in compound set on a hill near the town of Istra. Nikon wanted the entire world to be persuaded that Russia should be the center of the Christian faith. To achieve this goal, he set about building a replica of Jerusalem's Church of the Holy Sepulcher. This is the main structure within the monastery's whitewashed walls.[4]

The site was a focus for pilgrimage in pre-Soviet Russia, and after the railway was connected it attracted 35,000 visitors in 1913. The monastery was closed in 1918 and the buildings served as a museum during the Soviet era. The religious community of New Jerusalem Monastery was refounded in the 1990s and since 2002 the conservation of the site has been a project of the World Monument Fund. A 2009 presidential decree on restoration promised significant federal Russian funding, and in 2010 the site received 300,000 visitors. It is clear that the site continues to play an influential role in the public imagination of the Russian state. As then President Medvedev said when announcing federal funding for the project:

> "The New Jerusalem Monastery is unparalleled among the monuments of human history," Medvedev said. "It is deservedly regarded as a cultural phenomenon and it is the only successful attempt to produce an exact copy of the Holy Land," the president noted, adding, "By restoring our great spiritual centres, we are contributing to the revival of our roots and our values."[5]

PILGRIMS

Impressive at it was, the local reflection of Palestine at the New Jerusalem Monastery did not divert the masses of Russian pilgrims who made their way to Palestine as the transportation facilities improved. From peasant to Tsar, there was a deep attachment to Palestine and its holy city, Jerusalem. Shiploads of Russian pilgrims would cross the Black Sea on their way to Jerusalem, and for many of them it seems to have been an intensely personal journey. Montefiore describes the attachment in these terms: "every Russian believed that the pilgrimage to Jerusalem was an essential part of the preparation for death and salvation. As the poet Alexander Pushkin, the personification of Russia's soul, expressed this in 1836 . . . 'Is not Jerusalem the cradle of us all?'"[6]

4. "New Jerusalem Monastery to Be Restored."
5. Medvedev, "Speech to Trustees of the Foundation."
6. Montefiore, *Jerusalem*, 408.

Stephen Graham was a British adventurer and travel writer who travelled with a group of Russian pilgrims from Constantinople to Jerusalem in
February 1912. He travelled incognito, aided by his excellent Russian and
his rustic clothing, and he later published an account of his experiences:
With the Russian Pilgrims to Jerusalem.[7]

Graham's own photographs brought his prose to life for his readers,
but the prose was already quite vivid as can be seen in this description of a
renewal of baptism vows in the Jordan River:

> In a great miscellaneous crowd the peasants began to undress
> and to step into their white shrouds, the women into long robes
> like nightdresses, the men into full white shirts and pantaloons.
> Those who came unprepared stood quite naked on the banks.
> Then the priest when he had given the pilgrims time to prepare,
> began taking the service for the sanctification of the water. The
> ikons and the cross were ranged around a wooden platform over
> the water.[8]

Graham's account of the Easter celebrations at the Russian Cathedral in Jerusalem is equally vivid:

> Then at one on the morning we passed . . . into the Russian ca-
> thedral, now joyously illuminated with coloured lights, and we
> heard the service in familiar church Slavonic. And we all kissed
> one another again. What embracing and kissing there were this
> night; smacking of hearty lips and tangling of beards and whis-
> kers! The Russian men kiss one another with far more heartiness
> than they kiss their women. In the hostelry I watched a couple
> of ecstatical old greybeards who grasped one another tightly by
> the shoulders, and kissed at least a score of times, and wouldn't
> leave off.[9]

This devotion captured on film and described in purple prose around
one hundred years ago can still be witnessed in Jerusalem. Women from
across the Orthodox world—including Russia—are often to be seen blessing their own shrouds at the stone of anointing in the Church of the Holy
Sepulcher. Anecdotes circulating in Jerusalem today, suggest that a high
percentage of these Orthodox women die within twelve months of their

7. Graham, *With the Russian Pilgrims to Jerusalem*. See also the recent biography
of Stephen Graham by Michael Hughes, *Beyond Holy Russia*.

8. Graham, *With the Russian Pilgrims*, cited in Michael Hughes, *Beyond Holy
Russia*, 72.

9. Graham, *With the Russian Pilgrims*, 296, cited in Hughes, *Beyond Holy Russia*,
73.

pilgrimage to Jerusalem and the preparation of the shrouds for their own burial. This fits with Stephen Graham's description of the Russian pilgrims cited by Montefiore:

> Russian peasants, many of them women, often walked all the way from their villages southwards to Odessa for the voyage to Zion. . . . They brought their death shrouds and felt . . . 'that when they have been to Jerusalem, the serious occupations of their life are all ended. For the peasant goes to Jerusalem to *die* in a certain way in Russia—just as the whole concern of the Protestant centres around *life*.'[10]

We have already seen the description of the 1912 pilgrims by Stephen Graham. Montefiore describes the Russian presence towards the end of the nineteenth century as follows: "In Jerusalem, the streets glittered with the gold braid and shoulderboards of Russian uniforms, worn by princes and generals, while teeming with the sheepskins and smocks of thousands of peasant pilgrims, all encouraged by Nicholas who also despatched an ecclesiastical mission to complete with the other Europeans."[11] Long before Stephen Graham took his camera on pilgrimage from Russia to Palestine, we have precious archival images that illustrate and confirm the conspicuous presence of the Russian pilgrims in and around Jerusalem.

One such image is a photograph from the collection at the Russian Museum and Park Complex in Jericho that was opened in 2011 by Russian President Medvedev.[12] It shows a crowd of Russian pilgrims in front of the Dome of the Rock, and reflects a more relaxed state of affairs than prevails at the Haram as-Sharif these days.

A second photograph is from the Oregon State University collection. The image description, from an historic lecture booklet, reads:

> This picture is taken along the Jericho road looking west toward Jerusalem. The subject of the picture "Pilgrims" is one that has its place in all histories of religion. The present motley crowd is made up of a number of nationalities, but the majority are Russians. These have already been to the Jordon (sic) at their reputed places of the baptism of Jesus, and are now returning to the Holy City to partake in the festivities around the Holy Sepulchre which takes place at Easter.[13]

10. Montefiore, *Jerusalem*, 441.

11. Ibid., 409.

12. https://jacksdaily.files.wordpress.com/2013/10/img_9148.jpg.

13. http://commons.wikimedia.org/wiki/File:Russian_Pilgrims_Returning_from_the_Jordon.jpg.

POWERBROKERS

A convenient point to begin this section of our discussion is provided by Napoleon's military campaigns in Egypt and Palestine (1798/99). That unsuccessful military adventure was a dramatic turn in the confrontation between England and France at the time, and serves as a vivid illustration of the competition between European powers for influence in the Eastern Mediterranean. That competition in turn provides the larger context for Russian attempts to increase its own capacities to influence events in Palestine. For a detailed study of Russian interests in Palestine see the 1963 monograph by Stravou.[14] While the title indicates a focus on events between 1882 and 1914, the book includes a detailed discussion of earlier historical developments.

In the early decades of the nineteenth century we find moves by Britain, France, Germany and Russia to establish footholds in Palestine. Despite the occasional appeal to religious considerations, the competition between European powers was not primarily about religion, but more about trade routes—and access to oil supplies. The opening of the Suez Canal in 1869 was a major strategic development that greatly benefited British interests in the Mediterranean as well as other locations "East of Suez."

The joint Anglo-Prussian Bishopric created with the arrival of Bishop Michael Solomon Alexander on *HMS Invincible* in 1841 was driven largely by English and German concerns at French and Russian influence mediated via the Roman Catholic and Orthodox religious institutions in Palestine. Likewise, the establishment of the Palestine Exploration Fund in 1865 was as much about clandestine collection of intelligence on this strategic portion of the Ottoman Empire as it was about exploration of the Holy Land.

In 1844, before a formal Russian presence was established in Jerusalem, the British consul in the city observed with alarm the large number of Russians in the city at Easter time:

> The British consul warned London that 'the Russians could in one night during Easter arm 10,000 pilgrims within the walls of Jerusalem' and seize the city. Meanwhile the French pursued their own mission to protect the Catholics. 'Jerusalem', reports Consul Finn in 1844, 'is now a central point of interest to France and Russia.'[15]

Stravou summarizes the situation at the beginning of the nineteenth century as follows:

14. Stavrou, *Russian Interests in Palestine*.
15. Montefiore, *Jerusalem*, 409.

Until the end of the seventeenth century, one may speak of the purely religious interest of Russian rulers in the subjugated Christians. By the end of the eighteenth century, the Tsars had come to realize the political possibilities of championing Orthodoxy and protecting the Christians. Constantinople, the Holy Places, salvation of the human race—all these could come, perhaps, through the Russian Christ. This idea reached its highest expression during the second half of the nineteenth century, when political and economic necessities forced Russia's close attention to the Black Sea and the Straits.[16]

The Crimea War erupted in 1853. The three-year conflict was sparked by religious tensions in Bethlehem, but it was fueled by this long-running religious and national competition between Russia and the western powers of England and France.

The spark was the theft of the silver star from the grotto under the Church of the Nativity on 1 October 1847. The star had been a gift from (Catholic) France in the 1700s, and the theft was widely seen as an act by Orthodox clergy. Fights broke out between Catholic and Orthodox priests. So far there was nothing unusual about these ugly events, and nothing of international significance.

France claimed the right to replace the star (and also to repair the roof of the Holy Sepulcher in Jerusalem). Russia objected to this offer and asserted its traditional rights as protector of the Orthodox. The sultan was caught between opposing European powers: Russia to the North, and France to the West. Nicholas I of Russia saw an opportunity to expand Russian influence as Ottoman power declined. France and Britain were opposed to anything that would give Russia a greater influence over the Middle East.

France and England declared war on Russia on 28 March 1853, following the Russian invasion of Ottoman territory in the Balkans. There were 750,000 deaths among combatants, and the war ended in a major defeat for Russia. The Ottoman Empire was granted a brief reprieve from Russian encroachments due to the intervention by the English and French, who naturally consolidated their influence and power in the Middle East.

We get some idea of the rising European influence in the region from the list of European dignitaries visiting Jerusalem in the final decades of the nineteenth century. The Duke of Brabant (and future King Leopold II of Belgium) arrived in March 1855 and was the first European allowed to visit the Haram as-Sharif. He was followed just three months later by Archduke Maximillian, heir to the Habsburg Empire and a future Emperor of

16. Stavrou, *Russian Interests in Palestine*, 23.

Mexico. Prince Edward (the future Edward VII of England) visited Jerusa-
lem in 1862. His sons, Prince Albert Victor and Prince George (the future
King George V), followed in their father's footsteps in 1882. Grand Duke
Sergei Alexandrovich, the brother of Tsar Alexander III—with his consort,
Elizabeth Feodorovna, a German-born granddaughter of Queen Victoria—
visited Jerusalem for the consecration of the Convent of Mary Magdalene
in 1888. Finally, Kaiser Wilhelm II of Germany visited for several weeks in
October and November 1898.

After initially seeking to support the local Greek Orthodox clergy
in the face of incursions by Western Catholic and Protestant missions,
the Russians established their own ecclesiastical mission in Jerusalem. As
Vovchenko has shown,[17] one of the strategies adopted by the Russians as
they despaired of their traditional collaboration with the Greek Orthodox
clergy was to promote a sense of Arab nationalism. This created further
tensions with the Greeks who resented Russian promotion of nationalist
aspirations among the Orthodox Arabs.

In 1847 the Russians had made an unsuccessful attempt to establish an
ecclesiastical mission, without proper diplomatic approval, prior to Crime-
an War. This project was naturally cut short by the outbreak of the war, and
it was not until 1857 that the mission could return to Jerusalem—this time
with Ottoman recognition.[18] Stravou sums up the Russian strategy following its defeat in the Crimea War:

> The Peace of Paris of 1856 deprived Russia, among other things,
> of her monopoly as protector of Christians in the Ottoman
> Empire. The military defeat in the Crimea was a severe blow to
> Russian prestige in the Orthodox East. It was only natural that
> Russia would devise new methods of diplomacy to maintain her
> influence in the Ottoman Empire in accord with her traditional
> aspiration southward through the Black Sea. In this new phase
> of Russian diplomacy two procedures would be of use: estab-
> lishment of a new Russian Ecclesiastical Mission in Jerusalem,
> and building of a Russian merchant navy in the Black Sea . . .
> As for the second Russian Ecclesiastical Mission to Jerusalem, it
> was purely political in origin and purpose.[19]

The official task of these missions was organizing pilgrimages from
Russia as well as charitable and educational work among the Orthodox
Arabs. Between 1860 and 1864 the mission was able to establish a Russian

17. Vovchenko, "Creating Arab Nationalism?"

18. See the detailed discussion in Stavrou, *Russian Interests in Palestine*, ch. 2.

19. Ibid., 39–40.

Compound in Jerusalem on a prominent site opposite the Jaffa Gate. Here they established offices for the mission, the Russian consulate, a hospital, and pilgrim hostels with accommodation for 2,000 people. In time the compound would also include the Holy Trinity Cathedral, Jerusalem.

Meanwhile events in Russia would lead to an upsurge in anti-Semitism and trigger an exodus of Jews from Russia. Tsar Alexander II was assassinated in 1881, and Jews were suspected of involvement. This led to a series of anti-Jewish pogroms, and eventually the promulgation of the highly anti-Semitic "May Laws" of 1882. Between 1888 and 1914 two million Jews left Russia. While the vast majority of them went to the USA, a significant minority went to Palestine. As a result, by 1890 Jews comprised 25,000 of a total Jerusalem population of 40,000 people. For the first time since the destruction of the temple in 70 CE, Jews were a majority in Jerusalem.

The establishment of the Imperial Orthodox Palestine Society by Tsar Alexander III on 8 May 1882 took place in this context of internal anti-Semitism and international competition for influence in Palestine. Alexander III appointed his brother, Grand Duke Sergei, as president. The Imperial Orthodox Palestine Society especially encouraged pilgrimage to Jerusalem, but it also aimed to provide a "national character" for Russian activities in Palestine similar to the many Catholic and Protestant societies then active in the Holy Land.[20] A key objective for the Society was to promote "Autocracy and Orthodoxy" in order to save Holy Russia. As already noted, Sergei and his wife, Elizabeth, visited Jerusalem in 1888 for the consecration of Convent of Mary Magdalene on the Mount of Olives.

The Society acquired property throughout Palestine and launched an ambitious program of "good works" as described in detail by Stravou.[21] Stravou comments on the achievements in the first few years of its work:

> The first seven years were in many respects the most colorful of the Society's thirty-two years of active existence . . . As an organization it grew at an amazing speed, spreading its reputation into the far corners of the Russian Empire. In research and publication about the Holy Places, it soon ranked with the leading Western European Palestine societies. The pilgrims received the Society's immediate attention, and by 1889 annual pilgrimages more than tripled. Even in the most delicate issue of all, support for Orthodoxy in the Holy land, the Society by its untiring efforts prepared the ground for a future fruitful policy.[22]

20. See ibid., 62–63.
21. Ibid., see especially chs. 4 to 8.
22. Ibid., 88.

One tangible expression of the Society's success was its acquisition of properties across Palestine. The Imperial Orthodox Palestine Society purchased property in Hebron at the Oak of Mamre, at the summit of Mount of Olives, in Jaffa with the tomb of Tabitha, gardens in Jericho, a plot of land in Tiberias on the shores of the Sea of Galilee, the founding of the Convent at Ein-Karem, and a large site in Nazareth.

Russian activity in and around Nazareth was especially successful, and also serves as a case study for the wider program of the Imperial Orthodox Palestine Society. A prominent site located between the Greek Orthodox Church at Mary's Well and the Franciscan compound was acquired in the late 1800s. Here a substantial building (known locally as the "Moskubiyeh") was erected 1904 with accommodation for 1,000 pilgrims. The building also included a school, a pharmacy, and a hospital.

Russian activity in Nazareth took advantage of the large Orthodox population and had some success in reducing the loss of adherents to Western missionaries. Indeed the Russian schools were so successful that providing sufficient teachers to staff them became a challenge that was eventually addressed by the establishment of the Nazareth Teachers Training School.[23] The case of the Nazareth school for girls is indicative of both the strategy and its success.

> The Nazareth school for girls was a great success. It opened officially on October 3, 1885 with twenty-seven students from twelve to seventeen years of age. Nazareth was the choice for the schools, because of its strategic location to other schools of the Society and because of the opportunity to compete with other foreign mission schools there. The Russian school for girls grew at an amazing speed. A month after opening, enrollment rose from twenty-seven to ninety, and the following month it reached 120. This was largely the result of the zeal of the teachers, led by a Russian lady, Maria Semenovna, who had special pedagogical training in Moscow. Assisted by two native teachers from Beirut, the Russian teacher upset the enrolment of missionary schools in Nazareth. By the end of the first academic year, the enrollment was 283 students, and she wrote to the Society that the English schools there could not compete and had closed down, the teacher leaving Nazareth.[24]

All this was to change with the outbreak of World War I and then the revolution of October 1917. Russian pilgrimage to Palestine stopped and

23. Ibid., 113–14.
24. Ibid., 112–13.

the Russian institutions in the Holy Land were divided between those loyal to Moscow and those associated with the Russian Church in Exile. In the case of Nazareth, the Moskubiyeh became an administration building for the British Mandate authorities and later for Israeli civil authorities. Today it is a police station, with a post office in one corner.

Amin Saleem Jarjura (1886–1975) is a good example of the impact of the Russian presence on the local population. He was born in Nazareth on 10 November 1886 and educated at the Russian School, where he would later serve as a teacher. According to the website of the Knesset in Jerusalem,[25] Jarjura served in the Ottoman army during WW1 although his family do not have any memory of that military service. He studied Law in Jerusalem, and taught at El-Rashidia College in Jerusalem between 1922 and 1926. After serving as a lawyer in Haifa and Nazareth he was elected as an Arabic Member of the first Knesset (1949/1951) and served on a number of parliamentary committees. After losing his seat in the Knesset in 1951 he secured election as Mayor of Nazareth, serving in that role from 1954 to 1959. He died in Nazareth on 20 August 1975. As a child he spoke fluent Russian as well as his native Arabic. As the decades passed he will have acquired fluency in English and later in Hebrew. One of his granddaughters, Suhair Nusair, is my Arabic teacher.

REVIVAL OF RUSSIAN INTERESTS IN JERUSALEM

Alain Gresh has argued that Russia is poised to exercise new influence in the Middle East, an area where—as we have seen already—it has strong historical links.[26] Gresh notes some of the factors that give Russia a "strong hand" to play in this region: Russia is a local player with a shared common interests on many issues, Russia is now freed from its former ideological alliances that constrained it as late as the 1980s, Russia is no longer seen as a "purveyor of Revolution and Atheism," there is a large Russian immigrant population within Israel (including senior members of the current government), and Russia has a cadre of former diplomats and military advisors with excellent Arabic skills and extensive networks of contacts. Finally, like Europe, Russia is benefiting from rising anti-American attitudes in the Middle East. While this analysis was published in 1998, it still seems to ring true with current dynamics in the region.

In a more recent discussion, Yakob Rabkin has compared the different ways in which three non-Western nuclear powers (Russia, China and

25. www.knesset.gov.il/mk/eng/mk_eng.asp?mk_individual_id_t=345.

26. Gresh, "Russia's Return to the Middle East."

India) relate to the Middle East in general and the Israel-Palestine conflict in particular.[27] Rabkin notes the significant proportion of Russians in Israel (almost 25% of the non-Arab population) and the attention that each government has invested in the relationship since diplomatic relations were resumed only in 1991 after having been terminated following the 1967 war. Rabkin notes that one unique feature of the Russia-Israel relationship is the broad demographic in each country that values the relationship.[28]

Meanwhile, both Russia and Israel are quietly working to establish close links of a kind Russia has not enjoyed in Jerusalem for 100 years. In Jerusalem, the Russian Compound is being returned to Russia as part of a wider set of actions to normalize relations and restore pre-1948 property rights. Indeed, the Imperial Orthodox Palestine Society still operates. It is now led by Sergei Stepashin, a former Russian prime minister and security-police general. This is not as glamorous as a grand duke, but he is still a high-ranking official with good connections within the Russian elite. Stepashin is quoted in *The Economist* as offering this frank assessment of the geopolitical stake: "A Russian flag in the center of Jerusalem, in such close proximity to the Holy Sepulchre, is priceless."[29]

The new image of Vladimir Putin, as an Orthodox champion in the struggle against Western dominance may come as a shock to many in the West, but it resonates with historical Russian interests in the region. Indeed it has deep roots in Russia's own sense of herself. As in ancient Rome so in its aspiring successor, we see the power of religion to act as social glue for an empire that is both multi-ethnic and multifaith. Politics, scriptures and religion intersect in the Middle East, and most especially in Palestine, as Melik Kaylan observes with not a little discomfort.

> Look at the Middle East now. Putin and Assad have maneuvered to become the explicit protectors of Eastern Christianity *in situ*. Moscow is back as their shield and Orthodoxy's patron. He didn't sidle up to the Russian church in recent years purely for domestic reasons. He knew the unforgotten historical alignments just below the surface from Moscow out through the Balkans, through the Caucasus, past Turkey to the Holy Land.[30]

27. Rabkin, "Russia, China and India and the Israel-Palestine Conflict."

28. Interestingly, a similar point was made in an opinion piece published just as this chapter was being finished. See Basharat, "Israel's Russian-Arab Bond."

29. "Where Piety Meets Power."

30. Kaylan, "We Abandon Mideast Christians."

WORKS CITED

Ateek, Naim, Cedar Duaybis, and Tina Whitehead, eds. *The Bible and the Palestine-Israel Conflict*. Jerusalem: Sabeel, 2014.

Basharat, Oudeh. "Israel's Russian-Arab Bond: Stronger Than the Politics of Hatred." *Haaretz*, 29 December 2014.

Graham, Stephen. *With the Russian Pilgrims to Jerusalem*. London: Macmillan, 1913.

Gresh, Alain. "Russia's Return to the Middle East." *Journal of Palestine Studies* 28.1 (1998) 67–77.

Hughes, Michael. *Beyond Holy Russia: The Life and Times of Stephen Graham*. Cambridge: Open Book, 2014.

Israel Knesset. "Amin-Salim Jarjora." http://www.knesset.gov.il/mk/eng/mk_eng.asp? mk_individual_id_t=345.

Kaylan, Melik. "We Abandon Mideast Christians: They Fall Prey to Putin's Charms." *Forbes*, 9 May 2014.

Medvedev, Dmitry Anatolyevich. "Speech to Trustees of the Foundation for Restoring the Resurrection New Jerusalem Monastery." *Moscow Top News*, 20 Oct. 2008.

Montefiore, Simon Sebag. *Jerusalem: The Biography*. London: Phoenix, 2012.

Moran, William L. *The Amarna Letters*. Baltimore: Johns Hopkins University Press, 1992.

"New Jerusalem Monastery to Be Restored." http://www.moscowtopnews.com/ ?area=postView&id=734—cut.

Rabkin, Yacov M. "Russia, China and India and the Israel–Palestine Conflict." *Holy Land Studies* 12.1 (2013) 9–24.

Stavrou, Theofanis George. *Russian Interests in Palestine, 1882–1914: A Study of Religious and Educational Enterprise*. Thessaloniki: Institute for Balkan Studies, 1963.

Vovchenko, Denis. "Creating Arab Nationalism? Russia and Greece in Ottoman Syria and Palestine (1840–1909)." *Middle Eastern Studies* 49.6 (2013) 901–18.

"Where Piety Meets Power." *The Economist*, 17 December 2009

7

OF POSTCOLONIAL ISLAM

Garry W. Trompf

OVER TWENTY YEARS AGO, at a University of Sydney conference, I had occasion to be lecturing on Islam with theologian Rev. Dr. Alan Loy and Arabist Dr. Ahmad Shboul.[1] I highlighted that most of the Islamic world had fallen under Western domination, particularly between the World Wars. I was reminded that in my schoolboy atlas (dated 1940) lay a point of great excitement that British red was splashed around the globe, including Palestine-Transjordan, Bahrain, Qatar and Kuwait (Protectorates), Aden (almost all a Protectorate, now part of Yemen), British Somaliland, Zanzibar and Anglo-Egyptian Sudan, Malaya and Brunei (also a Protectorate), with Egypt and Iraq not long before having their times of Great Britain's aegis. An as yet undivided India (including Kashmir) contained a vast Muslim population under the British *Raj*. As if in a sports competition, yellow for France came second, across northwestern Africa and over to Lebanon, Syria and French Somalia; Italy third, with Libya, Eritrea (50% Muslim), Italian Somaliland, and also Albania (nearly 69%); and Holland looking fourth, when Indonesia—albeit with the largest Muslim populace of all!—was

---

1. Alan Loy was a leading figure in the establishment of the United Theological College at North Parramatta, Sydney, which was to become a component of Charles Sturt University; see Barnes, *Doing Theology in Sydney*, 21–23, 47–59. Ahmad Shboul became Associate Professor in Arabic and Islamic Studies and was the longest stand-ing teacher of Islamics in the history of the University of Sydney; see Shboul, "Ahmad Shboul: Biography."

counted.[2] The main conclusion of my lecture was that a great religious tradition—the one that expanded so spectacularly across the Afro-Asian world in the name of Allah—had been humiliated. It confirmed in me that I was working at something highly significant when, after our respective lectures, Dr. Shboul came up to me and asked: "Why haven't Western scholars acknowledged this fact?" and I realized how easily my own youthful chauvinism could have translated into a kind retarded imperialist myopia.

On the way to giving the lecture on which this chapter is based, I chanced upon a postgraduate student from Gaza, one I was helping, and told him of my topic. "And what do you think?" was his immediate reaction, "Is Islam colonialist?" Of course I knew immediately that his reaction was issuing from a very special context, from a very confined Arabo-Islamic space blocked in by "neo-colonial" Israel. I was tempted to be provocative, to remind him of the Muslim blind spot—"the missing piece: Islamic imperialism"—the Arab takeover of North African, Eurasian and Iberian lands in that massive early mediaeval change of the world's religio-political configuration in over little more than a century (630–750).[3] Instead I simply spoke to the Palestinian situation: "Was not the Ottoman empire colonialist? So that the Arabs wanted to throw off unwanted Muslim overlords during the First World War?"[4] And it is in this and other military efforts at dismantling the Ottoman Empire that the historical analysis of this paper properly begins.

When it comes to the complete collapse of the Ottomans, it did not just involve letting in European powers to have Mandate control over territories previously held by the Turks (with one set of colonial arrangements replacing a former one, through the Treaties of Versailles and Sèvres),[5] but also of generating a crisis in what remained of Turkey itself. It was within Turkey's internal crisis conditions that highly symbolic religious institutions of Islam came to be very seriously disturbed, and finalizing the disintegration of an empire that once ruled from near Vienna to Baghdad and the Yemen, and across northern Africa as well, meant the terrible loss of a huge entity that had been keeping a sense of Islamic unity alive. Indeed, in Is-

2. Brodie, ed., *Collins Australian Clear School Atlas,* esp. 2–3.

3. Karsdh, "Missing Piece," ch. 7.

4. For help on the Ottomans in Europe see van Meurs, "Development of an Administrative Class in South-East Europe"; and on the Levant, see Karpat, *Studies on Turkish Politics and Society,* pt. 2; and for attempts in sub-Saharan Africa, see the recent symposium organized by Cornell University's Mostafa Minawi, " 'Other' Colonialism"; David Murphy, *Arab Revolt 1916–18.*

5. League of Nations treaties: Versailles (1919), arts. 22, 434; Sèvres (1920), and Mandate Papers (1922), class A.

tanbul (conquered, fable city of Byzantine Constantinople) the Ottoman
Sultan had been guardian of the most crucial sacred offices of mainstream
(or Sunni) Islam; namely, the Caliphate, which he embodied in himself; the
Head of the highest Religious Authority (Turk. *Seyüislam*); the titular head
of the Islamic school system (*mederese*); and the Sunni Religious Brotherhoods (*tarikat*). But the last Sultan (Mehmed VI), unfortunately allied to
the losers in the Great War, suffered the same sort of ignominy faced by the
last German Kaisers (of Germany and Austria-Hungary). Indeed Turkey
was at the forefront of modernization and secularization among Muslim
countries when, from 1923, under the revolution led by heady nationalist
Mustafa Kemal Ataturk, a new Republic of Turkey was declared. The Sultan
was deposed, the Caliphate could not long continue, the religious school
system was replaced by state one, *Shari'a* law giving way to Western-style
legal codification, and the Brotherhoods driven underground. Public affairs
were to be carried on in Latin not Arabic script, using the Western solar not
traditional lunar calendar, meters not cubits, and with Sunday as a public
holiday. They were all moves striking at the heart of a long-inured "Muslim way"; borne out of internal fractures in the Islam's very power-center,
where former ideologues had been protesting that nationalism was foreign
to the true religion, and would never concede—because of the unity their
empire conveyed—that the Ottomans were ever colonialist like the Europeans. Globally speaking, now that the Cold War is basically behind us, we
might say that this imperial collapse and these portentous reactions, mark
the beginning of the "contemporary world" as it has eventually emerged for
all of us.[6]

Emergent modern Turkey, then, looked to be releasing itself from
complicity with empire yet at the same time from Islam as an established
religion (though not from Islam itself). It might seem to have been the
first Muslim country to have entered the socio-political condition of "postcolonial Islam." And are we not to be relieved that the Muslim world more
generally successfully negotiated its way through the Ottoman tragedy and
European interference and recovered with a flurry of new nationhoods?
Looking at the Near and Middle East, with North Africa, *inter alia* political independence arrived for Egypt (in 1922, but only relatively speaking),
Iraq (1932), Lebanon (1943), Trans-Jordan (1946), Pakistan (1947), Libya
(1951), Tunisia and Sudan (1956), Syria (1958, after a 25-year period),
Morocco (1959), Somalia (1960), Kuwait (1961), Algeria (1962, after war

---

6. For background, e.g., Lord Patrick Kinross, *Atatürk*; Toprak, "Religious Right,"
630–31. Please note many Muslim authorities postings against nationalism (as *haram*
or contrary to Islam), and that debate in which Arab intellectuals attack the Ottomans'
imperialism while others (esp. Turks) deny they were colonialist.

with France), Bahrain and Qatar (1971), Western Sahara (1976), the Central Asian states (1991), Eritrea (1993), Palestine (2014, at least holding permanent UN-observer status), with Saudi Arabia freed from outside interferences in 1926 and 1970 respectively and Afghanistan still standing undefeated.[7] Does not this altogether constitute an enormous statement of post-colonial Islam, and sufficient redemption from a temporary humiliation?

Appearances are deceptive, however, not only because the psychological scar of Allah's Dar al-Islam (the house or territories of Islam) having been subordinated at all, but also because of serious sacrifices made to "the Islamic way" through "modern (Western-dominated) politics." Of course it is not as if Muslim forces had never experienced worrying territorial losses to Western forces before the fall of the Ottoman Empire: from the expulsion in Iberia, the liberation of Ethiopia, to the repulsions from eastern Austria, Hungary and Transylvania in the "high" and "later" Renaissance, lands were lost to Allah that never should have been, for He promises *falah* (success) unless believers are defective, and, as Bernard Lewis has argued, troubles eventually mounted for the Ottomans in North Africa (especially after Napoleon's Egyptian campaign) and in Europe (during nineteenth-century conflicts, especially with Russia). The Turkish empire had become "the sick man of Europe," and in Lewis's terms there had been a long preliminary decline to Islam's first truly great "crisis," the diminishment which we have just been addressing.[8] Ever since bring "brought low," and in spite of the decolonization process, how many Muslim authors wrote addressing the question: what has brought about Islam's decline? Indeed, not a few were to say of the decay, however multi-layered, that it above all involved "moral degeneration," "loss of dynamism," a "rise of dogmatism and rigidity," before any "decline in intellectual scientific activity," "decline of agriculture," "exhaustion of mines," or "internal revolts and disunity."[9]

Surely, however, the Islamic world experienced an extraordinary resurgence in the post-War period, emblematized politically by Egypt's President Abdel Nasser's nationalization of the Suez Canal in 1956, the formation of the Middle Eastern-dominated organization for coordinating the petroleum market (OPEC) in 1960, the successful Turkish invasion of Cyprus in 1974, and speedy modernization, urbanization and engagement *vis-à-vis* the Western world? During the Cold War various Islamic states seemed able

7. For guidance, see Lapidus, *History of Muslim Societies*, pt. 3; cf. Feldman, *Fall and Rise of the Islamic State*.

8. Thus Lewis, *What Went Wrong?*; C. Stavrianos, ed., *Ottoman Empire*; Bentley and Ziegler, *Traditions and Encounters*, chs. 28, 30, 33.

9. Quoting here Mikailu's review of Chapra's *Future of Economics* as highly indicative.

to play off the two super-powers to their own advantage. Why, when it came to cultural-religious affairs, were there not great Muslim intellectuals and their schools—Iqbal, Nursi, Maudoodi, Taha, etc.—enriching Muslim life and in learned conversation with Western currents of learning? Were there not democratic energies burgeoning, as if a new "Spring" of cultural freedoms was also in the air? Certainly, by the turn of the millennium, leaders in the West might be gratified that Islamic nations were "developing," readier to do business in the "international market-place," and becoming members of the "global village." But dissatisfactions were constantly lurking, as if Islam had rebounded only to enter a "second crisis." There was always the fear of mimicking and of losing religious integrity by being trapped under the weight of Western commercial hegemony and tastes.[10] In some not atypical academic, yet "emic" or insider Muslim accounts, Islam was still in "general decay." Macroscopically,

> the political fall of the Muslims was conditioned by factors both internal and external. As the external factors were almost in all cases due to interferences of Europeans, so the internal factors in almost all cases were due to the intellectual, moral and spiritual bankruptcy of Muslims themselves. Thus, primarily the Muslims were responsible for their decadence.[11]

But because they were no longer "in the vanguard of knowledge," they lapsed into irrational and authoritarian solutions.[12] For all the excitements of modernity, did not the disappointments keep mounting? No curtailing of Israel, no real solution in strife-torn Lebanon, indeed no end to further external interference and/or internal division in virtually every "Muslim land."

As is well known, resurgence came from unexpected quarters. Not from within the context of the Sunni majority but out of the Shi'a minority—with the 1979 Iranian Revolution. No one can gainsay the importance of this event for the whole Islamic world, because it is a distinctly religious reaction to a global secularizing tendency that looked to be sucking all collective religious vitality down its drain. Month by month, the champion of the Revolution, the Ayatollah Mostavi Khomeini, having dramatically returned from exile in Paris like Lenin from Zurich, whittled off the threatening remnants of the Shah Reza Pahlavi's regime and judiciary, closed down

---

10. Sayyid, "Empire, Islam, and the Postcolonial," 129–31 on "double decolonization"; cf. Davutoglu, *Civilizational Transformation,* 26 et passim.

11. Tariq, "Ideological Background of Rationality in Islam," 51.

12. Ibid. For a related perspective with prospectus, cf. Sillah, "Islamic Futures after the Desert Storm," 20; cf. pro-Israeli Melbourne academic theologian Durie, "Islam's Second Crisis." See also Allawi, *Crisis of Islamic Civilization,* esp. chs. 7, 10–11.

the organizations and outlets of the leftists (who had initially supported the Revolution), and inaugurated a dramatic social Puritanism, with the *hijab* (headscarves) to be compulsorily worn in public by women, wine bottles piled up and smashed in the streets, and strict Shari'a punishments reinstituted (such as death by stoning for adulterers).[13] The leadership's political rhetoric was one of total resistance against the West, with Khomeini labelling The United States as "the Great Satan"; and national political arrangements took on a sharply de-secularizing aspect. The constitution of new Islamic Republic of Iran mirrored Plato's ideal Republic—which was understandable considering the impact of Platonic philosophy on the Shi'a theologies of "higher knowledge" (*'irfan* or *gnosis*)—with the final earthly authorities being the body of high-clerical jurisprudential Guardians, who could veto any legislation issued by the Parliament or even by the top Ayatollah).[14] And the effects were electrifying across Islam, bringing Sunni and Shi'a thinkers and activists into surprising and lively concord for half a decade or more. Iran set a tone for revolutionary religious change to restore Islam in an un-contaminated form.

As is well known, however, the amicableness wore thin, because it did not translate into Persian-Arab alliances. First, it immediately destroyed the British-initiated 1955 Baghdad Pact (or Middle East Treaty Organization) between Britain, Iran, Iraq, Pakistan and Turkey. Then followed the grueling Iraqi-Iranian war (1980–88), both sides declaring *jihad* (sacred war that should not apply between Muslim brothers), and by 1992 the newly independent secular (Sunni-majority) Azerbaijan, a key neighbor, declared against political Islam and favored relations and weapons deals with Israel rather than Iran (whose government was in any case friendlier with nearby Christian Armenia). Fears steadily grew about the Ayatollah "Khomeini's covert dream" to foster a Shi'a arc from Iran, via majority Shi'ite Iraq and Asad's (minority-Shi'a-run) Syria, over to the Pro-Iranian Hezbollah-dominated parts of eastern Lebanon (on Israel's borders). These fears intensified when the United States toppled Saddam Hussein and forced a "confessionalist democracy" on Iraq in 2003, i.e., a government inevitably dominated by the country's Shi'ite majority (instead of being run more through tribal alliances). Sunni-Shi'a tensions reached their greatest intensity in Iraq and in consequence have badly affected relations between the two great divisions of Islam for the last decade.[15]

13. Bazzi, "Relationship between Mysticism and Politics."

14. For initial guidance, Keddie, *Religion and Politics in Iran.*

15. Esp. Hero, *Longest War;* Schaffer, *Borders and Brethren,* chs. 4–5 (noting that the Azerbaijani cultural complex reaches into Iran, making up a western province that spawns many of the nation's leaders, who are of course Shi'ite!); Trompf, "Of Shi'a

By the turn into the third Christian millennium most of the energies for a resurgent, religiously purified Islam world devolved on the prospects of the Muslim Brotherhood, a fast-growing Sunni network in the Near (as against strictly Middle) East and North Africa.[16] The Brotherhood was founded in Egypt as early as 1928, and today, with over 2,000 branches in the country and proffering the first democratically elected Presidential candidate (Mohammed Morsi, in 2012), has been most politically successful there. But it is also the most international and widespread of Muslim political organizations, growing massively in the Arab-speaking countries (except Saudi Arabia) over the last 25 years. This increase has arisen particularly out of grassroots reaction to Western interferences in the Islamic world (especially foreign military presence in Iraq and Afghanistan), inspired by the testy motto: "The Qur'an is our law; jihad is our way."[17] Despite its official eschewing of violence (as stated in 1949), Egyptian members of the Brotherhood were involved in attempting to kill Abdel Nasser (1965), the revolutionary founder of the modern Egyptian Republic, and in the successful assassination of Nasser's successor Anwar Sadat (1981); and since the 1980s it has found it hard to shake off associations with "terrorism." Although originally supporting Nasser's concerns to lift the disadvantaged, the Brotherhood has consistently rejected any compromise with political structures and foreign ideologies (in Egypt's case of quasi-Socialism), insisting the state be grounded in the Qur'an and *Sunnah* (the latter being "the direct path" of teachings and example of Muhammad in the traditions or *hadith* about him and law or *shari'a* initiated from his time).[18] Needless to say, the Brotherhood thought the widespread introduction of "Western-style" parliamentary and judicial arrangements during the post-War independence rush through the Muslim heartlands spelt contamination, but the means to reaching its alternative goals became tempered by political realism from the 1990s.[19]

Importance"; Puelings, *Fearing a 'Shiite Octopus,* ch. 1; Osman, *Sectarianism in Iraq,* esp. ch. 6; Rizvi, "Political Mobilization."

16. Conventional distinctions between Near and Middle East have Levantine countries (including Jordan) as 'Near' (along with Turkey, and often Egypt), with Iraq and Iran, Arabia, etc. definitely 'Middle.' For background in International Relations (as distinct from History), Koppes, "Captain Mahan."

17. Background, esp. Mitchell, *Society of Muslim Brothers;* globalization, esp. Rubin, ed., *Muslim Brotherhood.*

18. For grounding, Zollner, *Muslim Brotherhood.* Al-Hudaybi succeeded Hasan al-Banna' the Brotherhood's founder.

19. See esp. Ranko, *Muslim Brotherhood,* chs. 5–6; Kandil, *Inside the Brotherhood.*

By now it will have become obvious that this chapter is not about post-colonial Islam in the senses made popular in cultural criticism or in more limited "liberal-critical" political analysis. Thus our concern is not much about Western misperceptions of Islam, "orientalizing" it and turning it into the "oriental-despotic" opposite to attained liberty in Western socio-political life.[20] Of course, we have to acknowledge that the "theft of history" always goes on when Islam is viewed in the dominant media as once super-seding the West yet now being a secondary player, or when the question of Islam as a security risk for the West is explained historically as a "clashing civilization" or one anti-modern and counter-democratic.[21] There is always lurking in the collective Western imaging of Islam a liberal paternalism that Europe and the United States have provided the blueprints, machinery, tools and exemplifications of a better way of organizing society for "greater happiness," but that Muslim nations have typically not managed to achieve desirable degrees of egalitarianism or avoid tribal and sectarian strife.[22] But the point of this chapter is to highlight an internal Islamic tension between those who are generally more accepting of what has been left over from the colonial period, with a preparedness to work out future socio-political problems in terms of what has been immediately inherited from "modern-izing processes," and those who want a fresh start with a revived Islamic basis, including those who prefer that the pristine Muslim arrangements should be restored. Of course the images of the "primitive ideal" can differ widely. All the criticism that might be levelled against foundational Islam from colonially associated Westerners, particularly allegations of violence, can be reckoned quite inapplicable. Thus it becomes false to make anything bad of the initial expansion of the Muslim faith by territorial takeover: Islam would have expanded peacefully anyway and the initial use of the sword might even be considered a mistake. Certainly today, as the great modern Kurdish theologian Said Nursi and his Nurculuk supporters have averred, true faith and true *jihad* should have nothing to do with armed coercion (cf. *Qur.* 2: 256).[23] In one extreme attempt at such "soft" post-colonial discourse Pakistani interfaith activist Imam Abdul Mujahid insists that Muhammad

20. On the history of the discourse of Oriental Despotism, Trompf, *Idea of Historical Recurrence*, vol. 2, chs. 7–9; and for post-colonial critiques, e.g., Said, *Orientalism*; Cavaliero, *Ottomania*, esp. ch. 14 (historical); Salzman and Divine (eds.), *Postcolonial Theory*, esp. ch. 14 (contemporary).

21. E.g., Goody, *Theft of History*, chs. 3–4, 7: Huntington, *Clash of Civilizations*, esp. chs. 9–12.

22. E.g., Pryce-Jones, *Closed Circle*.

23. E.g., Ozalp, "Peace and Military Engagement"; Turner, "Reconsidering Jihad."

"never killed anyone," and "only after God's command to defend his peace sanctuary . . . did he pick up arms."[24]

The post-colonial Islam addressed in this chapter, expectedly, is one that idealizes a recovery of Islam as a total way of life and thus allows back its full capacity as a traditional political and juridical force as much as a "separately religious" one, with a complete charge over human lives for their conforming to divine commands and *shari'a* rulings. Now, we confront here an important issue of distinction. In contemporary Islam we can presently find plenty of examples of intense Muslim revivalism, in the form of powerful social movements, and yet they have ostensibly disengaged themselves from politics while still concentrating on revivifying Islam as a complete life-way. The biggest and most internationally-spread among them is the twenty-million-strong Tablîgh Jamâ'at, founded in India in 1927, and generally accepted in the literature as "an apolitical, quietist movement of internal grassroots missionary renewal," teaching a life free from the ills of the material world, yet also well known in the Pacific region for "planting" Islam in Papua New Guinea.[25] And various other "revival movements" or "traditionalist Islamic activisms" like this now compete in the Asian, and noticeably Southeast Asian, "religious market-place."[26] What is typically imaged as worthy of revival is the original *Ummah* or Congregation of Muhammad's time but also the early period of the first four—"rightly guided"—Caliphs, who were Abu Bakr, Umar, 'Uthman, and 'Ali.[27] Significantly, a stress on avoiding compromise applies in such revivalist cases we have in mind here, but the avoidance is of worldliness through the willful re-creation of a "true spiritual community," one uncontaminated by any effects of the historically imperial and contemporary globalizing West. The issue of distinction needing confronting, then, is between post-colonial Islamic energies in Islam that present as "more spiritual" and those as "totalist"—insisting that the nexus of what we call religious and socio-political be preserved in the original spirit of Islam.[28]

24. Mujahid, "Avenging the Prophet."

25. Metcalf, "'Traditionalist' Islamic Activism"; cf. Ali, *Islamic Revivalism,* ch. 7; Flower, "Conversion to Islam in Papua New Guinea," ch. 4.

26. See, e.g., Ali, ed., *Modern Islamic Movements,* esp. pts. 4–5.

27. J. Ali, *Islamic Revivalism,* 253–54.

28. Totalist is an epithet popularized by Michel Foucault for "the colonization of the self by the self" through the insidious influence of Christianity and its "pastoral power" in generating behaviour deterrence. I use the term here in a related way to cover the capacity of any religious outlook and life-way to incorporate all aspects of existence, while eschewing Foucault's dreadful para-Nietzschean 'slippage' in reifying negatively and privatively the tradition that, with the obvious help of the Graeco-Roman classics, Judaism and Islam, has bequeathed us the richest and most diverse body

Naturally those holding the totalist position feel more confident that their effort at recovery is more genuine. But naturally again the totalist thrust most confidently manifests in countries where Muslims are already in the majority, while spiritual revivalism belongs more to minority conditions or to such a state as Indonesia, where Islam (or any one religion) is constitutionally debarred from being an "official establishment." That comparison, though, has made commentators suspect that spiritual revivalists are like "totalists-in-waiting," and it has been noted, as a key example, that the Tablighis come from the same ideological stable—the so-called Deobandi—as the Taliban, who present a totalist front in Afghanistan and Pakistan, both countries Muslim by majority and with "Islamic Republican" constitutions.[29] In broad theological terms any Sunni group emphasizing the recovery of the original Islam and rejecting newer theological interpretations can be read as "Salafis," literalist, strict, puritanical and ready with the rhetoric of *jihad* (as "struggle" of the faithful [*Mu'min*]).[30] Spiritual-revivalist and totalist types as we have characterized them, therefore, might also both be described as "Islamist" (the term better deployed than "Fundamentalist," which even in its generic usage has the lingering colonial suggestion of old-fashioned or outmoded religion in resurgence). Islamism denotes the keeping of Islam as a complete daily way of life, yet in all realism revivalists, often only small within Muslim populations in given countries in any case, can only pretend towards the revitalization of *al-din* or their practiced religion and not the overhaul of the state or society generally.[31] To have the confidence to go further, and to alter existing socio-political structures to reconstitute pristine Islam (according to a preconceived and programmed imaging) demands immense political clout or the availability of weaponry to pull it off. Although in the minority, the Taliban had the power to attempt a radical alteration in Afghanistan after the Soviet withdrawal (1992–2001), it could never unite the country and its ambitions were utterly thwarted by the invasion of the US-initiated Coalition of the Willing after 9/11.[32] The Muslim Brotherhood in Egypt, especially after the dislodging of President

---

of insights about the cosmos and the human tradition so far to hand. For assistance, Evens, *Anthropology as Ethics*, ch. 11. The distinctions between 'political Islam' and 'engaged Muslims,' or between "top-down" and "bottom-up" strategies of "reformist" or "neo-Fundamentalist" positions, have also been touted, but does not bring the clarity to the situation I am identifying here. Cf. Alatas, "Ideology and Utopia in the Discourse on Civil," ch. 9.

29. Metcalf, "'Traditionalist' Islamic Activism"; Alexiev, "Tablighi Jamaat," 9–10.

30. Consider Meijer, *Global Salafism*.

31. For guidance, Calvert, *Islamism*; Martin and Barzegar, eds., *Islamism*.

32. Olesen, *Islam and Politics in Afghanistan*; Abbas, *Taliban Revival*, esp. chs. 4–7.

Hosni Mubarak in the Arab Spring in 2010–11 had a much greater chance, but when their candidate Mohamed Mosei gained power by freer elections in 2012, backed by a virtual majority of the Brotherhood in parliament, it was precisely many Egyptians' "collective fear" of their agenda for a serious Islamization of Egyptian society that brought on the reactive military coup of July 2013.[33] One could be tempted to conclude that the failures of Sunni "Islamist"-Salafi energies, particularly in Egypt, fueled those ready to take desperate measures elsewhere, especially when the Shia Asad regime faltered and the theatre of civil war in Syria beckoned entrance—for however much the Iranian Revolution showed new possibilities, Salafic sensibilities were always against Shi'ite (and also Sufi) heresies, and so, by 2014, with sectarian strife burning fiercely in the heart of the Fertile Crescent, Sunni hatred of Shi'ism was intense and ready to block "the Ayatollah's dream" as one imperative, and to create a new space for the expansion of Sunni reactionary energies.

What I am dubbing the totalist version of Islamism seeks nothing less than the recovered glory of Islam, envisioned through the lens of the early foundations of the faith. As the most published leader of the Muslim Brotherhood in Egypt, Mustafa Mashhur, has put it, the movement's goal is that

> The Islamic *Ummah* . . . can regain its power, be liberated and assume its rightful position which was intended by Allah, as the most exalted nation among men, as the teachers of humanity . . . know your status, so that you firmly believe you are the masters of the world, even if your enemies desire your degradation . . . it should be known that Jihad is . . . not only for the purpose of fending off assaults . . . by Allah's enemies, but for the purpose of realizing the great task of establishing an Islamic state, strengthening the religion and spreading it around the world.[34]

This is a classic statement of post-colonial Islam, when it is considered that not a skerrick of past degradation from colonial interferences should remain, and that a socio-political system should be established that entirely does away with the (basically Western) enemy's continuing means of degrading the true religious way of life. This is thus also the perfect statement of a totalistic solution, of an authentically all-embracing Islamism, not a reduction of Islam to an enlivened spirituality among spiritualities.

What more precisely are thought to be the inimical means of degradation? One would not be blamed for starting with the realities of the

---

33. Wickham. *Mobilizing Islam;* Tadros, *Muslim Brotherhood,* esp. chs. 2–3; Davis and Robinson, *Claiming Society for God,* ch. 2.

34. Mashhur, *Jihad Is the Way,* vol. 5: *The Laws of Da'wa,* 1.

allegedly free but obviously Western-dominated global financial market. For, how much more readily can the destruction of New York's Trade Towers on September 11, 2001 be explained, when one considers the absolute hypocrisy often forced upon high-playing Muslim plutocrats by unearned moneymaking (contrary to most Islamic rulings bearing on usury and related issues, as Osama bin Laden strongly signaled)?[35] But here, using a key set of examples, I will concentrate on legal systems in Islamic countries. For, the extraordinary situation has arisen that virtually every Islamic nation possesses a legal system that is affected by European institutions (and thus by the colonial period), and so the full application of Shar'ia, in its possible "full expressions" according to different schools of Islamic law, are limited by later-coming reforms from outside influences, or those based on European principles meant to restrain the arbitrary power of rulers, secure the independence of the judiciary from politics, and abandon "old barbaric" forms of punishment (such as beheading, stoning and lashing, or the personal right to avenge for the death of one's father).

Thus, surprise, surprise, the very country whose revolution stimulated movements of totalist return to a full Islamic legal order, does not live under purely Muslim regulations. Iran's is a special combination of "Iranian Law" (inherited from a constitutional and judicial settlement developed between the 1906 and 1979 Revolutions) and "Islamic (or Shari'a) Law," which has been added after 1979 where considered necessary, to make up for the absence of distinctively Islamic elements (most notably traditional penalties, such as hand-severing for theft, and the stoning of adulteresses). And as years have passed the finely worded 1930s Civil (largely Napoleonic) Code has become the mainstay of the everyday running of the system (especially after setting up of Shari'a-focused local revolutionary Tribunals handed down too many arbitrary decisions). Iran also retains a parliamentary system, inspired by Western models when the corrupt Qajar "absolute" Shahdom was replaced by a "constitutional" monarchy. On strict Sunni estimates, moreover, the Platonic framing of the constitution, with members of the Supreme Judiciary (headed by the Supreme Ayatollah) acting as the "Guardians" of law and society, is an heretical deviation towards philosophy and away from the Qur'an.[36]

It will be a matter of difficulty even for well-educated Westerners interested in international affairs to work out how various nations in the

35. For background, Kureshi and Hayat, *Contracts and Deals in Islamic Finance*; see bin Laden, *Messages to the World*, 6.

36. Arjomand, "Shi'ite Jurists and the Iranian Law and Constitutional Order," 15–56; Amirshahi et al., "Iranian Legal System"; cf. as background, Bayat, *Iran's First Revolution*; Enayat, *Law, State, and Society on Modern Iran*, esp. ch. 5.

Islamic world have come to have the legal systems they possess. As a rule of the thumb, where British imperial control was strong, Common Law shows up, as in Bangladesh and Pakistan (with the latter making additional provisions for Islamic rulings); where France had its colonies, expect the influence of the French Civil Code (*Le Code Napoléon*), as in such North African states as Morocco and Algeria, and also Syria and to a lesser extent Jordan. Where Soviet rule left its imprint, the secular flavor of legal provisions will be stronger (as in Azerbaijan or Uzbekistan); and where modern Socialist thought has staked a claim, one must look out for signs in legal institutions of modernization, radicalizing efforts at equality before the law, and political populism (or calls to the national unity of a people as if working unification amounts to a democracy). The Leftist Ba'athist ("Resurrection") Party has been famous for its impact in these terms on "post-colonial" Syria and Iraq, and it became the catalyst for a short-lived regional union of Egypt and Syria (as the United Arab Republic, 1958–61) to create a consolidated Arab front against European manipulations, especially with regard to emergent Israel. In Egypt, Syria and Iraq, necessary "revolution" and Socialism were claimed to be compatible with Islamic values, and yet the political discourses of Nasser's revolution, and those involving Hafez al-Assad and Saddam Hussein in Syria and Iraq respectively, were more secular and nationalistic than Islamic (except *in extremis*). The only Muslim country opting for a Communist order (outside the old Eastern bloc) has been South Yemen, now in constant strain after unification with the North. In virtually all cases of post-colonial state-building, the term Republic has been chosen for the political form. Turkey was the first to adopt this term (*Türkiye Cumhuriyeti*), its legal system having strong Swiss and German input (because of prior dealings with the Germanic world), and for nearly twenty years had significantly chosen bi-cameral parliamentary arrangements (Grand National Assembly and Senate) by 1961. The bi-cameral system has been common, the French/American denomination of Senate most used to refer to the Upper House, with "Democratic Republic" gaining in official currency.[37] All this makes it very obvious that the post-colonial Islamic world has been increasingly *engagé* with globalizing political tendencies away from the traditional governances of the mediaeval and early modern centuries. More pertinently for our argument, they stand in the way of those hoping to recover an idealized, pristine Islam as the necessary solution to Islam's ills and as the best goal for humanity's future.

---

37. Documentation of the many details is not possible here. For guidance, e.g., Otto, *Sharia Incorporated*; Arjomand, ed., *Constitutional Politics in the Middle;* Hearnshaw and Montgomery, "Myth of Post-Soviet Muslim Radicalization."

It would be unwise to proceed further without considering the important case of Saudi Arabia. Would it not stand as a beacon for those who hope for a truly revivified Islam? It has managed the holy places and the enormous pilgrimage process (*hajj*) efficiently, publicly beheading those leading rebels who dared to take over Mecca's Great Mosque in 1979. It retains a monarchical political form that in January 2015 saw the untrammeled succession of king Abdullah by king Salman. The Saudis reign under Shari'a law, and they have sponsored the long-inured conservative brand of the tradition known as Wahhabism, that can be taken as one version of Salafism (itself a crucial minority in the country also going under that name).[38] For all these appearances, however, all those who quest for a pure Islam would rate the Saudi regime a chief *contaminant*. Even in majority Muslim opinion outside the general scope of Islamism, the house of Saud presents a problem as a usurping dynasty (against the Hashemite line), as a patently corrupted royal family, and as deeply entrenched in Western, especially United States capitalist networks and military policies. Despite its service to the worldwide Islamic following as custodian of their holiest sites of Mecca and Medina and pilgrim arrangements there, the Saudi leadership is pronouncedly Arabian (and thus "nationalistic") in its outlook.[39] It has been natural for those at the extremist end of things to announce their vexation. In the very words of the millenarian leader of the 1979 seizure of the Great Mosque, Juhayman al-Otaybi (of the influential Saudi family of Najd), the "al-Saud dynasty had lost its legitimacy . . . is utterly ostentatious . . . has destroyed Saudi culture by an aggressive policy of Westernization," with its Wahhabist religious backers misguidedly supporting the monarchy and forgetting "the Last Judgement." Juhayman's call was "a return to the original ways of Islam, among other things a repudiation of the West, an end of education of women, the abolition of television, and the expulsion of non-Muslims from the Arabian Peninsula."[40] And was not Osama bin

---

38. Esp. Vassiliev, *History of Saudi Arabia*, chs. 2, 10, 15–16, 20–21.

39. See, e.g., Safran, *Saudi Arabia;* cf. Lacey, *Inside the Kingdom*. Note that (*inter alia*) the destruction of Muhammad's house at Mecca to make way for a supermarket has produced adverse accusations, even of sacrilege, around the Muslim world; e.g., Musaji, "Saudi Destruction of Muslim Historical Sites."

40. Esp. Wright, *Sacred Rage*, 152; Commins, *Wahhabi Mission*, 63. For background, Profanter et al., *Saudi Arabia and Women*, 17 (education for females after 1960); Rugh, "Saudi Mass Media and Society in the Faisal Era," 125–27 (television introduced by the US Air Force in 1955).

Laden's deliberate choice of a simple, austere life-style above all a resound-
ingly negative statement against the Saudi luxury in which his own family
had been trapped?[41]

The essential point has been made. The Muslim world has undergone
thousands of intricate accommodations in modern history, especially in the
political sphere, and especially because of Western imperial intrusions. As it
turns out, the great majority of citizens in post-imperial (or post-colonial)
conditions accept what has resulted, and subsequent generations accept
what they have "inherited" as a "given." In the semi-traditionalist ethos of
the Muslim world anyway, what is decided at the top, unless it very ad-
versely affects daily life, is borne as Allah's provision. What I have called
"David Hume's law" applies: empires rise and fall and regimes change, and
when the fighting is over people want to get on with their business.[42] And
we can hardly say accommodation is a recent development in Islamic history. It has necessarily applied to institutional arrangements because of wars
and invasions. This is famously the case with the Caliphate. The Caliphate
is the last piece of the jigsaw puzzle that demands our attention, because it
is above all in evoking the four rightly guided Caliphs that purist Islamists
create a special ideological branding for themselves. But it cannot be said
this is a yearning for the return of the Caliphate after its abolition by the
Atatürk government in 1924 (see above); for that was the *Ottoman* Caliphate in particular, an introduced fixture. The end of the original line of Caliphs is conventionally put at 1258 CE (the Mongol siege of Baghdad), at the
end of what has been typically conceived by scholars over the years as the
end of the "Islamic Golden Age."[43] After that, the traditional question of the
Caliphate had to go into abeyance, and in any case, even before this terrible
rupture there were so many different governments by Muslim rulers that the
general tendency had been to separate the work of government from that of
the *ulama* or religious authorities (mostly also jurists).

Facing reality, the extraordinary influential Ahmad bin Taymiya
(1263–1328) of Harran (now southern Turkey) insisted that for Muslims,
despite the effects of the Mongols, *shari'a* should remain central to everyday
life. Taymiya framed the necessary project for the future: since "true Caliphs" had not ruled since the early days of Islam (i.e., the Umayyads, who

41. Arnett, "Interview with Osama bin Laden." Bin Laden's connections had been
with the Arabian version of the Muslim Brotherhood called Sahwa, who have always
chosen, however, to keep a low political profile under the Saud regime.

42. Trompf, *Historical Recurrence*, vol. 2, ch. 8, sect. 6. For Muslim teaching on
accepting government, start with Ibn Batta al-'Ukbari, *Kitâb al-Sharb wa 'l-ibâna 'alâ
usûl al-sunna wa 'l-diyIana* (960s) in Laoust, *La profession de foi d'Ibn Batta*.

43. E.g., Bobrick, *Caliph's Splendor*.

had been usurped by the Abbasids as early as 750 CE), Muslim governments could now only be defined by the self-inscription of rulers as followers, and thus in Taymiya's almost unanimously accepted "new concept of state and society . . . the *'Ulama* rather than the Caliphs became the principal actors," so that now "Sultan and scholar" became the "key figures" in the social order.[44] For the purists who do not want to be involved in politics (at least at this stage), this longstanding readjustment can be accepted for pragmatic reasons. For those who want the nexus between religion and governance to be re-forged, however, there is an impatience for a truly Islamic state reflecting the time of the first four "greats," and thus always in the back of hopeful minds is the return of the Caliphate in a pristine form. In what place it should be re-instated is a hotly contested debate under the present circumstances. Those accepting the Ottoman Caliphate as valid will look to Turkey, seeking to undo Atatürk's secularist agenda, which has treated Islam as a "scapegoat" in the creating of social turmoil.[45] Others look to Mecca, but Jerusalem is another (more eschatological) possibility, considering the corruption of the Saudis and the hope that Israel will collapse "a second time" (*Qur.* 17: 8, cf. 104).

When the democratically elected government of the Muslim Brotherhood in Egypt did not produce dramatic results for the impatient, and what Islamization policies it had were foiled by the July 2014 military coup, frustrations boiled over and cadres of those Sunnis espousing and waiting for drastic change in a total Islamic order converged on Syria, where civil war had raged since 2011 and an heretical Shi'a regime beckoned overthrow. A coagulating effect around the movement known as Islamic State in Iraq and as-Sham (ISIS) produced the most outstanding effects, an alliance with military successes not just in Syria but across the soft Syrian-Iraqi border ("the breaking of the [nationalist] borders") to the great city of Mosul. The most powerful symbolic gesture was in doing what the Muslim Brotherhood, which originated and centered on Egypt, was unable to do—not just found an "Islamic State," but declare a Caliphate (*Ramadan* 2014). It was putatively the polity and Caliphate of pristine Islam returned ("the generation of the Caliphate"), with its office-holder, Abu al-Baghdadi, preaching from the Grand Mosque al-Nuri in Mosul in a strange, artificial and wooden-like Arabic meant to imitate the first of the four rightly-guided ones, Mohammad's friend Abu Bakr. At last it was time to say again in historical reality, "You are the best nation produced [as an example] for mankind. You

44. Lapidus, *History of Islamic Societies*, 184.

45. E.g., Mowla, *Judgment against Imperialism*, 287 (Istanbul); Blunt, *Future of Islam*, 207 (Mecca); cf. Ahrari, *New Great Game in Muslim Central Asia*, 75 (quotation).

enjoin what is right and forbid what is wrong and believe in Allah [(*Qur.* 3) Al 'Imran, 110]," for "Allah has promised . . . to grant them succession [to authority] on earth just as He granted it to those before them ([*Qur.* 24] An-Nûr 55]."[46] This was not the first time that an attempt to recover or establish a Caliphate from Mosul,[47] and in that context of course the goal to re-forge the golden link with the past would be the taking of Baghdad, an attempt immediately made but forestalled by opposing Iraqi forces (with foreign, largely US assistance from the air).[48] But despite the setback, and there were more to come, and despite initial rejection by other radical movements, including al Qaeda, the establishing and rhetoric has come to stand, in all its literal recall of warrior conquests from early mediaeval days, as the most uncompromising expression of post-colonial Islam to date. Even the heavy *jizya* tax is imposed on non-Muslims, something that has been abandoned in Muslim-majority nations around the world, and the main target for executions in Mosul as the current center of the storm has been Shi'i "heretics." Extremist Nigerian and Libyan advocates of a restored Caliphate were ready to pick up the tag.

And this, to conclude, is where Australia and Australian Muslim communities come into the picture. The Australian Muslim majority is Sunni and accommodating to the nation of Australia and the way of life its major socio-political institutions have been projecting. But young Australian Muslims are readily exposed to the projection of an Islam that is not supposed to have national borders and to an ideal that, akin to Christian primitivism and impulses to reenact the early church, produces sectarian hopes of restoring an original Islam. That many in the majority believe this is a promise to be fulfilled by Allah, at first through the agency of an appointed Director (*al-Mahdi*), when the globe shall feel the converting power of the divine, before the final return of Jesus, Moses and Mary, hardly prevents a minority thinking of taking matters into their own hands.[49] The same sociology has applied for Judaism, Christianity, Zoroastrianism and other traditions with millenarian components in their beliefs. The millenarian moment provides twin opportunities to fulfil the consummation of a collectively visioned myth- or macro-history and effect final retribution—the "ultimate

46. Quotation of IS posts adapting the Qur'an, trans. van Ostaeyen, "Islamic State."

47. Consider the career of Abu Muhammad Nasir al-Dawia al-Taghlibi (d. 969); Kennedy, *Prophet and the Age of the Caliphates,* 265–70.

48. Esp. Weiss and Hassan, *ISIS: Inside the Army of Terror.* Cf. Mitchell, "Caliphate: Islamic World's 'Dream come True.'"

49. For the basics, start with Miller, Vandome, and McBrewster, *Islamic Eschatology.* I leave aside discussion of suicide acts as in any sense fulfilling Islamic *shari'a*; for orientation, J. Ali, "A Sociological Analysis of Muslim Terrorism," ch. 7.

payback"—against the enemies of God.[50] When the moment is seized, and has now been with up-to-the-minute firepower and technology, the call to be part of a cosmic scenario can be all too attractive to idealistic youths, and those who have become jaded by a certain "Ozzie" directionlessness, with bitter elements of racism and Islamophobia. Religion (if I may be poetic and hypostatize it) always has a sting in its tail, and it hurts. Better to work for conditions of "a peaceable kingdom" that will make recourse to revolutionary violence an utter self-betrayal.

WORKS CITED

Abbas, Hassan. *The Taliban Revival: Violence and Extremism on the Pakistan-Afghanistan Frontier.* New Haven: Yale University Press, 2014.

Ahrari, Mohammed E., with James Beal. *The New Great Game in Muslim Central Asia.* McNair Paper 47. Washington, DC: INSS, 1996.

Alatas, Syed F. "Ideology and Utopia in the Discourse on Civil Society in Indonesia and Malaysia." In *Islam and Politics in Southeast Asia*, edited by Johan Sarvanamuttu, 165–181. Abingdon: Routledge, 2010.

Alexiev, Alex. "Tablfighi Jamaat: Jihad's Stealthy Legions." *Middle East Quarterly* 12.1 (2005) 9–10.

Ali, J. "A Sociological Analysis of Muslim Terrorism." In *Sacred Suicide*, edited by James R. Lewis and Carole M. Cusack. Farnham, UK: Ashgate, 2014.

Ali, Jan A. *Islamic Revivalism Encounters the Modern World: A Study of the Tablīgh Jamā'at.* Delhi: Sterling, 2012.

Ali, Muhammad M., ed. *Modern Islamic Movements: Models, Problems and Prospects.* Kuala Lumpur: Noordeen, 2000.

Allawi, Ali A. *The Crisis of Islamic Civilization.* New Haven: Yale University Press, 2003.

Amirshahi, Hassan et al., "Iranian Legal System." amirshahlaw.com.

Arjomand Saïd Amir, ed. *Constitutional Politics in the Middle East, with Special Reference to Turkey, Iraq, Iran, and Afghanistan.* Oñati International Series in Law and Society. Portland, Or.; Hart, 2007.

———. "Shi'ite Jurists and the Iranian Law and Constitutional Order in the Twentieth Century." In *The Rule of Law, Islam, and Constitutional Politics in Egypt and Iran*, edited by Arjomand and Nathan J. Brown. Albany, NY: State University of New York, 2013.

Arnett, Peter. "Interview with Osama bin Laden." CNN, March 1997. Now in "Focus on Saudi Arabia" (2003). www.justresponse.net.

Barnes, Geoffrey. *Doing Theology in Sydney: A History of the United Theological College 1974–1999.* Adelaide: Openbook, 2000.

50. See Trompf, ed., *Cargo Cults and Millenarian Movements;* Trompf, "Millenarism." On applying Ernest Troetsch's model of Christian sectarian to Islam, see Ali, *Islamic Revivalism*, ch. 1; cf. Troeltsch, *Social Teaching of the Christian Churches*, vol. 1, esp. 331–33, and vol. 2, passim.

Bayat, Mangol. *Iran's First Revolution: Shi'ism and the Constitutional Revolution of 1905–1909*. Studies in Middle Eastern History 136. Oxford: Oxford University Press, 1991.

Bazzi, Emad. "The Relationship between Mysticism and Politics in the Personality of Ayatollah Khomeini." PhD diss., University of Sydney, 2002.

Bentley, Jerry, and Herbert Ziegler. *Traditions and Encounters: A Global Perspective on the Past*. New York: McGraw-Hill, 2014.

bin Laden, Osama. *Messages to the World: The Statements of Osama bin Laden*. Translated by James Howarth. New York: Verso, 2005.

Blunt, Wilfred C. *The Future of Islam*. Cambridge: Chadwyck-Healey, 1998.

Bobrick, Benson. *The Caliph's Splendor: Islam and the West in the Golden Age of Baghdad*. New York: Simon & Schuster, 2012.

Brodie, F. Thomas, ed. *Collins Australian Clear School Atlas*. Melbourne: Collins, 1940.

Calvert, John. *Islamism: A Documentary and Reference Guide*. Westport, CT: Greenwood, 2008.

Cavaliero, Roderick. *Ottomania: The Romantics and the Myth of the Islamic Orient*. London: Taurtis, 2013.

Commins, David. *The Wahhabi Mission and Saudi Arabia*. New York: Tauris, 2009.

Davis, Nancy J. and Robert V. Robinson, *Claiming Society for God: Religious Movements and Social Welfare*. Bloomington: Indiana University Press, 2012.

Davutoglu, *Civilizational Transformation and the Muslim World*. Kuala Lumpur: Mahir, 1994.

Durie, Mark. "Islam's Second Crisis: The Troubles to Come." *The Middle East Forum*. Feb. 17, 2014. www.meforum.org/3750.

Enayat, Hadi. *Law, State, and Society on Modern Iran: Constitutionalism, and Legal Reform, 1906–1941*. New York: Palgrave, 2013.

Evens, Terry M.S. *Anthropology as Ethics: Nondualism and the Conduct of Sacrifice*. Oxford: Berghahn, 2008.

Feldman, Noah. *The Fall and Rise of the Islamic State*. Princeton: Princeton University Press, 2008.

Flower, Scott. "Conversion to Islam in Papua New Guinea." In *New Religious Movements in Oceania*, ed. Trompf [Spec. issue of] *Nova Religio* 18.4 (2015), ch. 4.

Goody, Jack. *The Theft of History*. Cambridge: Cambridge University Press, 2006.

Hearnshaw, John and David W. Montgomery. "The Myth of Post-Soviet Muslim Radicalization in the Central Asian Republics." 2014. Chatham House Research Paper. Russia and Eurasia Programme. chathamhouse.org)

Hero, Dilip. *The Longest War: The Iran-Iraq Miliary Conflict*. London: Routledge, 1991.

Huntington, Samuel P. *The Clash of Civilizations and the Remaking of the World Order*. New York: Simon & Schuster, 1996.

Kandil, Hazem *Inside the Brotherhood*. London: Polity, 2014.

Karpat, Kemal H. *Studies on Turkish Politics and Society: Selected Articles and Essays*. Social, Economic, and Political Studies of the Middle East and Asia 81. Leiden: Brill, 2004.

Karsdh, Efraim. "The Missing Piece: Islamic Imperialism." In *Postcolonial Theory and the Arab-Israel Conflict*, edited by Philip C. Salzman and Donna R. Divine. London: Routledge, 2008.

Keddie, Nikki K. *Religion and Politics in Iran: Shi'ism from Quietism to Revolution*. New Haven: Yale University Press, 1983.

Kennedy, Hugh N. *The Prophet and the Age of the Caliphates: The Islamic Near East from the 6th to the 11th Century.* Harlow, UK: Pearson, 2004.

Kinross, Lord Patrick. *Atatürk: The Rebirth of a Nation.* London: Phoenix, 2003.

Koppes, Clayton R. "Captain Mahan, General Gordon and the Origin of the Term 'Middle East.'" *Middle East Studies* 12.1 (1976) 95–8.

Kureshi, Hussain and Mohsin Hayat, *Contracts and Deals in Islamic Finance: A User's Guide to Cash Flows, Balance Sheets, and Capital Structures.* Wiley Finance Series. Singapore: Wiley, 2015.

Lacey, Robert. *Inside the Kingdom: Kings, Clerics, Modernists, Terrorists, and the Struggle for Saudi Arabia.* London: Arrow, 2010.

Laoust, Henri. *La profession de foi d'Ibn Batta.* Damascus: Institut Français de Damas, 1958.

Lapidus, Ira M. *A History of Islamic Societies.* Cambridge: Cambridge University Press, 1988.

League of Nations treaties: Versailles (1919), arts. 22, 434; Sèvres (1920), and Mandate Papers (1922), class A.

Lewis, Bernard. *What Went Wrong?* New York: Oxford University Press, 2002.

Martin, Richard C., and Abbas Barzegar, eds. *Islamism: Contested Perspectives on Political Islam.* Stanford: Stanford University Press, 2010.

Mashhur, Mustafa. *Jihad Is the Way,* vol. 5: *The Laws of Da'wa.* Translated by Palestinian Media Watch. palwatch.org.

Meijer, Roel. *Global Salafism: Islam's New Religious Movement.* New York: Oxford University Press, 2013.

Metcalf, Barbara D. "'Traditionalist' Islamic Activism: Deoband Tablighis and Talibs." *Social Service Research Council* no. 1 (2004) 1. essays.ssrc.org.

Mikailu, Aminu S. Review of M. Umer Chapra's *The Future of Economics: An Islamic Perspective* in *Hamdard Islamicus* (Karachi) 24.4 (2001) 91.

Miller, Frederic P., Agnes F. Vandome, and John McBrewster. *Islamic Eschatology.* Saarbruucken: VDM, 2009.

Minawi, Mostafa. "The 'Other' Colonialism: The Ottoman 'Scramble for Africa' at the End of the 19th Century." Social Science Institute, Artuklu Mardin University, Turkey, 4 Dec., 2014.

Mitchell, Chris. "Caliphate: Islamic World's 'Dream Come True.'" *CBN News,* 2 Feb., 2015.

Mitchell, Richard P. *The Society of Muslim Brothers.* Oxford: Oxford University Press, 1969.

Mowla, Khondakar G. *The Judgment against Imperialism, Fascism and Racism against Caliphate and Islam.* Bloomington, IN: AuthorHouse, 2008.

Mujahid, Abdul M. "Avenging the Prophet Who Banned Revenges." *Highway: Quarterly Journal of the Gordon Uniting Church* (Feb. 2015) 30–31.

Murphy, David. *The Arab Revolt 1916–18: Lawrence Sets Arabia Ablaze.* London: Osprey, 2008.

Musaji, Sheila. "Saudi Destruction of Muslim Historical Sites." *The American Muslim.* www.theamericanmuslim.org.

Olesen, Asta. *Islam and Politics in Afghanistan.* Nordic Institute of Asian Studies Monograph Series 67. Richmond, UK: Curzon, 1995.

Osman, Khalil F. *Sectarianism in Iraq: The Making of State and Nation since 1920*. Routledge Studies in Middle Eastern Democratization and Government 5. London: Routledge, 2015.

Otto, Jan M. *Sharia Incorporated: A Comparative Overview of the Legal Systems in Twelve Muslim Countries in Past and Present*. Amsterdam: Amsterdam University Press, 2010.

Ozalp, Mehmet. "Peace and Military Engagement in the Qur'an and the Actions of the Prophet Muhammad." Sydney: Australian Catholic University, 2015. www.cofhslism.catholic.edu.au.

Profanter, Annemarie et al. *Saudi Arabia and Women in Higher Education and Cultural Dialogue: New Perspectives*. CRISSMA Working Paper 18. Milan: CRISSMA, 2010.

Pryce-Jones, David. *The Closed Circle: An Interpretation of the Arabs*. London: Dee, 2009.

Puelings, Jelle. *Fearing a 'Shiite Octopus'; Sunni-Shia Relations and the Implications for Belgium and Europe*. Egmont Papers, 35. Gent: Egmont Royal Institute for International Relations, 2010.

Ranko, Annette. *The Muslim Brotherhood and Its Quest for Hegemony in Egypt: State Discourse and Islamist Counter-Discourse*. Politik und Gesellschaft des Nahen Ostens. Wiesbaden: Springer, 2012.

Rubin, Barry, ed. *The Muslim Brotherhood: The Organization and Policies of a Global Islamic Movement*. New York: Macmillan, 2010.

Rugh, William A. "Saudi Mass Media and Society in the Faisal Era." In *King Faisal and the Modernisation of Saudi Arabia*, edited by Willard A. Beling, 125–27. London: Croom Helm, 1980.

Safran, Nadav. *Saudi Arabia: The Ceaseless Quest for Security*. Ithaca, NY: Cornell University Press, 1988.

Said, Edward. *Orientalism*. London: Routledge and Kegan Paul, 1978.

Sajjad Rizvi, "Political Mobilization and the Shi'i Religious Establishment (*Marja'iyya*)," *International Affairs* 86.6 (2010) 1313–29.

Sayyid, Salman. "Empire, Islam, and the Postcolonial." In *The Oxford Handbook of Postcolonial Studies*, edited by Graham Huggan, 127–41. Oxford: Oxford University Press, 2013.

Schaffer, Brenda. *Borders and Brethren: Iran and the Challenge of Azerbaijani Identity*. Cambridge, MA: Belfer Center for Science and International Relations, Harvard University, 2002.

Shboul, Ahmad. "Ahmad Shboul: Biography." *Aust Lit*. austlit.edu.au/austlit/page/6819181.

Sillah, Mohammad B. "Islamic Futures after the Desert Storm." *Hamdad Islamicus* 14.4 (1991).

Stavrianos, Leften S., ed. *The Ottoman Empire: Was it the Sick Man of Europe?* New York: Rinehardt, 1957.

Tadros, Mariz. *The Muslim Brotherhood in Contemporary Egypt: Democracy Redefined or Confined?* London: Routledge, 2012.

Tariq, M. M. "The Ideological Background of Rationality in Islam." *Al-Hikmat* 28 (2008) 51.

Toprak, Binnaz. "The Religious Right." In *The Modern Middle East: A Reader*, edited by Albert H. Hourani, Philip S. Khoury and Mary C. Wilson. London: Tauris, 1993.

Troeltsch, Ernst. *The Social Teaching of the Christian Churches.* Translated by Olive Wyon. London: Allen & Unwin, 1912.

Trompf, Garry, ed. *Cargo Cults and Millenarian Movements: Transoceanic Comparisons of New Religious Movements.* Religion and Society 29. Berlin: de Gruyter, 1990.

———. *The Idea of Historical Recurrence in Western Thought,* vol. 2: *From the Later Renaissance to the Dawn of the Third Millennium.* Berkeley: University of California Press (forthcoming).

———. "Millenarism: History, Sociology, and Cross-Cultural Analysis." In *Millennium,* edited by Hilary Carey [Spec. issue of] *Journal of Religious History* 24.1 (2000) 120–23.

———. "Of Shi'a Importance." In *Resistance of Cultures: The Battle for Heritage in a Globalizing World,* edited by Vladimir Ionesov and Garry Trompf. Samara: Samara Society for Cultural Studies, 2017 (forthcoming).

Turner, Colin. "Reconsidering Jihad: The Perspective of Bediüzzaman Said Nursi." *Nova Religio* 11.2 (2007) 94–111.

van Meurs, Wim. "The Development of an Administrative Class in South-East Europe." In *Ottomans into Europeans: State and Institution Building in South-East Europe,* edited by Alina Mingiu-Pippidi and van Meurs. New York: Columbia University Press, 2010.

van Ostaeyen, Pieter. "The Islamic State Restores the Caliphate." pietervanostaeyen.wordpress.com.

Vassiliev, Alexei. *The History of Saudi Arabia.* London: Saqi, 2015.

Weiss Michael, and Hasssan Hassan. *ISIS: Inside the Army of Terror.* New York: Simon & Schuster, 2015.

Wickham, Carrie R. *Mobilizing Islam: Religion, Activism, and Political Change in Egypt.* New York: Columbia University Press, 2003.

Wright, Robin. *Sacred Rage: The Wrath of Militant Islam.* New York: Simon & Schuster, 2001.

Zollner, Barbara H. E. *The Muslim Brotherhood: Hasan al-Hudaybi and Ideology.* New York: Routledge, 2009.

8

A SUITABLY ENGLISH ABRAHAM

Emigration to Australia in the Nineteenth Century

Mark G. Brett

FOLLOWING THE LEGAL ABOLITION of slavery in the British Empire in 1833, the morality of colonization came to the fore for the English churches, especially among the evangelicals and Quakers who had worked on the abolitionist cause. During the 1830s it is not difficult to find anti-colonial religious literature, and even the Colonial Office in London exhibited a social conscience that was in some respects unparalleled in subsequent Australian history.[1] The assumptions that had governed the settlement of New South Wales, Van Diemen's Land and Western Australia were no longer considered sufficient, and there was a deliberate shift in government policy.[2] In this chapter we will explore the biblical motifs adopted within this humanitarian movement, both in new legal initiatives and in the more popular literature supporting emigration at the time. While the biblical typology of a Promised Land emerged within the Australian colonial imagination of the 1830s and 1840s, this study describes the distinctive features of its reception through the figure of Abraham.

With the arrival of the new Whig government in Britain in April 1835, two key figures emerged in the activities of the Colonial Office, Lord

---

1. See Carey's account of the "anti-colonialism" of the mission societies in the 1830s, notably including the defence of Maori sovereignty, in *God's Empire,* 322–28.

2. Reynolds, "South Australia," 24–32.

Glenelg and James Stephen. Undersecretary from 1836 to 1847, Stephen set the tone of his policies when he condemned the 1823 landmark legal case in America, *Johnson v. McIntosh*, in which Chief Justice John Marshall had established the modern secularized version of the doctrine of discovery.[3] Marshall's judgment was summarily dismissed along with the international jurists who disguise injustice with "the most decorous veil which legal ingenuity can weave."[4] Stephen argued that the English initiatives in Canada and Australia set new and better standards for addressing the rights of Aboriginal peoples.

South Australia had been established as a free colony under a new piece of legislation in 1834, the *South Australian Colonization Act*, but in February 1836 the king's Letters Patent placed a new condition on the actual process of settlement:[5]

> PROVIDED ALWAYS that nothing in those our Letters Patent contained shall affect or be construed to affect the rights of any Aboriginal Natives of the said Province to the actual occupation or enjoyment in their own Person or in the Persons of their Descendants of any Land therein now actually occupied or enjoyed by such Natives.

Accordingly, the Resident Commissioner in South Australia was instructed:

> You will see that no lands which the natives may possess in occupation or enjoyment be offered for sale until previously ceded by the natives to yourself. You will furnish the protector of the aborigines with evidence of the faithful fulfillment of the bargain or treaties which you may effect with the aborigines for the cession of lands.[6]

Similar strictures preserving Aboriginal land rights were explicitly incorporated into the *South Australia Amendment Act* of 1838 but they are missing from the *Waste Lands Act* of 1842, which superseded previous arrangements for the alienation of land in all the colonies, including South Australia. Thus one would need to conclude that this particular window

---

3. *Johnson v. McIntosh* (1823), 21 U.S. (8 Wheaton). See especially Robertson, *Conquest by Law*; Miller, Ruru, Behrendt, Lindberg, *Discovering Indigenous Lands*; Echo-Hawk, "Colonialism and Law," 148–205; cf. Ford, *Settler Sovereignty*.

4. James Stephen, memorandum to the parliamentary undersecretary, 28 July, 1839, cited in Knaplund, *James Stephen and the British Colonial System*, 89.

5. Brennan, "Disregard for Legal Protections," 90–121. *South Australia Amendment Act* of 1838 includes a provision in the same terms provided by the king in the Letters Patent of 1836. See Act 1 and 2 Victoria, Cap 60, *Coming to Terms*, 390.

6. Quoted in Brennan, "Disregard," 101.

in colonial law remained open for around seven years, and only in South Australia, during which time no treaties at all were negotiated.

The existence of this historic window may be attributed in part to the influence and advocacy of the so-called "Clapham Sect," who had earlier been active in the abolitionist movement. The humanitarian aspirations of the reformers at this time are clearly reflected in a submission from the Aborigines' Protection Society in 1840, which proposed an ideal system of colonial legislation:

> That such system of legislation shall be based upon the dec-
> laration of the indefeasible rights of every people (not under
> allegiance to any other power) to the natural rights of man
> comprehending,
>
> 1. Their rights as an independent nation. That no country or
>   people has a right by force or fraud to assume sovereignty
>   over any other nation.
>
> 2. That such sovereignty can only be justly obtained by fair
>   treaty, and with their consent.
>
> 3. That every individual of a nation whether independent or
>   owing allegiance to any other power has a rights to personal
>   liberty, and protection of property and life.[7]

This kind of advocacy provided support for the Treaty of Waitangi in New Zealand (1840).[8]

In her discussion of religious writings on colonization in the nineteenth century, Hilary Carey has also drawn attention to some of the tracts that promoted the right kind of emigration around this time. While issuing stern warnings against the obvious evils of the colonies, we find no moral qualms in this pious genre of literature about the cause of emigration itself. A collection of these tracts re-published around 1852 were given the title *The Emigrant's Friend*, and presented as a small volume that would make a profitable "companion for the voyage."[9] The decision to emigrate is acknowledged in the first tract as a difficult one to make, but it may be supported by divine providence, as for example in the biblical precedent where God says to Abraham:

---

7. Motte, *Outline of a system of legislation*, 13–14.

8. See the overview provided by Knaplund, *James Stephen and the British Colonial System*, 66–94.

9. Religious Tract Society, *Emigrant's Friend*. The publication itself is undated, but library catalogues suggest 1852 as a likely date for the whole re-published collection.

"Get thee out of thy country, and from thy kindred and from
thy father's house, unto a land that I will shew thee," Gen. xii.1.
There is therefore nothing unlawful in emigration; it is one great
means of peopling the earth, and causing the ground to yield its
fruits for the sustenance of man and beast.

Carey finds in this passage an implicit acknowledgement of moral
qualms, but also a swift dismissing of the "ethical questions that had weighed
so heavily in the colonization of New Zealand."[10] *The Emigrant's Friend* is
much more concerned about the evils of alcohol, apostasy, and the pursuit
of material wealth than about the natural rights of Indigenous people. Accordingly, such tracts might be interpreted as susceptible to Edward Said's
influential critique of the moral blindness towards Canaanites in Israel's
founding narrative.[11]

While Carey provides a useful description of the religious character of
Britain's imperial expansion, one must also be careful to avoid some of the
misleading generalizations that are often asserted in postcolonial biblical
studies, as if there were no significant differences between the hermeneutics of Puritans in Massachusetts and the convict colonies of New South
Wales or Van Diemen's Land. Israel's exodus and conquest narrative was
indeed adopted in support of several colonization projects, but this particular metanarrative had little relevance in the convict settlements of early
nineteenth century Australia. The Puritan paradigm of the "New Israel"
was absent from the original motivations for Australian settlement,[12] and
it only became potentially relevant in supporting the cause of emigration.

Even in the tract mentioned above, *The Emigrant's Friend* (1852), we
find advice to the reader that conflates the peaceful model of Abraham with
the model of Joshua:

One of the first duties, and one of the highest privileges, too, on
entering a new habitation, is to set up an altar for God. . . Holy
men of old, wherever they went, made it their first concern to
build an altar to the Lord that they might worship him, Gen. xii.
7,8; xiii. 4. And the Lord dwelt with them and blessed them, and
made them a blessing. Joshua nobly resolved, whatever others
might do, "As for me and my house, we will serve the Lord,"
Josh. xxiv. 15.

10. Carey, *God's Empire*, 309, referring to *Emigrant's Friend*, 2.

11. Said, "Michael Walzer's Exodus," 161–78; cf. the review of subsequent literature in Masalha, "Reading the Bible with the Eyes of the Canaanites."

12. Cf. Rose, "Rupture and the Ethics of Care," 205; Brett, "Feeling for Country," in
response to Ann Curthoys, "Whose Home?"

One could regard this example as the exception that proves the rule: the only aspect of Joshua's character that is relevant to the argument is his similarity to eirenic Abraham's gift of reciprocal blessings.[13] The interest is selectively focused on Joshua as the ideal religious man, not the warrior. The significance of this selective hermeneutic emerges more clearly in other literature from the period that could properly be regarded as emigration propaganda.

Produced by the Religious Tract Society, this *Emigrant's Friend* makes no reference to a specific colony and simply advises a holy separation from the surrounding evils—evils that are to be found primarily among fellow settlers. But there is no mistaking the peculiar self-understanding of the South Australian colony reflected in a secular booklet published in 1848, *The Emigrant's Friend: or Authentic Guide to South Australia.*[14] This work presents itself as a practical guide for prospective colonists, covering a broad range of topics like climate, history, soil quality, animals, employment opportunities, and recommended provisions for the journey. The booklet highlights the need for "good character," and documented evidence of such was required when seeking the provision of free passage from an emigration agent. There was no financial support available for emigration to Van Diemen's Land, it was noted, and again the reasons relate to the requirement of good character: "The country is overrun with desperate bush rangers, and even the convicts, who are well disposed, destroy that feeling of safety and good manners, which so essentially distinguish South Australia." Similarly, describing New South Wales, the author suggests that in light of its convict origins "a moral contamination has spread over the colony."[15]

The ethnic identity of the intended audience of this booklet is clearly English, as is indicated by a taxonomy of strangers to be encountered in South Australia:

> There are very few natives, and these are perfectly harmless. Until lately there were no Irish in the Colony, and very few Scotch: but as many as 4,000 Germans, who live mostly together, and although the men are somewhat idle, smoking all day long, yet the women among them are very hardworking, and make the best nurses and servants.[16]

13. The passing acknowledgment of Indigenous people in Gen 12:7 seems to imply that their presence offered no insurmountable moral challenge.

14. *Emigrant's Friend.*

15. Ibid., 26.

16. *Emigrant's Friend*, 13. On the subsequent politics of race in Australia see especially Lake and Reynolds, *Drawing the Global Colour Line.*

Consistent with this distancing comment on the German population, the author neglects to mention Lutheran congregations when it comes to listing the churches in the colony.

An earlier and more comprehensive work on South Australia was provided by John Stephens in his 200-page book *The Land of Promise* (1839), which in spite of its evocative title has little in the way of an explicit theological argument for emigration. Stephens does however draw attention to Clause 22 of the colony's Constitution, which prohibited the emigration of convicts to South Australia, highlighting the absence of moral pollutions.[17] And "an Irish writer" is quoted in passing as having suggested that "in South Australia, at least, the climate of Paradise appears to have survived the fall."[18]

Moreover, we find in this earlier volume a more explicit sensitivity to the plight of Indigenous peoples in the colonies, and on this issue, setting South Australia apart. Stephens argues

> that the colonization of South Australia by industrious and virtuous settlers, so far from being an invasion of the right of the aborigines, is a necessary preliminary to the displacement of the lawless squatters, the abandoned sailors, the runaway convicts, the pirates, the worse-than savages, that now infest the coast and island along that extensive portion of New Holland, and perpetrate against the defenseless natives crimes at which humanity revolts. For the purpose of securing to the natives their proprietary right to the soil, wherever such right might be found to exist, special instructions were given to the colonial commissioner, in which it was laid down as a principle, that, of the colonial lands placed by Parliament at the disposal of the commissioners, no portion of which the natives might possess in occupation or enjoyment, should be offered for sale till ceded by the natives to the colonial commissioner. That officer was required to furnish the protector with evidence of the faithful fulfillment of the bargain or treaties which he should effect with the aborigines.[19]

Writing this in 1839, Stephens is still hopeful that the Letters Patent might be put into effect, but as already noted, that window seems to have closed with the *Waste Lands Act* of 1842. Citing a parliamentary speech from 1838, Stephens could claim that South Australia was established "without

17. Stephens, *Land of Promise*, 30.

18. Ibid., 46.

19. Ibid., 69.

bloodshed, violence and injustice" and that "there is not a single soldier in
the colony of South Australia."[20]

While clearly lacking the piety of *The Emigrant's Friend* that was produced by the Religious Tract Society, Stephens seems nevertheless to have
secularized and moralized the narratives of scripture, grafting in assorted
allusions to classical Western literature in order to produce a vision for the
birth of a new nation. "The awful emigration of Noah, and the promise that
painted his horizon," Moses, the Tyrians at Carthage, and Aeneas all figure
in this vision.[21] Reflecting on Captain Hindmarsh's commissioning on 28
December 1836 as the first governor of South Australia, Stephens finds reason to cite the *South Australian Record*:

> To the emigrant who was present at the formal assumption of
> the new country, and believed, according to the justest hope,
> that he was assisting at the foundation of a new people, every
> occurrence of the day was more momentous than if they had
> been awaiting in the royal bed-chamber the birth of a future
> king. They were ushering into existence a whole nation.[22]

Given that the settlement of New South Wales was some half a century
in the past, and the foundation of Australia as an independent nation was
a century in the future (if that is the import of the *Statute of Westminster*
1931), this might well be considered a prophecy of biblical proportions. It is
also a prophecy that exhibits all the irony of a settler sovereignty, projecting
an emigrant nation separate from its imperial homeland.[23]

Writing in a similar vein to John Stephens' *Land of Promise*, the influential Baptist George Fife Angas has been described as an "apostle for
emigration."[24] Already in 1832 Angas had joined the South Australian
Land Company, and he later became a member of the colony's first Legisla-
tive Council. A Dissenter, Angas promoted freedom of religion and it is
perhaps not surprising that he found a model in William Penn:

> If I can get pious people sent out to that land the ground will be
> blessed for their sake and if justice be done to the aborigines as
> was done by William Penn then we shall have peace in all our

---

20. Ibid., 210. On the initial absence of police, see Pike, *Paradise of Dissent*, 283–85.

21. Stephens, *Land of Promise*, 100.

22. Ibid.

23. On the tensions between the South Australian foundation as a colony and "national" aspirations, see further Foster and Nettlebeck, "Proclamation Day."

24. Pike, *Paradise of Dissent*, 129.

borders for I reckon that the principle of God's Government will apply to South Australia as elsewhere.[25]

Along with many others at the time, Angas was mindful of the frontier violence that had taken place in Van Diemen's Land, and his humanitarian attitudes were more in tune with the Quaker model of colonization in Pennsylvania. In the passage above, Angas implicitly links the Quaker example with the story of Abraham, suggesting, as John Stephens did, that this is the kind of immigration that yields blessings for the land and peaceful congress with the Indigenous people.

Another exponent of free emigration to the Australian colonies who deserves to be mentioned in this context is the Presbyterian John Dunmore Lang. Lang espoused a Promised Land typology on many occasions, while making quite clear that this did not include a right of conquest that might be extracted from the book of Joshua. This point is demonstrated even in his published sermon from 1838 *National Sins* where he configures Indigenous people with a "Gibeonite" typology, alluding to the wrongful killing of the Indigenous Gibeonites by King Saul in 2 Samuel 21:

> Let us ask ourselves seriously and in earnest, whether, as the European colonists of this territory, we can lay our hands upon our hearts, and plead *not guilty* concerning the Gibeonites, I mean the wretched Aboriginal inhabitants of this land? Alas! We are verily guilty concerning these our brethren; for not only have we despoiled them of their land, and given them in exchange European vice and European disease in every foul and fatal form, but the blood of hundreds, nay of thousand of their number, who have fallen from time to time in their native forests, when waging unequal warfare with their civilized aggressors, still stains the hands of many of the inhabitants of the land![26]

In her detailed research on John Dunmore Lang's biblical hermeneutics, Meredith Lake concludes that "Lang deliberately avoided applying the Promised Land narrative to the colony in a way that sanctioned the violent dispossession of Aboriginal people. In his usage, it was not a narrative of conquest and extermination at the expense of the land's prior inhabitants as Edward Said suggested."[27] She also concludes, however, that Lang was actually unusual among the nineteenth century clergy in promoting a Promised

---

25. Quoted in Hodder, *George Fife Angus,* 107–108, from a letter of June 4, 1835.

26. Lang, *National Sins,* 13–15.

27. Lake, *Spiritual Acres,* 295.

Land typology, perhaps in part because the Abrahamic hermeneutic was regarded by some as preposterous.[28]

Nevertheless, it is clear from John Stephens' *The Land of Promise* that a secularized biblical vision was indeed considered plausible, if only in South Australia.[29] And it is in South Australia that we find aspirations that overlap most clearly with the Priestly portrait of Abraham in Genesis—the ancestor who respected the traditional owners of the land, and who entered into treaties with them, rather than claiming as Joshua did a right of conquest.[30] Here in the 1830s and 1840s we find an Abraham typology that suited the advocacy of the Aborigines' Protection Society. As history unfolded, however, the legal concept of "waste" land was to prevail over the natural rights of Aboriginal people as economic interest relentlessly came to the fore.

Not only did the South Australian administration fail to negotiate any treaties with Aboriginal people, but around the same time, the Colonial Office rejected a treaty initiative in the area that was to become the colony of Victoria. In 1835, John Batman negotiated what he understood to be a treaty in Port Phillip (the site of the later city of Melbourne), and while he was styled "the Tasmanian Penn" in the local press at the time, he was not an agent of the Crown and therefore not authorized to make a treaty. The complexities in this case are similar to those in *Johnson v. McIntosh*, since in the American case the leading question was also whether a private company could treat with the Indians.[31] Nevertheless, whatever Batman's personal limitations might have been, it remains unclear why the Colonial Office in London did not continue to press for valid treaties in Victoria and South Australia.

Writing in 1858, the former Undersecretary James Stephen discussed the justice of colonization not by acknowledging that Aboriginal rights that had been disrespected in the 1830s and earlier, but by celebrating the kind of government that could work economic miracles, and disprove the "dismal science" of Thomas Malthus. The gloomy economic predictions of the Reverend Malthus turned out to be false, according to Stephen, because he had not anticipated the "commercial enfranchisement" wrought by the

---

28. See the dismissive response to Lang's Abrahamic pretentions in *Australian Quarterly Journal* vol.4 (1828), 331; Lake, *Spiritual Acres*, 264, 275, 289–90, 302; Brett, *Decolonizing God*, 10.

29. See further Davison, "Narrating the Nation in Australia."

30. On the Priestly origins of this paradigm in biblical theology see Brett, "Priestly Dissemination of Abraham," 24–44; Wöhrle, "Un-Empty Land," 189–206; cf. Habel, *Land is Mine*, 115–133.

31. See further Attwood, *Possession* and Boyce, *1835: Founding of Melbourne*.

abolition of slavery and colonial self-government.[32] In effect, it seems that the wealth of the suitably English Abraham outweighed the exemplary engagement with Indigenous people.[33]

In conclusion, a detailed study of the Australian emigration literature from the early nineteenth century illustrates a distinctive pattern in the reception of the biblical figure of Abraham: while the biblical metanarrative links the Promised Land with conquest themes, and has on these grounds been condemned by postcolonial biblical critics, it is the Abrahamic Promised Land typology that is associated most closely in the 1830s with the advocacy of treaties and with the condemnation of settler violence against the traditional owners of the land. It appears, however, that this acknowledgement of Indigenous natural rights was steadily overwhelmed by economic interests, by the rise of social Darwinism,[34] and by an increasing skepticism towards the very idea of human rights.

WORKS CITED

Attwood, Bain. *Possession: Batman's Treaty and the Matter of History.* Melbourne: Miegunyah, 2009.

Boyce, James. *1835: The Founding of Melbourne and the Conquest of Australia.* Melbourne: Black, 2011.

Brennan, Sean. "The Disregard for Legal Protections of Aboriginal Land Rights in Early South Australia." In *Coming to Terms: Aboriginal Title in South Australia,* edited by S. Berg, 90–121. Kent Town: Wakefield, 2010.

Brett, Mark G. *Decolonizing God: The Bible in the Tides of Empire.* Bible in the Modern World 16. Sheffield: Sheffield Phoenix, 2008.

———. "Feeling for Country: Reading the Old Testament in the Australian Context." *Pacifica* (2010) 137–156. [Response to Ann Curthoys, "Whose Home? Expulsion, Exodus and Exile in White Australian Mythology."] *Journal of Australian Studies* 61 (1999) 1–18.

———. "The Priestly Dissemination of Abraham." *Hebrew Bible and Ancient Israel* 3 (2014) 24–44.

Carey, Hilary. *God's Empire: Religion and Colonialism in the British World, c. 1801–1908.* Cambridge: Cambridge University Press, 2011.

Davison, Graeme. "Narrating the Nation in Australia." Menzies Lecture 2009, Menzies Centre for Australian Studies, King's College, London.

Echo-Hawk, Walter R. "Colonialism and Law in the Postcolonial Era." In *Coming to Terms: Aboriginal Title in South Australia,* edited by S. Berg, 148–205. Kent Town: Wakefield, 2010.

32. Stephen, "Colonization as a Branch of Social Economy," esp. 288 and 297.

33. See also Lang's invocations of Abraham's wealth, discussed by Lake, *Spiritual Acres,* 280.

34. See, e.g., Evans, Saunders and Cronin, *Race Relations in Colonial Queensland,* 81–82; Kenny, *Lamb Enters the Dreaming,* 295.

Evans, R., K. Saunders, K. Cronin. *Race Relations in Colonial Queensland: A History of Exclusion, Exploitation and Extermination.* 2nd ed. St Lucia: University of Queensland Press, 1988.

Ford, Lisa. *Settler Sovereignty: Jurisdiction and Indigenous People in America and Australia, 1788–1836.* Cambridge: Harvard University Press, 2010.

Foster, Robert, and Amanda Nettlebeck. "Proclamation Day and the Rise and Fall of South Australian Nationalism." In *Turning Points: Chapters in South Australian History*, edited by R. Foster and P. Sendziuk, 48–62. Kent Town: Wakefield, 2012.

Habel, Norman. *The Land Is Mine: Six Biblical Land Ideologies. Overtures to Biblical Theology.* Minneapolis: Fortress, 1995.

Hodder, Edwin. *George Fife Angus: Father and Founder of South Australia.* London: Hodder & Stoughton, 1891.

Kenny, Robert. *The Lamb Enters the Dreaming: Nathanael Pepper and the Ruptured World.* Melbourne: Scribe, 2007.

Knaplund, Paul. *James Stephen and the British Colonial System, 1813–1847.* Madison: University of Wisconsin Press, 1953.

Lake, Marilyn, and Henry Reynolds. *Drawing the Global Colour Line: White Men's Countries and the Question of Racial Equality.* Melbourne: Melbourne University Press, 2008.

Lake, Meredith. *Such Spiritual Acres: Protestantism, the Land and the Colonization of Australia, 1788–1850.* PhD diss., University of Sydney, 2008.

Lang, John Dunmore. *National Sins the Cause & Precursors of National Judgements: A Sermon preached in the Scots Church, Sydney on Friday November 2, 1838, being the day appointed by his Excellency, Sir George Gipps, as a Day of Fasting and Humiliation on account of the late calamitous Drought.* Sydney: Tegg, 1838.

Masalha, Nur. "Reading the Bible with the Eyes of the Canaanites: Neo-Zionism, Political Theology and the Land Traditions of the Bible." *Holy Land Studies* 8 (2009) 55–108.

Miller, Robert, Jacinta Ruru, Larissa Behrendt, and Tracey Lindberg. *Discovering Indigenous Lands: The Doctrine of Discovery in the English Colonies.* Oxford: Oxford University Press, 2010.

Motte, Standish. *Outline of a System of Legislation, for securing protection to the aboriginal inhabitants of all countries colonized by Great Britain; extending to them political and social rights, ameliorating their condition, and promoting their civilization.* London: Murray, 1840.

Pike, Douglas. *Paradise of Dissent: South Australia 1829–1857.* Carlton: Melbourne University Press, 1957.

Religious Tract Society. *The Emigrant's Friend: A Selection of Tracts, Being a Companion for the Voyage, and a Manual of Instruction in His New Home.* London: Religious Tract Society, 1852(?).

Reynolds, Henry. "South Australia: Between Van Diemen's Land and New Zealand." In *Turning Points: Chapters in South Australian History*, edited by R. Foster and P. Sendziuk, 24–32. Kent Town: Wakefield, 2012.

Robertson, Lindsay G. *Conquest by Law: How the Discovery of America Dispossessed Indigenous Peoples of Their Lands.* New York: Oxford University Press, 2005.

Rose, Deborah Bird. "Rupture and the Ethics of Care in Colonized Space." In *Prehistory to Politics*, edited by T. Bonyhady and T. Griffiths. Melbourne: Melbourne University Press, 1996.

Said, Edward. "Michael Walzer's Exodus and Revolution: A Canaanite Reading." In *Blaming the Victims: Spurious Scholarship and the Palestinian Question*, edited by E. Said and C. Hitchens, 161–78. New York: Verso, 1988.

Stephen, James. "Colonization as a Branch of Social Economy." Reprinted in Paul Knaplund, *James Stephen and the British Colonial System, 1813–1847*, 281–98. Madison: University of Wisconsin Press, 1953.

Stephens, John. *The Land of Promise*. London: Smith, Elder, 1839.

The Emigrant's Friend: or Authentic Guide to South Australia, including Sydney; Port Phillip, or Australia Felix; Western Australia, or Swan River Colony; New South Wales; Van Diemen's Land; and New Zealand. J. Allen, Warwick Lane Paternoster Row; D. Francis, Mile End Road, 1848.

Wöhrle, Jakob. "The Un-Empty Land: The Concept of Exile and Land in P." In *The Concept of Exile in Ancient Israel and Its Historical Contexts*, edited by E. Ben Zvi and C. Levin, 189–206. Berlin: de Gruyter, 2010.

9

BLESSINGS AND CURSES IN THE PENTATEUCH AND IN THE CONTEMPORARY CONTEXT

Grahame Rosolen

BLESSINGS AND CURSES ARE themes prevalent in the Pentateuch. The Hebrew word *barak* (ברך) appears 166 times in the Pentateuch and may be translated to mean bless and also to mean curse.[1] There is a reciprocal symmetry with the use of blessings and curses as they appear together in several key narratives within the Pentateuch. The ambiguity inherent in *barak* creates difficulties for translators but elegantly caters for those situations when what appears to be a blessing transforms into a curse and vice versa. Other situations may be viewed as a blessing or a curse depending on the perspective adopted. Some key places in the Pentateuch which illuminate aspects of the nature of blessings and curses are contained in the narratives of Abraham (Genesis 12), Jacob (Genesis 32) and Joseph (Genesis 39), the interplay between Balak and Balaam (Numbers 22–24) and the speeches of Moses to Israel (Deuteronomy 30).

---

1. Mitchell, "Meaning of ברך." The Hebrew word *arar* (ארר) appears less frequently and means to execrate.

ALGORITHM OF BLESSING IN THE PENTATEUCH

Some parts of the Pentateuch lend themselves to a logical mapping in the syntax of computer science which has algorithmic constructs such as "*if then else*" statements and "*while*" statements.[2] The speeches of Moses in Deuteronomy have this character: *if you* do this *then* you will receive blessing, *else* you will receive the opposite of blessing which is a curse. Or in the case of the "*while*" statements; *while* you do this you will be blessed. Blessing will occur while continuing to do certain actions which are periodically checked and *if* the actions cease *then* the blessing will not continue and will potentially be replaced by a curse. An example of this algorithmic description of blessing is recorded at the end of Deuteronomy in Moses' final speech to Israel as they prepared to enter the Promised Land. The alternatives are stark: life and blessings or death and curses.

> See, I have set before you today life and prosperity, death and adversity. *If* you obey the commandments of the Lord your God that I am commanding you today, by loving the Lord your God, walking in his ways, and observing his commandments, decrees, and ordinances, *then* you shall live and become numerous, and the Lord your God will bless you in the land that you are entering to possess. But *if* your heart turns away and you do not hear, but are led astray to bow down to other gods and serve them, I declare to you today that [*then*] you shall perish; you shall not live long in the land that you are crossing the Jordan to enter and possess. I call heaven and earth to witness against you today that I have set before you, life and death, blessings and curses. (Deut 30:15–19; italics added)[3]

Although the algorithm of blessing is a useful structure for understanding some aspects of divine blessing and establishing patterns of behavior to avoid divine curses, it is not sufficient to understand it. There is a danger of seeking to utilize the blessing of God or manipulate it for specific purposes or to try and divert or capture blessing. There are several examples in the narratives of the Pentateuch which highlight the futility and consequences of attempting to subvert the blessing of God and of ignoring God as the source of blessing. Those who focus on seeking a blessing and ignore the source may find they have obtained a curse.

There are numerous references in Genesis to Joseph as being blessed by God. For example, the narrative about Joseph's time as a servant in

---

2. Kernighan and Ritchie, *C Programming Language*.

3. Unless indicated otherwise, all biblical quotations are taken from the NRSV.

Potiphar's house and then in the Egyptian prison is framed by the text indicating the favor and blessing of God that was bestowed on Joseph.

> From the time that he made him overseer in his house and over all that he had, the LORD blessed the Egyptian's house for Joseph's sake; the blessing of the Lord was on all that he had, in house and field. (Gen 39:5–6)

> The chief jailer paid no heed to anything that was in Joseph's care, because the LORD was with him; and whatever he did, the LORD made it prosper. (39:23)

Earlier in Genesis Joseph's brothers were not enamored with Joseph's blessed status and sought to intervene and subvert this blessing by killing him. Joseph is ultimately sold into slavery and then, following the episode with Potiphar's wife, he ends up in prison. From this predicament Joseph becomes an important official in Egypt and he ultimately saves from starvation his brothers and their families and hence the people chosen by God. Despite the efforts of human intervention, the blessing bestowed by God on Joseph and also on the descendants of Abraham prevails. Indeed, Joseph recognizes this in his response to his brothers at the end of Genesis.

> But Joseph said to them, 'Do not be afraid! Am I in the place of God? Even though you intended to do harm to me, God intended it for good, in order to preserve a numerous people, as he is doing today. (Gen 50:19–20)

It is significant that Joseph recognizes that the blessing comes from God. Any attempt to subvert the role of God with regard to blessings and curses will not succeed. In the Pentateuch those human actions which are intended to harm or curse those blessed by God are transformed into blessing. There is a strong element of election in the blessing of those whom God chooses to bless.[4] This is particularly evident in the blessing of Abraham in Genesis.

> Now the LORD said to Abram, "Go from your country and your kindred and your father's house to the land that I will show you. I will make of you a great nation, and I will bless you, and make your name great, so that you will be a blessing. I will bless those who bless you, and the one who curses you I will curse; and in you all the families of the earth shall be blessed." (Gen 12:1–3)

In Genesis 12 Abraham is chosen by God as the recipient and conduit of blessing. In the last clause it is what others do to Abraham that is

4. Westermann, *Blessing.*

the catalyst for the blessings or curses that flow. Again the source of the blessings and curses is God. The zeal with which blessings were sought by the descendants of Abraham for at least the first several generations is well documented in the Pentateuch. These characters act as conduits for the blessing of God. When Abraham gives his nephew Lot the first choice over land, Lot chooses what in human terms seems to be the best land, blessed by abundant natural resources. However, problems soon arise and Lot ends up fleeing the land and his wife is turned into a pillar of salt. Abraham experiences less difficulty in what appeared to be the less blessed environment. Lot seeks to capture the blessing for himself at the expense of others and ultimately it turns into a curse.

Isaac and his wife Rebekah have favorites and different views as to which of their sons should carry the blessing. Receiving the blessing is considered so important that Rebekah secretly conspires with Jacob to ensure that Isaac confers the blessing on Jacob. The principal concern of Jacob in executing this plan is not the fear of the reaction of his father or brother, should the plan be discovered, but rather his fear of receiving a curse.

> "Perhaps my father will feel me, and I shall seem to be mocking him, and bring a curse on myself and not a blessing." His mother said to him, "Let your curse be on me, my son; only obey my word, and go, get them for me." (Gen 27:12–13)

The plan succeeds and Isaac is tricked into blessing Jacob. The significance of this is evident in the dismay of Isaac's response and Esau's desperation to receive a blessing.

> Then Isaac trembled violently, and said, "Who was it then that hunted game and brought it to me, and I ate it all before you came, and I have blessed him?—yes, and blessed he shall be!" When Esau heard his father's words, he cried out with an exceedingly great and bitter cry, and said to his father, "Bless me, me also, father!" But he said, "Your brother came deceitfully, and he has taken away your blessing." (Gen 27:33–35)

Isaac's response further highlights that the source of the blessing is from God. Once Isaac has passed the blessing to Jacob, even when done in error, there appears no opportunity to divert it. Furthermore the ending phrase of the blessing is the same as the blessing given to Abraham.

> Cursed be everyone who curses you,
> and blessed be everyone who blesses you! (Gen 27:29b)

The importance attached to receiving a blessing is further illustrated by Jacob in the account of him wrestling with the angel in Genesis 32.[5] Despite being injured Jacob would not let go of the angel until he received a blessing. There is further family politics in the passing of the blessing of God between generations when Joseph brings his two sons to Jacob for blessing. Jacob crosses over his hands to ensure that the younger carries the principal blessing. Jacob is reversing the intent of his own father Isaac by favoring the younger sibling and also going against the stated wishes of their father Joseph.

> When Joseph saw that his father laid his right hand on the head of Ephraim, it displeased him; so he took his father's hand, to remove it from Ephraim's head to Manasseh's head. Joseph said to his father, "Not so, my father! Since this one is the firstborn, put your right hand on his head." But his father refused, and said, "I know, my son, I know; he also shall become a people, and he also shall be great. Nevertheless, his younger brother shall be greater than he, and his offspring shall become a multitude of nations." So he blessed them that day. (Gen 48:17–20)

Balak is an example of a character from the Pentateuch who sought to manipulate the blessing of God. Balak seeks to enlist the help of the renowned prophet Balaam whom Balak asserts has the capacity to direct blessings and curses for a fee.

> Now Balak son of Zippor was king of Moab at that time. He sent messengers to Balaam son of Beor at Pethor, which is on the Euphrates, in the land of Amaw, to summon him, saying, 'A people has come out of Egypt; they have spread over the face of the earth, and they have settled next to me. Come now, curse this people for me, since they are stronger than I; perhaps I shall be able to defeat them and drive them from the land; for I know that whomsoever you bless is blessed, and whomsoever you curse is cursed.' (Num 22:4–6)

There is an echo in the last clause of the promise made to Abraham in Genesis 12 and repeated in Genesis 27, but with a reversal. Balak sees Balaam as the arbiter and active catalyst for blessing or curses which has a flow-on effect to others based on what Balaam does. Balak has misunderstood both the source and conduit of blessing. In the promise to Abraham from God, Abraham is the passive catalyst for the blessing of others based on what others do to Abraham. Balak has made this fundamental reversal of the source

5. Zakovitch and Zakovitch, *Jacob.*

of the blessing and asked Balaam to provide a service which carries a huge risk. The stance taken by Balaam is consistent with a wise acknowledgement of the last part of the promise of blessing to Abraham. If Balak and Balaam were to take the promise of God to Abraham as seriously as Abraham did, then the prospect of cursing the people God has chosen to be a great nation would seem a particularly risky proposition. The stark "if then else" logic of Genesis 12:3 is a compelling warning. Indeed, Balaam replies to the envoys sent by Balak that no inducement would be sufficient for him to opt for the "else" outcome in Genesis 12:3.

> Balaam replied to the servants of Balak, "Although Balak were to give me his house full of silver and gold, I could not go beyond the command of the Lord my God, to do less or more." (Num 22:18)

God makes it clear to Balaam that Israel is a nation that is blessed as Balaam agrees to go with Balak's envoys. He saddles his ass and sets off on a long journey with instructions from the Lord to "do only what I tell you to do" (Numbers 22:20). The role of Balaam's female ass provides an interesting perspective on the interplay between human actions and the blessing of God. Kirova asserts that the heroine of the Balaam narrative is the ass.[6] Inversion, triple repetition and irony in the Balaam narrative all contribute to a compelling account.[7] Balaam as a famous prophet has the status of "one who sees."[8] His ass by contrast is a lowly beast suited to carrying loads under the control of her master. On three occasions it is Balaam who is blind to the angel of the Lord standing in his path and on each occasion his ass sees the angel ready to slay Balaam with a sword and intervenes. On the last time, where the angel of the Lord blocks the way, the narrative reaches a miraculous climax.

> When the donkey saw the angel of the LORD, it lay down under Balaam; and Balaam's anger was kindled, and he struck the donkey with his staff. Then the LORD opened the mouth of the donkey, and it said to Balaam, "What have I done to you, that you have struck me these three times?" Balaam said to the donkey, "Because you have made a fool of me! I wish I had a sword in my hand! I would kill you right now!" (Num 22:27–29)

Balaam has embarked on a pursuit that has made him blind to the dangers of participating in an attempt to manipulate the blessing of God.

6. Kirova, "Eyes Wide Open."

7. Moberly, *Can Balaam's Ass Speak Today?*; Moore, *Balaam Traditions*.

8. Wenham, *Numbers*.

Balaam's ass can see the danger and responds but Balaam's response is one of blindness and anger. Balaam asserts that if he was carrying his sword he would have killed the very beast that protected him. Balaam complains that the ass has made a fool of him, when in reality Balaam has made a fool of himself. The miracle of the ass speaking shows that a reversal has taken place. The ass becomes the wise one who sees and even speaks and Balaam is rendered the blind dumb ass. The reason given in the narrative for the angel of the Lord appearing is to oppose any attempt to subvert the blessing of God, an endeavor Balaam has rashly embarked upon.

> I have come out as an adversary, because your way is perverse before me. The donkey saw me, and turned away from me these three times. If it had not turned away from me, surely I would by now have killed you and let it live. (Num 22:32b–33)

The angel indicates that the ass would have been spared and so were Balaam to come under God's curse the ass would not be included. The ass has chosen not to be complicit in the manipulation of God's blessing and so avoids being caught up in a curse. The way that Balaam has chosen is one of seeking to meddle with the blessing of God and this way is one that leads to a curse. The ass sees this and tries to intervene. Balaam reverses this blessing of insight and curses his ass and threatens its life. However, the angel of the Lord intervenes, saves the ass and warns Balaam. The irony of being able to see is amplified in the narrative three times as Balak takes Balaam to different vantage points. At each vantage point Balaam has an improved view of the people he is asked to curse. The farce of sacrificial offerings is repeated with Balak's increasing sense of desperation. In the text of Balaam's oracles, the rubric of the prophet as one who sees with clear and uncovered eyes is repeated.

> The oracle of Balaam son of Beor,
>   the oracle of the man whose eye is clear,
> the oracle of one who hears the words of God,
>   who sees the vision of the Almighty,
>   who falls down, but with eyes uncovered. (Num 24:3–4)

Balaam has his eyes open to what God says but remains engaged with Balak's quest to curse Israel. Balaam claims his eyes are clear and open to see the vision from God but he was unable to see the angel of the Lord blocking his way and the dangers of this endeavor. Baskin quotes the views of the patristic fathers such as Origen who saw Balaam as a villain "who fights for the darker forces against the righteous."[9] This villainy may take the

---

9. Baskin, "Origen on Balaam."

characteristic of amorality because Balaam appears to do whatever suits his situation at the time. He will play along with Balak following him along the mountain tops and conducting sacrifices in a hopeless quest to have what is blessed by God cursed. Balaam specifically articulates the impossibility of Balak's quest in each of his oracles on Israel.

> How can I curse whom God has not cursed?
>   How can I denounce those whom the Lord has not denounced?
> For from the top of the crags I see him,
>   from the hills I behold him. (Num 23:8–9)

> Blessed is everyone who blesses you,
>   and cursed is everyone who curses you. (Num 24:9b)

Balaam understands that the election and blessing of these elect comes from God. In accordance with Gen 12:3 Balaam knows that seeking to curse Israel, those whom God has blessed, will only serve to bring a curse on him as well as Balak and the Moabites who seek to help them. Balaam asks "Let me die the death of the upright" (Num 23:10b) but he is participating in an activity that is not consistent with upright character. It is worth noting that later in Numbers and also in Joshua the killing of Balaam by the sword at the hands of the Israelite army is recorded.[10] Balaam overreached through participation in the attempt of Balak to curse the Israelites. The role of human actions in the blessing and curses of God is one where actions must be carefully considered. There is further allusion to Balaam's role and culpability as his name may mean "abuser of a people."[11] Later in the Pentateuch a conclusion derived by looking back on the Balaam narrative in the context of what has happened to God's chosen people is presented.

> Yet the LORD your God refused to heed Balaam; the LORD your God turned the curse into a blessing for you, because the LORD your God loved you. (Deut 23:5)

The text states a reversal is applied by God who transforms what in human terms was intended to be a curse into a blessing. God is both the source of blessing and the architect of the reversal. The motivation for this is cited as the love God has for his chosen people. As the Balaam narrative makes clear, the blessing comes from God and seeking to thwart the blessing of God or capture a blessing whilst acting in opposition to God will result in a curse.

---

10. Num 31:8; and Josh 13:22.

11. Radday and Brenner, eds., *On Humour and the Comic.*

> All who hear the words of this oath and bless themselves, think-
> ing in their hearts, "We are safe even though we go our own
> stubborn ways" (thus bringing disaster on moist and dry alike)
> the LORD will be unwilling to pardon them, for the LORD's anger
> and passion will smoke against them. All the curses written in
> this book will descend on them, and the LORD will blot out their
> names from under heaven. (Deut 29:19–20)

Most discussion of blessing and curses assumes it is clear what out-
comes constitute blessing and what constitute curses. The perspective that
one adopts has a significant role to play in characterizing situations as either
a blessing or a curse. In this sense the opposite alternative translations inherent in the polysemous Hebrew word *barak* cater for these possibilities.

BLESSINGS AND CURSES
IN THE CONTEMPORARY CONTEXT

In a contemporary context several authors have examined the ownership
of natural resources and discussed how this can be either a blessing or a
curse, or sometimes both.[12] Van der Ploeg provides empirical evidence to
demonstrate how abundant natural resources can be a curse or a blessing for
some of the nations who possess them. The blessing of these resources can
lead to the ability to fund programs in social areas such as health, education and welfare for the disadvantaged. However, this blessing of resources
may be a curse for some other areas of the economy as the inflow of wealth
influences foreign exchange rates which in turn makes other industries less
competitive and so they decline. This phenomenon is typically described as
Dutch disease.[13] In some economies the perceived blessings of rich natural
resources can lead to increased corruption, cost of living pressures, greater
and more widespread inequality, poverty, civil unrest and war.[14] Storey and
Hunter discuss the link between fossil fuel natural resources and the energy
they provide as a blessing to many people but a curse for others on a global
scale.[15] In particular, the contribution of fossil fuel burning to rises in sea
level is one factor resulting in the people of Kiribati being at risk of losing
their homeland. The existence and use of resources which are a blessing for
some have become a curse for others.

12. Van der Ploeg, "Natural Resources"; Li, "Corruption, Transparency and the
Resource Curse."

13. Van Wijnbergen, "'Dutch Disease'"

14. Abah, "When Blessing Becomes a Curse."

15. Storey and Hunter, "Kiribati."

The reliance on an apparent blessing which is temporary or subject to external influences can transform into a curse when circumstances change. A contemporary example is the Australian economy which generates considerable wealth through the export of mineral resources. During times of boom in the resources sector there are typically increases in capital inflow, increases in income and increases in government spending funded by increased taxation revenue. These financial blessings come along with the reduced competitiveness of some industries due to the appreciation of the currency.[16] In the contemporary Australian context the competitiveness of manufacturing has suffered as a consequence and so for these industries the resources boom is considered a curse.[17] During the boom cycle the trajectory of community expectations is set and this has consequences when the boom declines or comes to an end. A blessing may be amplified during the boom years to the point that when circumstances change and the blessing declines it is then replaced by an amplified curse. The gap between expectations and reality widens as the greater the boom the greater the subsequent bust. What appeared initially as a blessing has for many transformed into a curse.

The identification of a situation or outcome as a blessing or a curse is potentially problematic in some circumstances. The perspective of humanity is limited and what is often perceived as a curse may be a blessing and vice versa. Carson and Wakeley examine the role of mental illness in some famous historical individuals and conclude that the significant impact of their lives was made possible in part by the mental illness they suffered.[18] Their conclusion is that the benefits were considerable both to the individuals who suffered as well as to the communities they served. Through these difficulties enhanced insight and broader perspectives are cited as blessings of the conditions they suffered. A similar sentiment was expressed by a study of cancer patients some of whom noted "changes in meaning were seen as coming from the struggle rather than despite the struggle and, once learned, were carried forward in their lives."[19]

CONCLUSION

Some attributes of blessing and curses have emerged from considering various aspects of some key narratives in the Pentateuch. The Pentateuch

16. Corden, "Dutch Disease in Australia."
17. Cleary, *Too Much Luck*.
18. Carson and Wakely, "A Curse and Blessing."
19. Fletcher et al., "A Blessing and a Curse."

narratives assert blessing comes from God and this blessing will not be thwarted by human attempts to divert or overturn the election of God. Seeking to capture and control blessing out of self-interest can lead to what appears to be a blessing becoming a curse. Conversely events and situations contrived by human efforts to be a curse may be transformed into a blessing for those whom God has chosen. The categorization of situations as blessings or curses may differ depending on the perspective adopted. Those who focus on the blessing rather than the giver of the blessing and who seek to manipulate the flow of the blessing should consider the algorithmic choices articulated by Moses and to ponder the rhetorical question Joseph posed to his brothers, "Am I in the place of God?" (Gen 50:19b)

WORKS CITED

Abah, Betty. "When Blessing Becomes a Curse in the Niger Delta." *Women in Action* 2 (2009) 25–32.

Baskin, J. R. "Origen on Balaam: The Dilemma of the Unworthy Prophet." *Vigiliae Christianae* 37 (1983) 22–35.

Carson, Jerome, and Elizabeth Wakely. "A Curse and Blessing. (Impact of Mental Illness on the Lives and Achievements of Winston Churchill, Florence Nightingale, Charles Darwin, and Abraham Lincoln)." *History Today* 63.2 (2013) 10–16.

Cleary, Paul. *Too Much Luck: The Mining Boom and Australia's Future.* Collingwood, Vic.: Black, 2011.

Corden, W. "Dutch Disease in Australia: Policy Options for a Three-Speed Economy." *Australian Economic Review* 45.3 (2012) 290–304.

Kernighan, Brian W., and Dennis M. Ritchie. *The C Programming Language.* 2nd ed. Englewood Cliffs, NJ: Prentice Hall, 1988.

Kirova, Milena. "Eyes Wide Open: A Case of Symbolic Reversal in the Biblical Narrative." *International Journal of Nordic Theology* 24.1 (2010) 85–98.

Li, Mingcong. "Corruption, Transparency and the Resource Curse." *International Journal of Social Science and Humanity* 3.6 (2013) 572–75.

Mitchell, Christopher Wright. "The Meaning of ברך "to Bless" in the Old Testament." PhD diss., University of Wisconsin-Madison, 1987.

Moberly, R. W. L. *Can Balaam's Ass Speak Today?: A Case Study in Reading the Old Testament as Scripture.* Grove Biblical Series 10. Cambridge: Grove, 1998.

Moore, Michael S. *The Balaam Traditions: Their Character and Development.* Society of Biblical Literature Dissertation Series 113. Atlanta: Scholars, 1990.

Radday, Yehuda T., and Athalya Brenner, eds. *On Humour and the Comic in the Hebrew Bible.* Journal for the Study of the Old Testament Supplements 92. Sheffield: Almond, 1990.

Storey, Donovan, and Shawn Hunter. "Kiribati: An Environmental 'Perfect Storm'." *Australian Geographer* 41.2 (2010) 167–81.

Swore Fletcher, Barbara, Marlene Z. Cohen, Karen Schumacher, and William Lydiatt. "A Blessing and a Curse: Head and Neck Cancer Survivors' Experiences." *Cancer Nursing* (2011) 1.

van der Ploeg, Frederick. "Natural Resources: Curse or Blessing?" *Journal of Economic Literature* 49.2 (2011) 366–420.

van Wijnbergen, Sweder. "The 'Dutch Disease': A Disease after All?" *Economic Journal* 94.373 (1984) 41–55.

Wenham, Gordon J. *Numbers: An Introduction and Commentary*. Leicester, UK: Inter-Varsity, 1981.

Westermann, Claus. *Blessing: In the Bible and the Life of the Church*. Translated by Keith Crim. Overtures to Biblical Theology. Philadelphia: Fortress, 1978.

Zakovitch, Yair, and Valerie Zakovitch. *Jacob: Unexpected Patriarch*. Translated by Valerie Zakovitch. Jewish Lives. New Haven: Yale University Press, 2012.

10

[S]PINNING BALAAM AGAINST THE WALL

Anthony Rees

OVER THE LAST TEN to fifteen years, political commentators and concerned citizens have lamented the ever declining quality of Australian political discourse. This is a disease which seems to have infected every level of Australian politics. What was once an engaged ideological debate about policy, argued along party lines, has descended into a type of personality politics, where the ultimate goal is power, not service to the nation.[1] Rather than informed policy debates, Australian politics has become largely about popularity polls and leadership speculation. In recent times, this phenomenon has been clearly on display.

With the recent Prime Minister Tony Abbott's popularity at crisis levels, the Australian Liberal Party entered an internal war. A motion to spill the leadership was defeated, though the amount of support for the spill was

1. In the last couple of years, Australia has lost two great former political leaders—one from each side of the political divide—Gough Whitlam and Malcolm Fraser. Both were fierce combatants, and great personalities. The depth of emotional outpouring for these two men included a reflection on the way in which their political depth is absent in the current political climate, of which they were both critical. Indeed, Malcolm Fraser went so far as to resign membership of the Liberal party, and was an outspoken critic of the Abbott government. It was not uncommon to hear him referred to as the current Australian opposition, such was the lack of critical engagement by the actual opposition!

significantly higher than Abbott had anticipated.[2] Chastened, he publicly conceded that he needed to change, and declared that "Good government begins today"[3] However, it was very clear that Abbott was working on borrowed time, and that a change of leadership was inevitable. With an election less than two years away, the Liberal Party could not continue on this path. Within six months, Abbott's time was up, and Malcolm Turnbull moved successfully to take leadership of the Liberal Party, and so become Australia's Prime Minister.[4] When the ultimate goal is power, one does not head to an election with a lame leader, and the promise of irrelevance in the ensuing parliament. Given current polling, it would come as no shock for the Australian Labor Party to switch leader ahead of elections later this year.

The evidence of the rise of personality politics in Australia was most clearly displayed by the now famous Kevin07 phenomenon. Kevin Rudd, the media darling, who won a generation of young voters through his appearances on a popular television chat show, and an ability to present himself as a laid-back, jovial fellow (which, incidentally, turned out to be far from the truth).[5] This is not in any way to suggest that Kevin Rudd was short on policy: indeed, at the time, his stance on climate change and asylum seekers did tap into an element of our society for whom those issues were important. He declared climate change as the great moral concern of our time,[6] a statement which gave great hope to Australians, who suffer the effects of climate change acutely in our uniquely diverse nation. Drought, fires and flood, ever-increasing in intensity, are very much a part of normal Australian experience, these days.[7] The decline in Rudd's popularity, perhaps because of his failure to turn such ambitious discourse into legislation that would pass through the parliament, and a looming election, saw the shift to his deputy, Julia Gillard.

This wasn't a shift of policy, but personality. Rudd's popular appeal waned as his language became more and more laden with jargon. The complexity of his speech contrasted sharply with the popular tone he had demonstrated previously, and which had won him such vast support.[8] In the face of electoral disaster, it was thought that a change in face would make a

---

2. Leslie, "Liberal Leadership Spill."

3. Griffiths, "Tony Abbott." This statement had many Australian wondering what had been happening up to this point!

4. Bourke, "Malcolm Turnbull defeats Tony Abbott."

5. See https://www.youtube.com/watch?v=rq8iw4-uB5E.

6. See https://www.youtube.com/watch?v=CqZvpRjGtGM.

7. Pitman, "Links between Global Warming and NSW Bush Fires."

8. Overington, "Kevin Rudd."

difference. Julia Gillard: Australia's first female Prime Minister, Labor's new hope. Of course, we know the story. After forming a minority government, and pursuing what was actually quite an ambitious policy program, the relentless badgering, name-calling and sexist taunts from the opposition gave way, to another change. Even Gillard's breath-taking misogyny speech[9] couldn't save her. Kevin Rudd emerged again, and after an initial bump in the all-important polls, Labor ran out of personality, and lost government.

But as we have seen, personality politics is hardly the sole-domain of the Australian Labor Party. In opposition, Tony Abbott assumed the leadership of the Liberal party in a carefully orchestrated execution of Malcolm Turnbull, some of Abbott's followers voting for Turnbull in an initial round of voting to ensure the demise of Joe Hockey, who would have beaten Abbott in a head-to-head ballot. Subsequently Abbot seemed to revel in his persona as the stern-faced, boot-camp martial operator, more comfortable in lycra than a tie, more likely to snarl than smile. Abbott is the face of conservative Australia: a serious, disciplined fellow, committed to fixing the mess in his own way. Stopping the boats, direct action, budget emergencies, and so on. Throw into the mix the newer faces of Clive Palmer and Jacqui Lambie, and the regular re-incarnations of Pauline Hansen and it is clear, personality trumps policy in Australian politics these days.

SPIN-DOCTOR

As a result of this decline in policy, and the importance of the protection of the personality figure on whose popularity success rides, a new class of political operator has emerged in Australian politics. This person is the "spin-doctor."[10] The spin doctor has two main tasks. The first is to be the spokesperson for policy, the second is to protect the reputation of the personality figure. For our purposes, the second task stands as the more important one. When politics is based upon the person of the leader, one of the most crucial aspects of political life becomes the protection of that figure's reputation. What we hear in the political rhetoric is how much support the leader has within the party, and how they have a vision for the nation, the state, whatever the case may be. It becomes important that in the presentation of policy which is not necessarily good news, that the leader not be subjected to too much exposure, whereby they might say something, or present in a way which might impact their popularity. And now I have sort of naturally progressed to the former point, which is that the spin doctor

9. Gillard, "Transcript." See also https://www.youtube.com/watch?v=SOPsxpMzYw4.

10. Harcup, "Spin Doctor"; Hogan, "Spin Doctor"; Stevenson, "Spin Doctor."

is charged with the responsibility of making unpalatable things, palatable; of turning pain into the national interest, of finding the small glimmer of positivity in an otherwise bleak situation, and making that the main thing, all the while trumpeting the value of the leader.

So a crucial question becomes, who is the spin doctor? Who plays this now important role in Australia's public life? I want to suggest that there are two types of spin-doctor. The first type is the low-ranking parliamentarian: perhaps a minor minister, or a back bencher from a safe party seat, who have little to lose. Indeed, the chance to appear as the leader's spokesperson is quite an opportunity for the otherwise unknown politician, and a chance to impress their constituents back at home with their public appearances. These characters take heat for the leader, repeating well-learnt party-lines over and over, sometimes not even coming close to answering the questions put to them. They might get slammed in the media, but they are unimportant and the press moves on quickly. Their pain, should they feel any, is short-lived, but their message remains. Coming from safe seats, they are not really under major threat. They are both expendable and re-usable. And perhaps, for their faithfulness, they might one day receive a cabinet position. As Stevenson suggests, they are employed to give a favorable view of events[11] even when such a positive view runs contrary to experience.

The second sort of spin doctor is the party outsider, with a huge following, and for whom saying ridiculous things is more likely to be positive than negative. I'm talking of media personalities: in particular, talk-back radio hosts, and newspaper columnists. To be clear, I am not suggesting that these people are in the employ of the party. That would be unethical. But no reasonably minded person could possibly believe that the Australian media is unbiased in its coverage these days. Numerous newspaper pages could be held up to demonstrate the truth of that. I don't want to suggest that this is necessarily new, but I do think that the ideological positions of media outlets are much more obvious today than ten years ago. These media characters are paid to be controversial. Their job is to mobilize a particular sort of person, to agitate for a particular ideological position. They tap into people's fear and anxiety and provide a space for what is often the worst aspect of our society (and here I mean attitudes, not people). Their game is the championing of one and the trashing of another, of polarity, of difference, of essentialism. There is no room for debate, no room for negotiation, no comprehension of nuance. Things are black and white. Pick your side, and be ready for the ridicule if you choose poorly. For this breed of spin doctor, the leader is almost messianic. To speak against them is heresy, to

11. Stevenson, "Spin Doctor."

vote against them, lunacy. And this is often cast in Nationalistic terms. If you are on our side, you are for Australia, you are a patriot. If not, you're a traitor, and an idiot.

Obviously, there is a difference in the way these two sorts of spin-doctor operate, and the audience to which they speak. After all, the only people who read a columnists' piece are those that buy their paper, and often that clientele is already invested in the narrative that is taking place. Likewise, the great majority of people who listen to talk-back radio do so because the host affirms or gives credibility what they already believe. The role of these spin-doctors is to develop a greater level of agitation, to mobilize people, emboldened by the affirmation of their beliefs. They can afford to push beyond the extremes, in order to make the reality seem more moderate than it really is. They are really preaching to the converted. Crucial to their value is that as outsiders, the party can always distance themselves from the spin-doctors if things go bad, if there is a public backlash to something too extreme. But the parliamentarian has a slightly different role, because their appearance is likely to have a broader audience. In as much as they are actually likely to face questions, and at least give the illusion of dialogue, they cannot really afford the same level of extravagance, and they have to guard themselves against going too far. If they over-step the mark, there can be political consequences for them, in a manner that the radio-hosts and newspaper identities are protected from. Nonetheless, what brings these two together is their role in twisting reality, in the presentation of something that isn't quite real: of distortion, displacement and deceit. No wonder our commentators and concerned citizens are in lament at this sad state of affairs. Style has replaced substance; presentation has trumped policy. Diversionary stories are trumpeted to bypass attention on matters of importance.[12]

BALAAM, A SPIN-DOCTOR

Having laid out some context, what I want to do is turn to the scriptures for an example relating to this sort of practice. I'm not claiming that this is a like-for-like situation. I'm suggesting that we use a feature of the present practice of politics in Australia as a way of looking at a particular piece of scripture. The text I want to turn to are the prophetic oracles of Balaam in Numbers 23 and 24. For the sake of our experiment, Balaam is our spin-doctor. Exactly who is he?

Balaam is a Mesopotamian prophet who in Num 22 is hired by the Moabite King, Balak, to curse the surrounding Israelites in order to protect

12. Hogan, "Spin Doctor."

his Kingdom going the same was as his surrounding neighbors (Num 22:5–6).[13] Balaam is historical figure. There is an extra-biblical inscription from Deir-Alla, dated to around 800 BCE which gives evidence of his standing as a noted diviner within the region. Likewise, Micah (an eighth-century contemporary) makes reference to him, though this is the only positive reference to Balaam in the scriptures (Micah 6:5). Balaam is one of the bad guys, par excellence. This is not to suggest that the oracles of Balaam necessarily have him as their source, but rather, there is a historical tradition which is utilized here for political purposes. So in terms of our spin-doctor profiles, Balaam fits reasonably comfortably amongst the second group. He has a strong reputation, is well known, has a large following, and the freedom and capacity to make big statements. As an outsider to the "party" he is not constrained by party-political concerns. He can simply claim to speak what God tells him to speak, and damn the consequences.

Balaam's position is a little complicated. He is employed by Balak to come and curse the Israelites. He is a gun for hire. This is what he does: he speaks, and things happen, and you can buy his words. These days, we call it cash-for-comment.[14] Sadly for Balak, Balaam seems to have a political pre-commitment. Let's briefly look at the four oracles:

In the first (Num 23:7–10), Balaam briefly sketches the events which led to him being in his position, and his claim that he cannot do what he has been engaged to do. He has a polarity set up between blessing and cursing. Balaam cannot curse what has been blessed (23:8). Further, we have an exaggerated account of Israel's size,[15] and the claim that the death of a son of Israel is the death of the upright. "Let my death be like his" (23:10).

The second (23:18–24) covers much of the same ground. But we also have here the announcement that would strike fear into Israel's enemies. Their God is like the horns of a wild Ox (23:22), an image of supernatural

13. Numbers 21 narrates the demolition of two kingdoms: the Amorite Kingdom of Sihon (21–32), and the Bashan Kingdom of Og (33–35).

14. Zinn, "Australian Radio Stars."

15. The census data which begins the book of Numbers postulates an adult male population of over 600,000, and so an overall population in excess of two million. This is clearly fanciful. If the seventy members of Jacob's family grew at the same rate as the rest of the population in Egypt, over four hundred years they would have grown to 10,000, some way short of the two million imagined in the census data! These numbers are not necessarily in view here. Even a mass of 10,000 people surrounding an ancient city would have seemed like a legitimate threat. However, the exaggeration is still in play. See Davies, "A Mathematical Conundrum."

strength,[16] and that Israel is like a lion,[17] not resting until it has devoured the bodies of its enemies (23:24).

The third (24:3–9) employs much the same material though it contains an unusual statement about how beautiful the tents of Israel are, likening them to palm groves, gardens and rivers (24:4–5). A reiteration of how much damage is going to be wreaked upon Israel's enemies follows, with a final kicker, "Blessed is everyone who blesses you, and cursed is everyone who curses you." Here we see an example of the dialectic which is common to the spin-doctor. Either one is in, or out. There is no room for nuance here.

The final oracle (24:15–24) forecasts the damage to be done to surrounding nations. The names of the nations and peoples are a mixture of known and unknown peoples and places, but the scale of the damage is catastrophic. Nations will perish forever, peoples will be taken captive, peoples' lands and livelihoods crushed and destroyed, but Jacob will prevail and rule (24:19). Interestingly, the nations mentioned largely correspond to the nations who come under other classical biblical prophetic judgement: Moabites, Edomites, Amalekites and Kenites all, at various points, are the subject of prophetic judgement.

We now consider the audience of Balaam's words. Are these proclamations of doom directed at Israel's enemies, the nations slated here for various forms of misfortune? Or do they serve some other purpose? Clearly, Balak is imagined as an audience, and a frustrated, even enraged one at that. The things he is paying Balaam to say are not being said! But these words are not for him, they are for Israel. Balaam is preaching to the converted, and painting a picture of Israelite dominance and prosperity at the expense of their enemies. This is nationalistic pomp, most perfectly captured in the promise, "blessed is everyone who blesses you, and cursed is anyone who curses you" (24:9b).

What we know of course, is that Israel never reached the grand heights Balaam so confidently forecast, never became the dust-cloud he imagined, and never ruled with the ferocity and entitlement that his oracles suggest. In short, what the biblical compilers have done is turn Balaam into a spin-doctor, twisting and distorting particular things in order to imagine an alternative reality. Why? Because in the face of their own imperial annihilation at the hands of Assyria, Babylon and the Medes, Israel needed to reassert their national identity, their history. The book of Numbers, from the first census (Chs. 1–2) onwards imagines an Israel some distance removed from any historical reality. The census numbers suggest a nation upwards of 2

16. Borowski, "Ox"; Borowski, "Wild Ox."
17. Borowski, "Lion."

million people, a complete impossibility on any number of scores. That immense mass of people is re-imagined in this cycle of chapters, creating the impression of an irresistible Israel, an all-consuming, all-powerful fighting juggernaut. But none of that is real. It's all spin.

As a spin-doctor, Balaam isn't delivering his own message, but the message of someone else. As we saw previously, Balaam is an historical figure whose international standing has been co-opted here for the purpose of lending external authority to the text. However, the inscriptions at Deir Alla which verify the historical veracity of Balaam are dated to the eighth-century, sometime after the events imagined in the book of Numbers. These words, later put into Balaam's mouth are clearly the work of Israelite writers, though identifying a time frame is complicated. The texts provide some historical markers, but not enough to make a firm hypothesis.[18] Levine suggests a time frame in the ninth century, drawing on the allusions to the Transjordan in the first two poems. Whatever the case, the poems do not internally identify the speaker, and the narrator fixes the identity as Balaam.[19] The texts seem to celebrate the "glory days" of the Transjordanian period, retrojecting these experiences into the wilderness period. This process takes place in the final redaction of the Torah which comes later again, highlighting some of the historical complexity which is involved in any analysis of these texts.

The irony of the story is that Balaam's prestige is brought to bear in order to give the account credibility. The famous Mesopotamian diviner's international reputation is required to give the ideology weight. And yet nationalistic anxiety makes it necessary to castigate Balaam, precisely because he is an outsider. Balaam is Israel's biggest cheer-leader, most enthusiastic supporter, yet he always remains outside the party. He is treated harshly in Israel's traditions, but his message remains. They pin him to the wall, just like his donkey does to him in chapter 22, but realize that to kill him off would be a mistake. Like the first sort of spin-doctor, he is both expendable and re-usable. And just as our perception of the spin doctor has changed, so that we see through the veneer of pretense, so too Israel's view of Balaam changed. In some sense then, Balaam is the ultimate, proto-typical spin-doctor. Or more accurately, Balaam is made into a spin doctor by a group desperately trying to sell a new narrative against the odds.

18. Levine, *Numbers 21–36*, 231.
19. Ibid., 239.

WORKS CITED

Borowski, Oded. "Lion." In *The New Interpreter's Dictionary of the Bible* edited by Katherine Doob Sakenfeld, 3:669–70. Nashville: Abingdon, 2008.

———. "Ox." In *The New Interpreter's Dictionary of the Bible,* edited by Katherine Doob Sakenfeld, 4:348–49. Nashville: Abingdon, 2009.

———. "Wild Ox." In *The New Interpreter's Dictionary of the Bible,* edited by Katherine Doob Sakenfeld, 5:848. Nashvile: Abingdon, 2009.

Bourke, Latika. "Malcolm Turnbull Defeats Tony Abbott in Liberal Leadership Spill to Become Prime Minister" (2015). http://www.smh.com.au/federal-politics/political-news/malcolm-turnbull-defeats-tony-abbott-in-liberal-leadership-spill-to-become-prime-minister-20150914-gjmhiu.html.

Davies, E. W. "A Mathematical Conundrum: The Problem of the Large Numbers in Numbers i and xxvi." *Vetus Testamentum* 45 (1995) 449–69.

Gillard, Julia. "Transcript of Julia Gillard's Speech" (2012). http://www.smh.com.au/federal-politics/political-news/transcript-of-julia-gillards-speech-20121009–27c36.html.

Griffiths, Emma. "Tony Abbott: PM Vows to Pass Leadership Test after Surviving 'Near-Death' Spill Motion" (2015). http://www.abc.net.au/news/2015-02-09/tony-abbott-says-good-government-starts-today/6080434.

Harcup, T. "Spin Doctor." In *A Dictionary of Journalism.* Oxford: Oxford University Press, 2014.

Hogan, M. "Spin Doctor." In *Key Concepts in Public Relations,* edited by M. H. Bob Franklin et al., 220–221. London: Sage, 2009.

Leslie, Tim. "Liberal Leadership Spill: As It Happened" (2015). http://www.abc.net.au/news/2015-02-09/liberal-leadership-spill3a-as-it-happened/6079418.

Levine, Baruch A. *Numbers 21–36: A New Translation with Introduction and Commentary.* Anchor Bible 4A. New York: Doubleday, 2000.

Overington, Caroline. "Kevin Rudd a Soft Target in Plea for Plain English." *The Australian.* http://www.theaustralian.com.au/news/kevin-rudd-a-soft-target-in-plea-for-plain-english/story-e6frg6n6-1225867940465.

Pitman, Andy. "Links between Global Warming and NSW Bush Fires" (2013). http://www.climatescience.org.au/content/395-links-between-global-warming-and-nsw-bush-fires.

Stevenson, A. "Spin doctor." In *The Oxford Dictionary of English.* 3rd ed. Oxford: Oxford University Press, 2010.

Zinn, Christopher. "Australian Radio Stars in Cash-for-Comment Scandal" (1999). http://www.theguardian.com/world/1999/nov/15/4.

11

SERVING MAMMON ON STOLEN LAND

Reading Luke 16 towards a Second Peoples' Hermeneutic

Karl Hand

Facts do not at all speak for themselves, but require a socially acceptable narrative to absorb, sustain and circulate them.[A]

The setting sun played on his brown temples and the evening sun ruffled his beard. The hunger in his eyes became rapaciousness as he looked down the long green valley. His possessiveness became a passion. "It's mine," he chanted. "Down deep it's mine, right to the centre of the world." He stamped his feet into the soft earth. Then the exultance grew to be a sharp pain of desire that ran through his body in a hot river. He flung himself face downward on the grass and pressed his cheek against the wet stems. His fingers gripped the wet grass and tore it out, and gripped again. His thighs beat heavily on the earth.

The fury left him and he was cold and bewildered and frightened at himself. He sat up and wiped the mud from his lips and beard. "What was it?" he asked himself. "What came over me then? Can I have a need that great?" He tried to remember exactly what had happened. For a moment the land had been his wife. "I'll need a wife," he said. "It will be too lonely here without a wife." He was tired. His body ached as though he had lifted a great rock, and the moment of passion had frightened him.[B]

A. Said, *Permission to Narrate*, 252.
B. Steinbeck, *To a God Unknown*, 8.

CHRIS BUDDEN CLAIMS IN *Following Jesus in Invaded Space* that the Australian church has "internalized the values of an invading society and its racist and class-based explanations and justifications of invasion,"[1] and that in fact, "the primary defining context for those who live in Australia is invasion."[2] If this is true then these internalized values must also inform our reading and preaching of scripture.

Drawing on Budden's second peoples' theology, I set out in this chapter to sketch a second peoples' hermeneutic of scripture. I turn to the parables of Luke, which are texts thickly interwoven with both imperial and colonial power relations, and are therefore rich in material for such a project.

SECOND PEOPLE'S HERMENEUTIC

I read from the perspective of a white colonial boy who was brought to Australia from England as a child by a family who believed strongly in the ideology that colonization had brought something wonderful to this land. Five years of ministry in a church with a regular outreach in public housing in the Waterloo area has made me deeply suspicious of that narrative. When, in 2013, my friend was beaten and falsely arrested for legally crossing the road at the Sydney Mardi Gras, and then subjected to ongoing trumped-up litigation by police for allegedly assaulting the very police who had beaten him,[3] the indigenous community spoke to us both about their experiences of daily police brutality and harassment, and I realized that our one-off nightmare experience was their ongoing reality. The colonial ideology of my childhood was completely destroyed.

I will begin by focusing on a specific historical experience, that of the theft of Aboriginal children from their mothers. While I am describing this experience primarily by listening to the voices of Aboriginal women who have spoken out on this issue, I assert that the experience of such mothers defines the white Australian subject differently to that subjectivity which arises from the myths of colonization. This different subjectivity is a better place of departure for scriptural reflection in Australia.

It is because of the myths of colonization, for instance, that we so often speak of the "stolen generation" in the past tense, even though the forced removal of children is currently more widespread than it has ever been in Australian history. In fact, as reports of child abuse and neglect in indigenous communities had dropped by 13% in 2010, the number of children

1. Budden, *Following Jesus in Invaded Space*, 7.
2. Ibid., 17.
3. Ozturk, "Police Assault Charges against Gay Activist."

being placed in care and protection orders rose from 34.8 to 51.4 per 1,000. Indigenous children were 7.6 times more likely at this time to be the subject of a protection investigation and 10 times more likely to be in foster care.[4]

An infamous example is the theft of 41 children from their mothers in Lightning Ridge in 2009,[5] only one year after Kevin Rudd's much cele- brated apology to the stolen generation. There is evidence that this situation is being covered up, as claimed by John Pilger, who has been an eyewitness to the living conditions of Aboriginal people in rural Australia from the 1970's until today. Pilger draws attention to the case of Olga Havnen, the coordinator general of remote services in the Northern Territory, who was sacked for publishing the information that $80 million a year was being spent on surveillance and removal of Aboriginal children, while only half a million was being spent on supporting those families, even though the primary reasons children are removed are directly related to poverty.

Money continues to be poured into the policing of Aboriginal people. In December 2013, Indigenous Affairs Minister Nigel Scullion announced that the federal government would recruit 400 new truancy officers to target remote communities, with programs that include daily home visits.[6] But impoverished Aboriginal mother Kelly Briggs says she has never been asked what would help her to get her kids to school regularly.

> Neither of my children would have missed days at school (ex- cept if sick of course) had there been programs in place that would have helped me. A simple lunch program for disadvan- taged kids. A school shoes payment plan for low income fami- lies. And on the odd occasion, a bus pickup for scorching hot or pouring rain days. Instead of addressing the problems that arise with poverty, the government has now put in place an initiative that employs truancy officers in Indigenous communities, at a cost of $24m.[7]

The consequence for a mother like Briggs is that, in her words

> In the back of my mind, I always hear the voice that says "don't ever let anyone know you're doing it tough, because they will take your kids from you" . . . The feeling of a cold hand of fear on the back of my neck, always present, can only intensify.[8]

4. Australian Institute of Health and Welfare, *Child Protection Australia 2011–12.*

5. "Wirringah Women," *Message Stick*, ABC1.

6. Metherell, "Government to Recruit Truancy Officers."

7. Briggs, "Aboriginal Mothers."

8. Ibid.

If Budden is correct that invasion is the primary context for Australian society, then white Australian readers of the Biblical text read from a subjectivity that is shaped by the practices of invasion such as those outlined above. The myths of settler-colonialism seek to cover over the truth, that we conquer indigenous people through the moral demonization of their culture, and then by aggressive over-policing. But if that is true then it is extremely difficult to talk about a postcolonial subjectivity in this place, because situations like Lightning Ridge make it clear that the colonial project is just as successful now as it has ever been.

Postcolonial theorists often attempt to address this issue by claiming that "post" need not refer to a stage after colonialism and imperialism, so long as the critical potentialities within these structures are analyzed,[9] but this claim demands an answer to the question of the feasibility of such potentialities. Colonialism is strengthening in Australia, and no credible vision of reconciliation is politically on the table.

Recently, a different paradigm has begun to emerge which addresses some of these problems. Namely, since 2007–08, books, international conferences and a journal dedicated to the area of settler-colonial studies have been published, which have set this apart as a specific field of inquiry. Lorenzo Veracini defines settler colonialism as a specific social situation in which indigenous populations are not conquered and ruled by a foreign metropole, but rather replaced by a settler society, which often ends up acquiring a state of its own, such as Australia did at Federation in 1901.

Settler colonial societies such as the USA, Canada, Australia and New Zealand are structurally distinct from true colonial states such as the British Raj in India. These colonial societies kept their indigenous populations alive because the purpose of the state was to exploit the labor of the indigenes, whereas settler colonial societies are seeking to acquire land, and therefore have tended to eliminate the indigenous populations. As Patrick Wolfe explains,

> The primary object of settler-colonization is the land itself rather than the surplus value to be derived from mixing native labor with it. Though, in practice, Indigenous labor was indispensable to Europeans, settler-colonization is at base a winner-take-all project whose dominant feature is not exploitation but replacement. The logic of this project, a sustained institutional tendency to eliminate the Indigenous population, informs a

9. Sugirtharajah *Postcolonial Criticism,* 12–13.

range of historical practices that might otherwise appear distinct—invasion is a structure not an event.[10]

I propose that in a settler-colonial society such as Australia, we cannot
speak of a postcolonial subject. Neither Australia nor any settler-colonial
state is in the process of decolonizing. Rather, the context of invasion defines the subjectivity of the white Australian as settler-colonist.

While the postcolonial project is one of restoration and rebuilding,
there is no such optimism in settler colonial societies. The best theological
hermeneutic that a white Australian can offer is one of prophetic lamenta-
tion and not reconciliation.

Furthermore, the language of post-colonialism in such a context could
actually be dangerous, because it is prone to being used as a white-wash. The
Australian state has adopted exactly such a faux-postcolonialism when it
changed the language used to describe the theft of children from "breeding
out the color" to "building stronger futures," but while the experience of
forced removal of children is no less traumatic under this new language, it
is all the more common.

This should give us pause to think about our rhetoric in a number of
areas. The very concept of "second peoples" is problematized by this because
it does not distinguish between second peoples who are settlers such as
White Australians, and those who come as immigrants after the settlement,
and recognize the sovereignty of the Australian state which they apply to
join. In this sense, the popular sentiment "we are all boat people" is inac-
curate. Boat people recognize the sovereignty of the society which they flee
to, but white Australia did not recognize the sovereignty of any indigenous
nations in Australia. A refugee, then, actually has more in common with an
Aborigine than he or she has with a white citizen, since both must recognize
the sovereignty of a foreign power, the Australian state, in order to be a part
of that society. As the Rainbow Spirit Elders describe, "the European invaders have desecrated this land and made us, the original custodians of the
land, dispirited refugees and outcasts in our own country."[11]

Awareness of our settler-colonial subjectivity exposes readings of Biblical texts which justify the policies aimed at the elimination of Aboriginal
people. Lukan parables are particularly relevant here. As tales of moral
uplift, they are potentially useful theme-texts for the demonization of Aboriginal culture.

Moral panic about the behavior of Aborigines is a bipartisan phenomenon in Australia. Take for instance Julia Gillard's "Closing the Gap" speech

10. Wolfe, *Settler Colonialism*, 163.

11. Rainbow Spirit Elders, *Rainbow Spirit Theology*, 44.

in 2013. She said, "I have a real fear that the rivers of grog that wreaked such havoc among indigenous communities are starting to flow once again."

But such concern for the moral condition of Aborigines is not so much a genuine response to the needs of Aborigines, as a distraction from the real causes of social problems among indigenous people. Such problems are maintained by the Australian state's criminalization of children from an early age, such as the 12 year old Aboriginal boy with no prior criminal convictions, who in 2009 when indigenous children between 10 and 14 were incarcerated 24 times more often than other children,[12] was arrested and jailed on charges of receiving a stolen Freddo Frog worth 70 cents.[13]

The Lost Son who scattered his resources on profligate living (Luke 15:11–32), read uncritically of colonial subjectivities, resonates with the criminalization of Aborigines. Moralizing interpretations of the Lost Son can be found at least as early as Augustine, who used the son's lost condition as an allegory of his own sinful past, and compares it to wantonness, spiritual darkness, and alienation from God.[14]

In a colonial context, such moralizing readings uphold the practices of colonization. This is illustrated well in the Australian context by a newspaper article from 1950 in *The Barrier Miner*, outlining a plan to give South Australian Aborigines a better deal. The plan was put together by the Protector of Aborigines (Mr. W. R. Penhall), who was also a Methodist lay preacher, and drew on his extensive experience of "grinning young" Aborigines from his congregation, which gave him both sympathy and an understanding of the Aboriginal mind.[15]

According to Mr. Penhall, even those full-bloods who had been raised as white from their earliest childhood would enter dream-like states during puberty in which they experienced an overwhelming desire to go "walkabout." Half-bloods seemed better equipped to resist the urge and so had a better chance of adapting, but it would take many generations to eradicate such urges from full-bloods. For such Aborigines, who were incapable of dwelling in houses, Mr. Penhall could only suggest that they should live in reserves, where their children could be supplied with a good education to help them accept the ways of the white man.

One Monday, the day after Mr. Penhall had preached about the Prodigal Son, he summoned a young Aboriginal "buck" to be punished for a misdemeanor, and the young man said to him that since he was repenting

---

12. Australian Institute of Health & Welfare, *A Picture of Australia's Children*, 118.

13. Farouque and Rimrod, "Boy, 12, to Fight Stolen Freddo Charges."

14. Confessions of a Sinner 1.18.

15. Brownrigg, "Age-Old Instincts Can't Be Changed."

and returning home, he should be treated with the same leniency as the younger son in the parable. Here we see the internalized equation of Aboriginal culture with profligate living and/or estrangement from God, and the more disturbing equation of forgiveness by the white man with a restored relationship with God. In a colonial reading of Luke, civilised white society waits, like a divine Father figure, for the Walkabout Son to return home from Aboriginal culture into its loving arms.

I propose a re-reading of the teachings of Jesus in Luke, based on the application of a settler-colonial hermeneutic to his teaching discourse in the travel narrative. It is within this context that Jesus is able to speak because both historically, and in the narrative world of Lukan parables, Jesus speaks with the voice of an Aborigine.

LUKE 16

I start with Luke 16 because of the grouping of relevant themes in this section, such as stewardship of land and money, and the hoarding of wealth in the face of poverty. I propose that the discursive and narrative logic of Luke 16 reveals and denounces the hoarding of resources through bureaucratic means in a way that, far from upholding such practices as the Northern Territory intervention and the over-policing of indigenous people in urban suburbs, exposes them as unjust.

As Veracini points out, the founding narrative of western civilization (the Aeneid) is a settler-colonial text, and the first Aborigines "were the people of Latium at the time when Aeneas and his companions arrived and settled in Italy."[16]

It seems entirely reasonable then to describe the Galilee of Jesus' time as a settler-colonial state also. Under Herod the Great, Palestine had been united under the indigenous temple-state in Jerusalem, which was colonial, but not a settler state *per se*. By Jesus' time, however, the land has been subdivided into a tetrarchy, and Herod Antipas had begun to build Greco-Roman cities such as Tiberius and Sephoris. This settlement of Galilee by Rome transformed the Galilean peasants into Aborigines.

Richard Horsley has said that in the first-century, Rome was consolidating its power in Galilee by transforming it into a "military-agribusiness complex," comparable to the "military-industrial complex" of American imperial expansion as described in the speeches of Dwight D. Eisenhower. Under Rome, retired soldiers from ranking and equestrian families would buy huge tracts of land and acquire slaves. They would then use the surplus

16. Veracini, *Settler Colonialism*, 98.

of their booty to foreclose on indebted peasants. The result of this process was that local peasants experienced land-displacement and either wage-labor or slavery. Horsley quotes Plutarch's claim that the provinces of Rome experienced "a rapid decline in the class of small-holders."[17]

All of these social problems were further exacerbated by the need to pay tribute to Rome. When in normal circumstances, peasant families struggle to maintain a subsistence level existence, increased taxation would drive peasants first into debt, then off their lands, and finally into slave or wage labor. So Horsley describes, "in the reign of Antipas in Galilee, villagers would have been heavily in debt, chronically hungry and distressed about the future."[18] In other words, they are Aboriginal people in a settler-colonial society.

Kenneth Bailey's interpretation of the parable of the Dishonest Manager (Luke 16:1–15) draws on mishnaic categories of tenancy to contextualize the economic situation of Jewish tenants on Roman occupied land. He describes three social layers of tenant farmers: The *aris/kablan* is a shareholding tenant who pays a rent as a fixed percentage of crop, the *hoker* pays a designated portion of the crop regardless of the yield, and the *soker* simply pays rent in money.[19] The social context of the L community which remembered these parables, and the rhetoric of their placement within the Lukan narrative are best understood in the context of this style of tenancy within the larger context of a settler-colonial society.

However, as John Nolland and others have pointed out, the internal logic of the material in Luke 16 is notoriously difficult to pin down. It is likely that the material has been organized in this order by the final redactor of Luke and yet the parables of vv. 1–8 (the dishonest steward) and vv. 19–31 (Lazarus and the Rich Man) seem to have been adjacent in the document from which Luke has sourced his parables.[20]

In between these parables, the final redactor has placed:

- A series of three sayings about unrighteous mammon (vv. 9–13);
- The Pharisees mocking Jesus' teaching (v. 14);
- Jesus responding to the Pharisees (v. 15);
- A saying about the law, John the Baptist and the kingdom of God (vv. 16–17);
- Jesus' ruling on divorce law (v. 18).

17. *Life of Tiberius Gracchus*, 8.
18. Horsley, *Jesus and the Powers*, 101.
19. Bailey, *Poet and Peasant*, 92.
20. Nolland, *Luke 9:21—18:34*, 796.

While redaction, literary and narrative criticisms have made considerable progress in understanding the relationship of these units to each other, I want to demonstrate that recognizing the Aboriginality of Jesus in a settler-colonial context not only makes better sense of this story, but also allows an Aboriginal voice to speak, and to condemn disempowering colonial narratives.

ABORIGINALITY OF JESUS

The easiest place to begin is the sayings about mammon, which at first glance are at least thematically apt, compared to the material in verses 16–18 which in particular seems quite out of place here, and worse yet, as Nolland points out, seems to have no intrinsic unity either.[21] It is not even possible to explain Jesus' ruling against divorce as an intensification of his affirmation of Torah observance in vv. 16–17, because as Luke Timothy Johnson points out, the Torah clearly allows divorce.[22]

The relationship between the parable (vv. 1–8) and the material on mammon (vv. 9–13) is most easily explained by the common theme of possessions. For instance, Kenneth Bailey suggests that verses 9–13 are a poem on Mammon, consisting of three chiasms, authored by Jesus himself. This poem, Bailey claims, was originally ahead of the parable of Lazarus and the rich man, but was moved alongside the parable of the Dishonest Steward by Luke, based on word associations between vv. 4 and 9, and also "as a corrective for the non-Oriental reader," who might misunderstand the parable to have encouraged dishonesty.[23]

Much redaction-critical research on Luke 15–16, however, queried the view of Bailey and most traditional commentators, that chapter 16 was a series of loosely connected traditions on the theme of wealth, and looked to the unfolding narrative of Jesus' interaction with the Pharisees in chapters 15 and 16 (and 18:9–14) to explain the unity of this section. The polemical attitude towards the Pharisees found here leads him to suggest the possibility that this narrative unity belongs to a document redacted before the final redactor of Luke-Acts, whose view of the Pharisees is generally more positive.[24]

In this hypothetical tract, Hickling suggests that the Pharisees have criticized Jesus because of his scandalous association with the "sinners,"

---

21. Ibid., 814.
22. Johnson, *Gospel of Luke*, 255.
23. Bailey, *Poet and Peasant*, 116.
24. Hickling, "A Tract on Jesus and the Pharisees," 265.

whom Hickling associates with the 'am ha-'aretz. Jesus has responded in chapter 15 with three parables of lost and found, in which he outlines what the Pharisees' true attitude to the 'am ha-'aretz should be, that they should "seek them out."[25] The following parable of the Unjust Steward makes it clear that not only should they not look down on such people, but they could learn something from the wisdom of such people.[26] Finally, the parable of Lazarus and the Rich Man associates the Rich Man with the Pharisees— both of them are "exalted before men," and both of them tend to seek after signs.[27] Like the Rich Man, the Pharisees are condemned.

Luke Timothy Johnson has reconciled the thematic and narrative suggestions very effectively in his Luke commentary. He begins by suggesting that the solution to the unity of the various sayings in 16:9–13 may lie in a lost mnemonic linkage, evidenced in the way that "faithful" and "reliable" recur frequently in the context of "the *mammon* of unrighteousness" and "unrighteous *mammon*,"[28] and on Joseph Fitzmyer's view that mammon is most probably the maqtal of 'mn (to be firm),[29] which could be translated as "something to rely on." He states, "If the etymology of 'mammon' as 'something to rely on' is correct, then the real key to the conjunction of sayings may be a bilingual pun on 'mammon/faith', which is no longer entirely available to us."[30]

However, when it comes to the trickier section in vv. 14–31 with the sayings about law and divorce leading up to the parable of Lazarus and the Rich Man, Johnson then notes that "it is easier, in fact, to make sense of the overall narrative function of this section than it is to figure out how its pieces fit together with internal logic."[31]

Johnson fits this narrative function into his larger understanding of Luke-Acts as a geographically determined prophetic structure,[32] in which Jesus' journey to Jerusalem functions as the occasion for the rejection of the prophet by Israel. The teaching given on the road is carefully demarcated as being directed to the crowd, the disciples and the Pharisees and lawyers. Those of the crowd who convert become disciples, but those who

---

25. Ibid., 254.

26. Ibid., 258.

27. Ibid., 257.

28. Johnson, *Gospel of Luke*, 243–57.

29. Fitzmyer, *Gospel according to Luke X–XXIV*, 1094–136.

30. Johnson, *Gospel of Luke*, 248.

31. Ibid., 254.

32. Ibid., 13–17.

reject Jesus, including the Pharisees, are given parables of warning.[33] In this context, Jesus has addressed the Pharisees in chapter 15 with regard to their complaint that he associates with outcasts, and in 16:1, he has turned to address his own disciples with positive *paraenesis* about possessions, concluding that one cannot serve both God and Mammon. It is at 16:14 that the audience changes. The Pharisees, who must have overheard this discussion, begin to mock his teaching because they are "lovers of money."

In Luke 16:14–31, then, Jesus turns to warn and condemn the Pharisees. In v. 15, he makes it clear that it is they who are the abomination despite their self-justification and exaltation in human sight. While *mammon* has been the unifying theme in the previous section, *bdelygma* (abomination) unifies what follows. Both the teaching about divorce and the emphasis on money in the parable are connected by the term *bdelygma*. Deuteronomy, Fitzmyer notes, has a similar set of connections when it uses *bdelygma* primarily for idolatry, but also for financial misdealing (Deut 25:26) and cohabitation with a former wife (Deut 24:4).[34] Jesus thus exposes the false legal piety of the Pharisees who pose as the protectors of the law, but are unable to keep its deep moral demands because of their love of money.[35]

To understand what is happening in this narrative within the context of the settler-colonial situation, it is necessary to view the characters from a sociological perspective, including the Scribes and Pharisees who are the targets of Jesus' polemic. As little as is known about the livelihoods and economic position of Palestinian Scribes and Pharisees from historical sources, Anthony J. Saldarini draws on a Lenskian model of agrarian societies to show that these literate groups would have functioned as retainers of the governing class.[36] That is, their primary social function would be to organize and structure society while being granted a degree of privilege in exchange. This is different from the post-industrial middle classes in that membership in the retaining class does not entail any additional status or power, since a retainer can be removed or replaced at no cost to the governing class—the retaining class is therefore forced to act in the interests of the governing class.[37]

If Jesus and the "sinners" of Luke's gospel are indigenous peasants, then within Luke's narrative the Scribes and Pharisees must be understood as agents of colonialism. However, they are also indigenous Palestinians.

33. Ibid., 164–65.
34. Ibid., 254–55.
35. Ibid., 260–621.
36. Saldarini, *Pharisees, Scribes and Sadducees,* kindle loc., 610–29.
37. Lenski, *Power and Privilege,* 243–48.

In Luke's narrative, they are even portrayed as indigenous Galileans, and closely associated with the local landed aristocracy (see for instance 14:1 where they are holding banquets),[38] although this is impossible to verify historically because in the gospel traditions the primary purpose in characterizing the Pharisees is to provide a negative foil for Jesus rather than to give an accurate history.[39] In fact the very presence of any Pharisee in Galilee itself is impossible to demonstrate on historical grounds as, for instance, Sean Freyne concludes that any presence of Pharisees in Galilee prior to 70 CE must have been "sporadic and unsuccessful" according to both Josephus and the rabbinic sources.[40] Luke's portrayal is also different to the portrayal of the Pharisees in the other synoptic gospels where they seem to be agents of the governing class in Jerusalem, or Josephus and the Gospel of John where they are only found in Jerusalem. The point, at the moment, is that in the text of Luke 16, understood in the context of first-century CE Palestine, the Scribes and Pharisees are indigenous people who are functioning as part of a bureaucracy in the interests of privileged locals whose loyalty must be with social order, and therefore are acting on the side of the military-agribusiness complex and of the settler-colonial state.

It should also be taken into account that Saldarini's functionalism gives the Scribes and Pharisees an overly simplistic role in the social structure of ancient Palestine. Richard Horsley notes that as indigenous Palestinians drawn from the peasant class, the Scribes were caught in the middle of the conflict between the Roman imperial rule and the commitment of the Judeans to their local traditions, of which the scribes were committed as custodians.[41] But, as Saldarini points out, in Luke, even though the Pharisees are portrayed with nuance, and will even collaborate with Jesus against Herod (13:31) the Pharisees are portrayed as having failed in their duties to the local indigenous people, and Jesus who is an intermediary with God[42] is presented as one whose patronage can be trusted, and this is the picture which is at the forefront in Luke 16.

An old Irish aphorism from the days of British occupation seems fitting (although it assumes a different, post-industrial economic system), "an

38. Saldarini further cites 5:17–26, 30–32; 6:7–11; 11:37–53; 14:1–3; and 15:2 as evidence for this view of the Pharisees in Luke, *Pharisees, Scribes and Sadducees*, Kindle loc., 1932.

39. See for instance a study of the Pharisees characterization as a literary device in the Gospel of Matthew that is highly applicable to Luke also by Davies, "Stereotyping the Other."

40. Freyne, *Galilee*, 319.

41. Horsley, *Revolt of the Scribes*, 122.

42. Saldarini, *Pharisees, Scribes and Sadducees*, kindle loc., 778, 1959.

English boss is a monster, an Irish boss is worse." This summarizes aptly the way that the Pharisees are portrayed in Luke 16, where Jesus (like a Galilean James Connolly) stands up to a group of people who have betrayed both their social class and their indigenous kin, and sold out to serve the system in the service of unrighteous mammon.

Once this social situation is understood, I claim that the narrative flow of the passage becomes much easier to understand. The situation described in 16:14–15, where the Pharisees who are "lovers of money" ridicule Jesus' teaching about mammon, makes sense of the inclusion of the sentences which follow, including Jesus' prohibition of divorce. That is, Jesus' response "plays them at their own game": he uses halakhic regulation and case law to construct power relationships. In doing so, he embarrasses the members of the Pharisee party and uncomfortably exposes the relationship between their "red-tape" and colonial oppression. This interaction only strengthens the point of the first parable—that both wealth and power should be used for the sake of people, not people for the sake of wealth and power.

CONCLUSION

Jesus the Aborigine has exactly the same point to make to white Australian readers as he does to the landed aristocracy of Galilee. In fact, this whole situation could be played out nicely in the Northern Territory or in Redfern, in which the relationships of power which arise from those "halakhic regulations" regarding porn, drugs, "grog," and the custody of children serve as a colonizing red-tape, whose function is to bolster the hoarding of resources by white Australians regardless of the content of the laws themselves. Once this is recognized, the rhetoric of Luke 16 becomes an Aborigine's powerful condemnation of the settler state and its bureaucrats.

As a program of redistributive justice[43] Budden calls for three projects: Reconciliation, Covenant, and Treaty, which would enable the creation of a more just social order including a reformation of the structure of race relationships in Australian society, self-administration and autonomy of land ownership.[44] While these projects would certainly join Jesus in dressing down the case-lawyers of colonial red-tape, the conclusion of Luke 16 pushes further still, calling for an even more radical social reversal as the good things Lazarus lacked in this life are taken away from the rich man and given to him.

---

43. Budden, *Following Jesus in Invaded Space*, 91–109.

44. Ibid., 154–57.

For instance, the project of Reconciliation in South Africa, for all its promise, has done little to dislodge the apartheid economy which creates the shanty-towns of Soweto. Why would we expect it to be more successful here? We have accumulated a debt of over two-centuries of "unpaid rent" on this stolen land, and Luke's eschatology promises us that the difference will be exacted either in this age, or in the age to come.

The rich man's single life-time of hoarding resources in Luke 16 pales in comparison to the hoarding of Australia's national resources by those second peoples privileged under British and then Federal Australian colonial rule. I conclude by questioning whether the vital structural and formal equality Budden outlines will be enough if unaccompanied by a Lukan program of social reversal and radical redistribution of material wealth. There can be no reconciliation apart from the eschatological banquet of Luke 14 in which the poor eat plenty while the rich are left outside in the cold.

WORKS CITED

Australian Institute of Health and Welfare. *Child Protection Australia 2011–12.* Child Welfare Series no. 55. Cat. no. CWS 43. Canberra: AIHW, 2013.

———. *A Picture of Australia's Children 2009.* Cat. no. PHE 112." Canberra: AIHW, 2009.

Attwood, Bain. "Law, History and Power: The British Treatment of Aboriginal Rights in Land in New South Wales." *Journal of Imperial and Commonwealth History* (2013) 171–192.

Bailey, Kenneth. *Poet and Peasant; and, Through Peasant Eyes: A Literary-Cultural Approach to the Parables in Luke.* Grand Rapids: Eerdmans, 1983.

Briggs, Kelly. "Aboriginal Mothers Like Me Still Fear that Our Children Could Be Taken Away." *The Guardian*, 21 January, 2014. http://www.theguardian.com/commentisfree/2014/jan/21/aboriginal-mothers-like-me-still-fear-that-our-children-could-be-taken-away.

Blake Brownrigg, "Age-Old Instincts Can't Be Changed—Giving S.A. Aborigines a Better Deal." *Barrier Miner*, 23 February 1950.

Budden, Chris. *Following Jesus in Invaded Space: Doing Theology on Aboriginal Land.* Eugene, OR: Pickwick Publications, 2009.

Dalton, Trent. "New Stolen Generation Fear 'Perpetuates Violence.'" *The Australian*, 2 February 2013. http://www.theaustralian.com.au/national-affairs/new-stolen-generation-fear-perpetuates-violence/story-fn59niix-1226567068427.

Davies, Margaret. "Stereotyping the Other: The 'Pharisees' in the Gospel according to Matthew." In *Biblical Studies/Cultural Studies,* edited by J. Cheryl Exum and Stephen D. Moore, 415–32. Journal for the Study of the Old Testament Supplements 266. Sheffield: Sheffield Academic, 1998.

Farouque, Farah and Fran Rimrod. "Boy, 12, to Fight Stolen Freddo Charges." *The Sydney Morning Herald,* Nov. 16, 2009. http://www.smh.com.au/national/boy-12-to-fight-stolen-freddo-charges-20091116-ihll.html.

Fitzmyer, Joseph A. *The Gospel according to Luke X–XXIV*. Anchor Bible 28A. Garden City, NY: Doubleday, 1985.

Freyne, Sean. *Galilee, from Alexander the Great to Hadrian, 323 BCE to 135 CE: A Study of Second Temple Judaism*. Wilmington, DE: Glazier, 1980.

Hickling, C. J. A. "A Tract on Jesus and the Pharisees?: A Conjecture on the Redaction of Luke 15 and 16." *Heythrop Journal* 16 (1975) 253–65.

Horsley, Richard A. *Jesus and the Powers: Conflict, Covenant, and the Hope of the Poor*. Minneapolis: Fortress, 2010.

———. *Revolt of the Scribes: Resistance and Apocalyptic Origins*. Minneapolis: Fortress, 2010.

Johnson, Luke Timothy. *The Gospel of Luke*. Sacra Pagina. Collegeville, MN: Liturgical, 1991.

Lenski, Gerhard E. *Power and Privilege: A Theory of Social Stratification*. New York: McGraw-Hill, 1966.

Metherell, Lexi. "Government to Recruit Truancy Officers in Indigenous Communities to Improve School Attendance." *ABC News*, 20 December, 2013. http://www.abc.net.au/news/2013-12-20/government-to-recruit-truancy-officers-in-indigenous-communitie/5168540.

Nolland, John. *Luke 9:21—18:34*. Word Biblical Commentary 35B. Waco, TX: Word, 1993.

Ozturk, Serkan. "Police Assault Charges against Gay Activist Bryn Hutchinson Dismissed." *Sydney Star Observer*, Nov. 28, 2013. http://www.starobserver.com.au/news/local-news/new-south-wales-news/police-assault-charges-against-gay-activist-bryn-hutchinson-dismissed/113500.

Pilger, John. "The Mass Removal of Indigenous Children from Their Parents Continues Unabated—Where Is The Outrage?" *The Guardian*, 22 March 2014. http://www.theguardian.com/commentisfree/2014/mar/21/john-pilger-indigenous-australian-families.

The Rainbow Spirit Elders. *Rainbow Spirit Theology: Towards an Australian Aboriginal Theology*. 2nd ed. Adelaide: ATF, 2007.

Saldarini, Anthony J. *Pharisees, Scribes and Sadducees in Palestinian Society: A Sociological Approach*. Grand Rapids: Eerdmans, 2001.

Said, Edward, "Permission to Narrate." In *The Edward Said Reader*, edited by Moustafa Bayoumi and Andrew Rubin, 243–66. New York: Vintage, 2000.

Steinbeck, John. *To a God Unknown*. New York: Penguin, 1995.

Sugirtharajah, R. S. *Postcolonial Criticism and Biblical Interpretation*. Oxford: Oxford University Press, 2002.

Veracini, Lorenzo. "Historylessness: Australia as a Settler Colonial Collective." *Postcolonial Studies* 10.3 (2007) 271–285.

———. *Settler Colonialism: A Theoretical Overview*. Palgrave Macmillan, 2010.

———. "'Settler Colonialism': Career of a Concept." *Journal of Imperial and Commonwealth History* 41.2 (2013) 313–33.

"Wirringah Women." *Message Stick*. ABC1. Sydney: ABC. 23 May 2010. http://www.abc.net.au/tv/messagestick/stories/s2906122.htm.

Wolfe, Patrick. *Settler Colonialism and the Transformation of Anthropology*. London: Cassell, 1999.

Wright, Jessica. "More Indigenous Children in Care." *The Age,* January 20, 2012. http://www.theage.com.au/national/more-indigenous-children-in-care-20120119–1q8i8.html.

12

IMMIGRANT AND REFUGEE

Paroikous, Parepidēmous and Politics in 1 Peter

Matthew Wilson

THE PHRASE *PAROIKOUS KAI parepidēmous* (1 Pet 2:11), most commonly translated "alien and stranger," implies that an aspect of socio-political status is in the mind of the author to the community addressed in 1 Peter. However, in the Australian context of theologizing on stolen land, and with the ongoing debate about further immigration, the manner in which people enter the country, and the people who are allowed to do so—what might be the implications of Jennifer Bird's proposed alternative of "immigrants and refugees" for a contemporary Australian audience?

1 Peter is a truly and clearly catholic—or general—epistle. The letter is addressed to communities following Jesus in what is now Asiatic Turkey. Acknowledging but avoiding the disputes about authorship and the precise ethnic composition[1] of the intended recipient communities, what is

---

1. Authorship of 1 Peter is contested. See Michaels, *1 Peter*, lxii–lxvii for a discussion of the authorship of the letter. For practical reasons this chapter will refer to the author of the epistle as "Peter," however this should not be taken to suggest that the author is convinced that Peter the Apostle was author or dictator of the epistle known as 1 Peter. The ethnic and social nature of the intended recipient community is also contested. Whilst many scholars interpret 1 Peter as a letter to a gentile community (the geographic location of the intended recipients would suggest this), the distinctly Jewish nature of 1 Peter and the arguments within it have led to a variety of suggestions including, but not limited to the notion that 1 Peter may have been written to a diaspora

relatively well attested is that this circular letter originates in Rome (theologically and rhetorically camouflaged as "Babylon") and addresses communities of followers of Jesus in Roman colonial Asia Minor. Asia Minor in the late first-century had been colonized over a period of centuries by Persians, Macedonians, Greeks and Romans. The area had absorbed Hellenistic language and culture as well as Roman imperial commerce and religion. The letter, according to Schüssler Fiorenza, is "sent from the imperial center, presenting itself as authoritative advice and admonition to good conduct and subordination to authority in the colonial public of the provinces."[2]

IMMIGRANT AND REFUGEE

1 Peter is infamously addressed to "resident aliens"—Peter, an apostle of Jesus, to the chosen *parepidēmois* of the diaspora in Pontus, Galatia, Cappadocia, Asia and Bithynia (1 Pet 1:1). The majority of English translations of the text highlight aspects of transience—the sense of the foreign, using terms such as "exiles of the dispersion," "elect who are sojourners," "elect strangers in the world," "chosen people who are living as foreigners," or simply "strangers." The linking of the more common Greek word *paroikos* with *parepidēmous* occurs in 1 Pet 2:11—"Beloved, I urge you as *paroikos kai parepidēmous* to abstain from the desires of the flesh that wage war against the soul." Here the communities of Jesus followers are referred to, in the more common English translation, as "aliens and strangers," "aliens and exiles," or "strangers and pilgrims." Jennifer Bird, in her work on 1 Peter, prefers to translate the phrase as "immigrants and refugees"[3]—a point to which we return shortly.

It is a matter of debate as to the precise ethnic nature of the communities to whom 1 Peter is addressed. The language of 1 Peter contains a plethora of metaphors and images that are clearly related to the covenant people of Israel—no more so than in the verses surrounding the "aliens and strangers" or "immigrants and refugees" with reference to the Holy and royal priesthood, a chosen race, a holy nation, the people of God. This section of the letter in particular is steeped in the language of the Hebrew Scriptures, the traditions of Israel and Judaism. More generally the letter is saturated with scriptural allusions and quotations (admittedly from Septuagintal rather than Hebraic forms). This led most exegetes before the 19th century to

---

of Jewish Christians, to proselytes, priests, god-fearers or Noachians (see Michaels, *1 Peter*, xlv–lv).

2. Schüssler Fiorenza, "1 Peter," 383.

3. Bird, *Abuse*, 63.

assume that the recipients were, like the assumed author Peter, ethnic Jews with a messianic bent now following Jesus. These people were now resident in Asia Minor following the dispersion from Roman Judea after the end of the Jewish War. However, in the last two centuries this understanding has largely been replaced by the view that the intended recipients were predominantly gentile converts. Though the letter portrays the recipients in terms of the covenant people, it does not mention Israel directly, nor does the text suggest these communities form a "new Israel." To the covenantal communities of the letter, Israel is not an "other" or former persona, it is rather a constitutive identity. Many exegetes and commentators today argue that the author has appropriated the language and status of covenantal Israel for a predominantly gentile audience. I tend to feel that Schüssler Fiorenza and a minority of other scholars have the stronger, though admittedly circumstantial, argument, and that the intended recipients are indeed communities of ethnic Jewish followers of Jesus.[4] This conclusion has some bearing on the interpretation of the letter, and of the implications of the address to the recipients as *paroikous kai parepidēmous*.

It has been common in some circles to read 1 Peter in a particularly pietistic manner. This constitutes a grievous misreading of 1 Peter in my estimation. Such a style of interpretation is aided by the twin identification of the intended audience both as "aliens and strangers (in the world)" and as of predominantly gentile ethnicity. Such a reading rests on the assumption that this particular New Testament text articulates an escapist "it will all be fine when you're dead" type of theology. It encourages the follower of Jesus to ignore the world's problems by waiting patiently to escape the world into the arms of a loving and welcoming God. Accordingly, readers are depicted as pilgrims and exiles on earth waiting to shuffle off this mortal coil. Along the way these dedicated followers of Jesus may suffer unjustly but stoically, reassured by the knowledge that after death they will be joining God in heaven. This view is nurtured by an unfounded assumption of a heaven/earth duality not present in 1 Peter, and it rests on these terms used repeatedly of the addressees of this letter in chapters 1 and 2; namely *paroikous kai parepidēmous*.[5]

The expression *paroikous kai parepidēmous* is used by Abraham (LXX Gen 23:4) to identify himself as a landless "resident alien and temporary visitor" among the Hittites. 1 Peter states "Since you are to be holy as God is holy" (1:16), and "since you call upon a Father who judges impartially according to each one's deeds, conduct yourselves with reverence throughout

---

4. See Schüssler Fiorenza "1 Peter," 388–89.

5. See Elliott, *A Home for the Homeless*, 21–58.

the time of your alien residence." Rather than understanding these terms as a linguistic phraseology of the period used to refer to foreigners and immigrants some commentators instead imagine that these terms describe the readers as spiritual pilgrims and exiles *on earth* rather than as persons who experience life as "aliens" within society. The follower of Jesus is thus interpreted as a soul which belongs in heaven but is somehow condemned for a time to endure the challenges and sufferings of human society on earth before redemption to their proper place and true spiritual home in heaven. They hold this view despite the fact that the qualifying expression "on earth" is nowhere to be found in the text of 1 Peter. Indeed, some translators, convinced of the presence of this pie-in-the-sky theology within the letter, go so far as to add the phrase to their translations.[6]

However, when the phrase *paroikous kai parepidēmous* is understood in context as a socio-political descriptor, it becomes clear that the intended audience of the letter find themselves disdained by their neighbors as "resident aliens and strangers" or as "immigrants and refugees" with no roots in, or ties to, the localities in which they reside. They have met with the ignorance, suspicion, and verbal abuse typically directed by natives and the political elite against those who do not share the history, traditions, customs, loyalties and deities of the local populace, or indeed, and perhaps more significantly, of the dominant Roman culture. As immigrants and refugees they are suspected and slandered: they are perceived as being a social and ethnic minority who are up to no good, a group involved in doing what is wrong, a group who are potentially—or actually—threatening the fabric of society through their different customs, beliefs, ideas and practices. Their actions are deemed culturally inappropriate and a threat to the favor of local gods and the well-being of their communities. Suspicion breeds slander. Slander in turn results in undeserved suffering. Thus undeserved suffering becomes the central theme of 1 Peter.

This notion of the social and cultural "alien" forms the basis on which Bird suggests her preference for translating the terms as immigrants and refugees. She, like Elliot before her, notes that both Greek terms are used as translations of the Hebrew *ger/gerim. Ger,* she argues, is often used in the Hebrew scriptures to refer to a hired hand or employee of a household—someone clearly not a family member, yet distinct from any slaves. She notes that Levites are instructed to be *gerim* amongst the rest of the Israelites and that *ger* is also used to refer to God's presence at times. Most notably, the Israelites are *gerim* during their time in Egypt.[7] Bird notes the strong

6. See Elliott, "Church as Counterculture."

7. Bird, *Abuse,* 63–66.

socio-political aspects of the term, and reminds us that to depoliticize our readings tends to downplay the desperation and degree of dispossession and disempowerment that often accompanies being in such a position.[8] For Bird, translating the Greek terms as "immigrant and refugee" highlights concerns of the lack of citizenship and belonging, the resultant bearing of the brunt of labor that sustains the region and its economy, and the continual state of being to a greater or lesser extent at any one particular time—at the mercy of the dominant socio-political elite. To contextualize Bird's argument to our current location, space and time—to be an immigrant/refugee is to be "unAustralian."

HOME WITH GOD

In the face of this situation which threatened the survival of the community, let alone its growth, the author of 1 Peter affirms the Jesus followers to be the elect and holy people of God. They are indeed immigrants and refugees—aliens and strangers—just as were their patriarchal ancestors Sarah and Abraham. Just like those patriarchal ancestors they have now been called by God to lead lives of holy non-conformity, to resist the pressures of cultural assimilation to other standards of behavior, and to be so engaged in holiness and the doing of good that even their detractors would be led to glorify God. Followers of Jesus, 1 Peter asserts, are immigrants and refugees in their wider society and should remain so. For in the household of God and the community of faith it is people such as these who have found a home with God. So the reader of 1 Peter is encouraged that as Christians we find ourselves called upon to concretize our notions of holy space, holy ground and holy community by practicing a holy non-conformity and by offering a home to the homeless, regardless of the consequences.

But in our present situation and our current Australian context do we really see ourselves as "immigrants and refugees" in a religio-socio-political sense? An understanding of Christian existence as immigrant and refugee is hardly representative of Christian main-streamers crowding the corridors of power, the elect, those chosen or ordained by God. "You are a chosen race, God's own special people called from darkness into light" (1 Peter 2:9)—a phrase which taken out of context and on its own might be more strongly suggestive of the divine right of kings, the power of imperialism and the innate superiority of a Judeo-Christian-Eurocentric socio-economic/political worldview rather than the plight of refugee or immigrant. Such a sectarian message comes across as strange and unsettling news to a church which has

8. Ibid., 64.

made its compromises with society. What are we to do today with 1 Peter's notion of holy nonconformity, its call to a superior morality which might even gain outsiders to the faith, its message of standing fast in God's grace and offering ongoing resistance to the powers that threaten to devour us?

The author of 1 Peter encourages the intended audience to live good lives (1 Pet 2:12) such as to be an example to those surrounding them. To a postcolonial theologian this is a message which elicits a mixed response. There is a certain wisdom in the author's suggestions of submission and conformity. It is certainly a valid response to a tense and sometimes difficult marginal socio-political position. It allows a minority community continued existence, even if it does not allow for it to flourish or enhance its equality within the wider society. It conforms to what political strategists in modern Australian election cycles call a "small target" strategy. Do as little as possible to attract negative attention to yourself whilst upholding as best you can the opinions and good of the wider society. It is a standard survival technique for marginal and minority groups throughout time and space.

However, this strategy also has its weaknesses, as the author of 1 Peter reminds his audience. This strategy does not prevent unjust suffering. "Who is going to harm you if you are eager to do good? But even if you should suffer for what is right, you are blessed" (1 Pet 3:13) the writer reminds the audience. With the adoption of such a strategy it can be expected that suspicion, social tension and persecution will continue. And so accusations have been made and will continue to be made that the advice of 1 Peter feeds into, rather than seeking to challenge and overturn, the dominant social paradigm. In these ways the colonized become complicit in their own colonization and oppression. Perhaps nowhere is this more strongly debated in studies of 1 Peter than in the commentary around the Haustafeln[9]—the household codes of 1 Pet 2:18–3:8. Submission and dignified silence towards masters and husbands may be a sound short term survival strategy, but it is highly questionable as to what is achieved in the longer term, or as to whether it is compatible with a prophetic or gospel challenge to justice, equity and righteousness.

So what exactly was the social situation of the communities to which 1 Peter was addressed? This again is a matter of debate, dependent somewhat upon the choices made as to the dating and authorship of the epistle. The communities in question were quite obviously non-indigenous to their present geographical location, and whilst they were equally obviously of a religiously sectarian nature it is not entirely clear as to exactly what this

9. See Balch, *Let Wives Be Submissive*, for extensive discussion of the household codes in the New Testament.

would have meant socially, culturally and economically for those being addressed by 1 Peter.

In Roman colonies the non-citizen, the resident alien—the immigrant or refugee—was a member of an institutionalized group which ranked lower than the citizen population and the freed persons.[10] Such "immigrants" were on one hand excluded from public office and honors. They had limited legal protection and were restricted in aspects of commerce, marriage and land tenure. They were allowed limited participation in cultic rites but excluded from priesthood and roles of civic responsibility. On the other hand, like the citizenry they were responsible for contributing to taxes, civic support, tribute and military service.[11] They were exposed to suspicion and hostility, and if they were as I suggest, ethnically a part of the Jewish diaspora, then in a post 70CE situation this would have added to the degree of suspicion and hostility at ethnic, religious and political levels.

However, centuries of colonization in Asia Minor had also led to deep social and political rifts between the indigenous peoples and the descendants of colonial powers. Elliot notes the socio-political dynamics in Roman Asia Minor were that the Hellenistic colonial group took over the areas of imperial administration, commerce and civic institutions.[12] Thus the basically Hellenistic culture of the cities was not changed by Rome, instead it was adopted and adapted. The result was a rich aristocratic class constituting Roman and leading local colonial families, with a colonial "middle" class of administrators and merchants consisting of the Hellenized colonial descendants and immigrants. Supporting these was a working class predominantly composed of the local indigenous population along with imported workers and slaves. Indigenous peoples formed the bulk of the working and lower classes. In contrast it was the colonial settlers and Hellenized citizenry who formed the vast bulk of the numerically much smaller middle and upper classes. Thus whilst the Jesus following communities of immigrants may well have been systematically institutionally and socially discriminated against by the Roman imperial system and the elite Hellenized colonial population, their socio-political status was probably significantly better than that of the indigenous population.[13]

10. Citizenship in this context refers to citizenship recognised by the Roman elite—not as we now usually presume of indigenous locality or affiliation by choice.

11. Schüssler Fiorenza, "1 Peter," 385.

12. Elliot, *1 Peter*, 94, relying on Rostovtzeff.

13. Schüssler Fiorenza "1 Peter," noting Prostmeier 386.

SECOND PEOPLES

In the contemporary Australian context an understanding of the followers of Jesus being socio-political immigrants and refugees strikes more than one chord. As Budden points out, the Christian church, and most of us within Australia, have come as second peoples—immigrants and refugees—to a land already inhabited and cultured by the first peoples of this land. Not only that, we did not arrive by invitation, but here we do theology on invaded and colonized space[14]. In Australia, the church has always had a vested interest in the politico-religious drama played out by the colonial enterprise. Too often the church has been the willing partner of the machinery of colonization—ideologically, politically, socially and religiously. Unlike the communities of Jesus-followers addressed in 1 Peter, the Australian church has not been (at least until very recently if at all) a marginal minority which challenges the dominant socio-political elite, but rather it has been a part of that elite, and usually a very willing part. Despite undoubted good will and positive intent, the church has not questioned its place as immigrant and refugee to see, or to seek, the experience of the "other." This applies both to the "other" who is indigenous to this land, and the "other" who, also immigrant and refugee, comes after, and is linguistically, culturally, ethnically, politically, socially or religiously "other" to the dominant socio-cultural group of colonial invaders.

Budden reminds us that within the European narrative, earth has been turned into "landscape" a thing which is external, other, outside, distant and separate to us—it becomes, in commercial terms, real estate. Once our concept of earth is so transformed land becomes something to be traded. Land can be bought, sold, occupied, invaded, dominated and stripped of its resources. Land becomes a thing subdued by lines on maps, fences on land, title deeds, infrastructure. It can then be organized into places of residence, manufacture, prisons, reserves, and even churches. We might find identity and enjoy a place in nation or culture which occupies a particular space at a particular time, but not in the country. For Indigenous Australians there is not this separation of earth and people—country is not the place someone chooses to live, but an integral part of who they are—the Aboriginal person is a living, thinking, breathing physical manifestation of their land. Thus invasion and colonization disorders country as it removes the story of country and redefines it within the context of the socio-political schema of the invader/colonizer.[15]

---

14. Budden, *Following Jesus in Invaded Space*, 6.

15. Ibid., 16–19.

Alongside considering what it may mean as being a religious community of "immigrants and refugees" to this land we need also to consider what it may mean to the way we theologize and act towards those who choose to become "immigrants and refugees" in this place in subsequent times. Australian history is not kind to the indigenous population, neither is it always kind to those who have chosen to become immigrants and refugees from places, ethnicities, religions and cultures outside the dominant colonial wave of Anglo-European immigration/invasion. Whether it be Irish Catholic, the Chinese of the Gold rush period, the pacific islanders subject to "blackbirding," Afghan cameleers, victims of the white Australia policy, or those who have, and continue to suffer indefinite detention as notionally "illegal immigrants" and seekers of refuge, the nation's treatment of those who come to this place who are not "us" but seem more like the "other" is at very best indifferent, and often significantly worse.

CONCLUSION

Paroikous kai parepidēmous—immigrant and refugee. Hauerwas, reflecting on the problem of suffering—a key theme of 1 Peter, reminds us that the only hope we will have is if we can place alongside our stories of pointless suffering a story of suffering that shows we have not been abandoned.[16] Where is God in the suffering? I believe that this is precisely what the author of 1 Peter is trying to achieve in reassuring the communities addressed in the letter—even though that reassurance may have its acknowledged weaknesses, and may seem inappropriate in a twenty-first-century post-colonial world. It is not a question that can be answered from the safety of socio-political dominance. It is not a question that can be answered from the position of the privileged or the perspective of the colonizer. It is rather, a question that must seriously reflect on and include the experience of the colonized, of the immigrant and the refugee. Here the adoption of Bird's preferred translation of the terms is helpful. To speak of immigrant and refugee—particularly in an Australian context—takes the reader clearly outside the pietistic context in which 1 Peter has often been read. It moves the reader to a place where the social and political struggle of the immigrant and refugee must be seriously considered. It moves the reader to a place where the rights and the experience of indigenous and immigrant must be considered alongside each other. It does not allow the reader the easy comfort of placing all such problems into the "too hard" basket of life in the sure and certain knowledge that the struggles of our human existence are meaningless in the face of

16. Hauerwas, *Naming the Silences*, 35.

an escape to the perfection of God's eschatological kingdom. If we are to understand ourselves as immigrant and refugee, then what we do here and now in this place truly matters in our search to follow Jesus.

This suggestion does not offer an unproblematic reading of 1 Peter. There remain difficulties with the text. How are the indigenous people of the Roman provinces addressed by the letter to be understood? What implications does this have for our own context today as we continue the struggle in Australia to read into our biblical understanding and our theology an appropriate appreciation of the suffering and struggle of indigenous voices? A Eurocentric reading from a place of dominance can no longer be considered a valid reading of any scripture, but particularly 1 Peter, in contemporary Australia. We can no longer pretend that the treatment of indigenous people is of no significance to biblical interpretation or our theology. Nor can we pretend that continued demonization of later immigrants from cultures and ethnicities other than the White-European-male and his worldview is irrelevant to how we read and interpret this and other texts. To read from the place of the immigrant and refugee—within a society of immigrants and refugees—allows a broader interpretation of the text of 1 Peter, one which permits indigenous, alien and refugee a voice.

The advice of the author of 1 Peter may well be tinged with Bhabha's notion of colonial ambivalence. It may well not stand up to the criticisms of feminist and liberationist critique. But unless we take seriously the call to live, and to experience what it is to be immigrant and refugee it becomes too easy to spiritualize in favor of preserving the dominant socio-political elite. It becomes too easy to pass off the challenge as something that belongs to the minority, the "other." But if we are the *paroikous kai parepidēmous*—the immigrant, the refugee—then that is not so easy, and the implications for how we treat the immigrant and refugee, the indigenous person, and the land on which we live come close to home.

WORKS CITED

Achtemeier, Paul. *1 Peter: A Commentary*. Hermeneia. Minneapolis: Fortress, 1996.
Balch, David L. *Let Wives Be Submissive: The Domestic Code in 1 Peter*. Society of Biblical Literature Monograph Series 26. Chicago: Scholars, 1981.
Bird, Jennifer. *Abuse, Power and Fearful Obedience: Reconsidering 1 Peter's Commands to Wives*. Library of New Testament Studies. London: T. & T. Clark, 2011.
Budden, Chris. *Following Jesus in Invaded Space: Doing Theology on Aboriginal Land*. Eugene, OR: Pickwick Publications, 2009.
Elliot, John H. *A Home for the Homeless: A Sociological Exegesis of 1 Peter. Its Situation and Strategy*. 1990. Reprinted, Eugene, OR: Wipf & Stock, 2005.

————. "The Church as Counterculture: A Home for the Homeless and a Sanctuary for Refugees." *Currents in Theology and Mission* 25.3 (1998) 176–85.

————. *1 Peter: A New Translation with Introduction and Commentary.* Anchor Bible 37B. New York: Doubleday 2000.

Hauerwas, Stanley. *Naming the Silences: God, Medicine and the Problem of Suffering.* Edinburgh: T. & T. Clark, 1993.

Michaels, J. Ramsey. *1 Peter.* Word Biblical Commentary 49. Dallas: Nelson, 1988.

Moy, Russell G. "Resident Aliens of the Diaspora: 1 Peter and Chinese Protestants in San Francisco." *Semeia* 90–91 (2002) 51–67.

Pattel-Grey, Anne. *The Great White Flood: Racism in Australia; Critically Appraised from an Aboriginal Historico-Theological Viewpoint.* American Academy of Religion Cultural Criticism Series. Atlanta: Scholars, 1998.

Prostmeier, F. R. *Handlungsmodelle im ersten Petrusbrief.* Forschungen zur Bible 63. Würzburg: Echter, 1990.

Schüssler Fiorenza, Elisabeth. "1 Peter." In *A Postcolonial Commentary on the New Testament Writings,* edited by Fernando F. Segovia and R. S. Sugirtharajah, 380–403. Bible and Postcolonialism 13. London: T. & T. Clark, 2007.

13

INDIGENOUS LANGUAGE LOSS

The Future of Gagana Sāmoa
(Samoan Language) in Diaspora

Terry Pouono

LANGUAGE DECLINE OR LANGUAGE loss is a worldwide reality that contributes to the diminishing authentic and increasingly ambiguous identity of indigenous groups as they are influenced by the language and dominant cultural values of the mainstream group. The decline of the Samoan language, or at least the threat of the language being lost to the pervading dominant English language in Aotearoa/New Zealand, is a concern not only shown by Samoans themselves, but by other ethnic minority groups whose languages are also under threat.

In the post-colonial period, the issue of language has been the converging point for new acts of colonization but also resistance. In resistance, the narratives of the dominant group who fosters hegemony are scrutinized by minority groups in the struggle for ethnic, cultural, and political autonomy. Conversely, this chapter looks at the gradual decline of Samoan-speaking Samoans in New Zealand and the imposing influences of the pervasive, invasive, colonizing forces of the diverse, complex world.

Despite the historical political struggles and attempts of the indigenous *Te Reo Maori*[1] for recognition, and the rapid increase of diaspora

---

1. Language of the indigenous Maori.

communities contributing to the multicultural complexion and linguistic diversity[2] in New Zealand, the English language remains the more universal and commonly spoken language in New Zealand. Coined by France Mugler and John Lynch[3] as the 'metropolitan language' of the colonial era, the English language is understood to create greater opportunities for regional and international access.[4] This colonial mind-set is still a persistent reality.

The cultures associated with ethnic minority languages are acknowledged within the multi-cultural fabric of New Zealand society today, though they play second fiddle to the dominant culture associated with the language of success and progression in western society. This colonial understanding is further justified in the revision of the New Zealand Curriculum by the Ministry of Education in 2007, which affirms the significance of literacy in English as a constitutive resource for appropriate understanding and participation in all aspects of life within New Zealand and the wider world. In that line of thought, English is branded as the 'global language'.[5]

GAGANA SĀMOA IN AOTEAROA / NEW ZEALAND

In certain pockets within the main cities of Auckland and Wellington, there are large populations of people from the Pacific Islands. Unlike the settlement of early civilizations throughout history, which settled in regions of fertile land, proximity to waterways and trade centers for means of survival, the island migrants were drawn to and settled in contexts of familiarity. It is in these regions today that you would find sites that attract Pacific peoples like takeaway shops, Kentucky Fried Chicken outlets (my personal favorite), island fashion stores, Chinese shops that sell cheap merchandise, island music and video outlets, and fruit shops that sell taro, green bananas and coconut cream. Also common in these pockets are numerous networks of Samoan churches that can be viewed as transplanted villages replicating the homeland. These areas are 'linguistic enclaves' where the languages of the Pacific people are spoken more frequently inside and outside the home.[6]

Today, the Samoan language is the third most spoken language in New Zealand,[7] behind English and Maori. The focus of this chapter addresses the inevitable. The issue for *gagana Sāmoa* (Samoan language) is not about

2. Howarth, "Globalising Literacy," 142.

3. France Mugler and John Lynch are scholars in Pacific languages.

4. Mugler and Lynch, *Pacific Languages in Education,* 3.

5. Howarth, "Globalising Literacy," 144.

6. Taumoefolau, Starks, Davis, and Bell, "Linguists and Language Maintenance," 24.

7. Fisher, "Samoan Language under Threat in New Zealand."

whether or not it will survive, but what needs to be done to slow down the gradual decline.[8] The decline of the number of New Zealand-born Samoans who could speak the Samoan language, as recorded in government statistics over a period of five years, has been gradual from 48% to 44%.[9]

There are many reasons for the decline. One is the increasing ratio of New Zealand-born Samoans.[10] The increasing population of first, second and third generation New Zealand-born Samoans, added to other changing social dynamics such as mixed marriages, the choice not to attend the Samoan church or Samoan-centered communal gatherings and a preference for predominantly English speaking homes[11] contribute to the decline. Simultaneously, the gradual decrease in numbers of the older migrant community who have either passed away or returned to Samoa adds to the dilemma. The elders are a crucial missing link to preserving the language as well as maintaining connections with family and community.[12]

GAGANA SĀMOA IS SACRED

The continuing effect of language loss holds repercussions for ethnic communities in many ways because language is crucial for preserving the vitality of cultures, traditions, epistemologies and values. From an anthropological view, the shared notion about the nature of language declares it as an essential feature to '. . . inform worldviews, shape verbal behaviors [sic], and contour social interactions. As such, they help construct social realities, personhood, identity, agency, aesthetic sensibilities, and sentiments.'[13] Crucial to this insight are the questions of language ideology: What is the function of language in the minds of the people? What is the value of language?

To the traditionalists who preserve the Samoan culture, traditions and customs, the Samoan language is integral for the survival and social cohesion of the core elements that define the binding together of the Samoan community in a diverse world. The Samoan language is a central facet of the Samoan identity. There is a saying, *E iloa le Sāmoa i lana tautala, tu ma*

---

8. Taumoefolau et al., "Linguists and Language Maintenance," 24.

9. Hunkin, "To Let Die," 204; Toloa, McNaughton, and Lai, "Bi-literacy and Language Development," 515–16. See also Hunkin, "A Frequency Based Word List," 16.

10. Fisher, "Samoan language under threat," A14. 2006 Census: 60% of the total Samoan population (131,100) are New Zealand born Samoans (78,660).

11. Hunkin, "To let Die," 207.

12 Taumoefolau et al., "Role of Second Language Acquisition," 46.

13. Tomlinson and Makihara, "New Paths," 18. Citing Kroskrity, *Regimes of Language*; Schieffelin, Woolard, and Kroskrity, *Language Ideologies;* Woolard and Schieffelin, "Language ideology."

lana savali. Metaphorically the saying denotes that the identity of a Samoan person is clearly grounded in the way one speaks, by one's moral conduct and respect for others. Samoan customs are abundant in gestures and uses of language that communicate rules for behavior and social conduct within the Samoan community. Acquiring a language is a strong marker of the affirmation of cultural identity because of the concomitant values and belief systems attached to that language.[14]

Language is more than just a collection of words. Language is a social phenomenon. Whether it is written, spoken, or expressed through signs, language is not an isolated entity from cultural or ethnic identity.[15] In other words, a culture without language is like a physical body with no skeleton. With a great sense of ethnocentric pride, the traditionalists regard the Samoan culture as morally and ethically superior to other cultures because it centers on mutual respect and reciprocal love. A lack of understanding or violation of these characteristics implies a deviation from accepted ways unique to the Samoan society.

Amituana'i-Toloa, a scholar in Pacific education, expresses the significance of the connection between Samoan language and identity thus:

> Language empowers, encourages, motivates and reinforces identities because it cups the ancient, past, present and future, thus, in the Samoan context, it stores within it the experiences, knowledge, wisdom, understanding and activities of home life that is habitually Samoan.[16]

In a diverse and complex world, language retention is crucial for the wellbeing and productivity of an ethnic group.[17] The 'ethnolinguistic vitality' of groups, an idea initially proposed by Giles, Bourhis and Taylor argues that the greater a groups' vitality, the more likely it is that the members of that group will use and maintain the language.[18] Vitality in this case may be defined by factors such as economic status, political representation and geographical concentration.

Inherent to Samoan belief, the Samoan language is a gift from God; a divine language entrenched in the Samoan culture. The vitality of the *gagana Sāmoa* is deeply entrenched in the spiritual *mana* of the language and culture. The survival of the Samoan language here is dependent on the vigor

14. Amituana'i-Toloa, "To Each a Language," 82.

15. Ibid., 81.

16. Ibid., 82.

17. Hunkin, "To Let Die," 203.

18. Giles, Taylor and Bourhis, "Towards a Theory of Language in Ethnic Group Relations," cited in Mugler and Lynch. *Pacific Languages in Education*, 229.

and strength of the community to preserve what is believed to be God given. Regardless of the profound insights advancing the value of the Samoan language, one fundamental component absent in existing academic literature is the idea that the Samoan language is 'sacred and divine.'

PENETRATING DOMINATION OF THE ENGLISH LANGUAGE

The initial Samoan language nest is the home, involving face-to-face instruction with the parents. Another significant site is the Samoan church where the Christian teachings in Sunday School are disseminated in the Samoan language. These places of activity are coined by John Dickie as 'educative sites'[19] that promote the instruction of the Samoan language, customs and cultural values. The Samoan home and church in this case, as 'communities of practice,'[20] serve two key objectives: first, to preserve the core values of the community through application of the ethnic language and enacting cultural practices; and second, to be places where members of the community are able to congregate and reconcile differing values circulating around society.[21] For ethnic minorities, the preservation of the native tongue reassures and regenerates cultural and religious zeal in a land considered as the new home. As a medium for cultural identity, it channels the values and history of an ethnic group on a continuum from the past traditions and locations, to the minds of the people in the present.

The penetrating domination of the English language infusing values and ideals upon the already ingrained Samoan 'ethnic personality' provides a pathway for hegemonic ascendency. The nature of the shift to the dominant dialect alludes to a sense of uniformity, which is a reversal of the social fabric of linguistically diverse New Zealand.[22] It raises the question, why are ethnic minority speakers vulnerable to losing partially, or completely, their mother tongue? One reason is colonial education via western forms of education in New Zealand schools. I call this the Big Monster! Indications from research have shown a language shift from bilingualism to monolingualism particularly with younger speakers.[23]

The Assimilationist Policy of the New Zealand Government in the latter stages of the twentieth century was developed with the intention

19. Dickie, "Samoan Students Documenting Their out of School Literacies," 247.

20. Ibid., 248. Citing Etienne Wenger, *Communities of Practice*.

21. Ibid.

22. Ibid., 249.

23. Taumoefolau et al., "Linguists and Language Maintenance," 23.

of devaluing the status of ethnic languages to a diminutive position. The implication was that ethnic languages were inferior and irrelevant in New Zealand society at the time. The objective of the policy was to aid migrant parents and their children to learn the English language faster.[24] This concept is also coined as 'linguistic imperialism' describing the structures of the dominant group as reflecting 'persisting colonial mentalities.'[25]

The teaching of the Samoan language and values in the early stages loses momentum to subtractive bilingualism as children become subjects of colonial encroachment to western education systems and on a broader scale, social life outside of the home and church. Subtractive bilingualism is apparent when the Samoan language is lost or on the decline, even before knowledge of the English language is fully developed.[26] Of great concern, is the fact that the phase happens so early in their lives, Samoan children lose crucial information at such a vital stage. For this reason, they end up playing catch-up when learning the new language. Grace, who investigated the process of language shift, alluded to the process of translation 'whereby a speaker says something in a different way, that is, in a different language . . . until the former way is forgotten.'[27] Tove Skutnabb-Kangas describes this as learning subtractively.[28]

Skutnabb-Kangas also employs a savage-like allusion referring to the dominance of the English language as having a 'killer-effect' impact on the subordinate languages.[29]

An even 'Bigger Monster' is the fluid process of globalization. More specifically, networks of communication, symbols and patterns that are circulated through various regions and throughout the whole world itself. The term 'cultural flows'[30] denotes elements and symbols that are transported through global networks; promoted through commercialization and/or media culture this affects cultures socially and economically at different levels. Global cultures based on production and consumption, have a homogenizing effect on clothing, food and entertainment. This forms cultural

24. Hunkin, "To Let Die," 203. Citing Splosky, "Samoan Language in New Zealand Educational Context."

25. Ibid., 208.

26. Taumoefolau et al., "Role of Second Language Acquisition," 50.

27. Taumoefolau et al., "Linguists and Language Maintenance," 26; Citing Grace, *An Essay on Language.*

28. Hunkin, "To Let Die," 208, citing Phillipson, "Realities and Myths of Linguistic Imperialism."

29. Hunkin, "To Let Die," 203.

30. Schreiter, *New Catholicity*, 54.

synchronization[31] or the sameness of cultures worldwide. Sports labels such as Nike and Adidas, McDonalds, and Coca Cola are examples of such global cultures.

I will use the American children's television series *Sesame Street* as a reference to symbolize the potent, persuasive influence of media culture that has invaded not only our Samoan home, but many others. *Sesame Street* has for many years amused our family by captivating our emotions, planted in our memories images of Muppet characters: Big Bird and his best friend Mr Snuffleupagus, Super Grover, Bert and Ernie, Oscar the Grouch and personalities such as Mr Noodle, Gordon, Susan, Bob and Maria. *Sesame Street* has educated our minds, taught me and my children the English alphabet, to count, to sing and many more things. As an audience we have been mesmerized by the colorfulness, and the vibrant, modern and relevant conceptions that are portrayed. It is the reason for the human alarm clock in the early hours of the morning: 'Daddy, turn on the TV! *Sesame Street* is on!'

Sesame Street exemplifies the social and cultural ascendency of media culture in promoting the 'global language' and continually evolving global cultural perceptions explicitly portrayed in its educational content, images communicated and cultural references. The effect of engaging with the global world opens channels to exploring worlds beyond the local context. Other than the possibility of conflicting values, media culture opens doors for engagement with various genres such as hip hop music, Hollywood movies, global sports teams and through social media we are able to enter the personal lives of people, even strangers around the world.

English as the dominant global language may not be seen as the pervasive 'killer language', but as an attractive proposition that cannot be ignored. It is the language that connects us with the world! The consequences of the resulting identity are referred to as 'Glocal identity.' This term denotes the process whereby 'globalization makes the local an aspect of the global and vice versa.'[32] It forces us to renew our thinking on the local, asking for new reflections on the local and the global.

Why are children learning the English language so quickly? The key here is the attitude and needs of the learner, from where the motivation to learn comes from. Dornyei reiterates this fact by stating that 'motivation is a significant aid to learning.'[33] The younger generation today, my children included, are fond of what is out in the world today mediated through me-

---

31. Mooney and Evans, *Globalization,* 56.

32. Witvliet, "Christian Identity in Cross-Cultural Perspective," 173.

33. Taumoefolau et al., "Role of Second Language Acquisition," 50, citing Dornyei (1998).

dia culture. I am reminded of Aesop's fables on the race between the tortoise and the hare. The hare is challenged by the tortoise to a race. The hare ridicules the tortoise and leaves the tortoise behind. Ending the story here to fit the direction of this essay, the English language and the dominant culture is like the hare; mediated to the minds and hearts of indigenous people at a rate that is rapid and powerful. The Samoan language, for many of its non-speakers, is like the tortoise . . . slow and, it would appear, ineffective.

TOWARDS PRESERVING *GAGANA SĀMOA*

In recent times there has been a shift in thinking by the New Zealand Government, from the Assimilationist Policy in the late twentieth century to seeing the benefits of biculturalism in schools. This initiative led to the development of bi-lingual schools and language programs where the Samoan language was taught in some secondary and tertiary institutions. Added to this, the passion and desire of the Samoan community to move forward generated the development of language nests (*Aoga Amata*).[34] Consequently, a great number of projects have been implemented in the Manukau region in South Auckland to cater for the large Pacific population.[35] It is not surprising that Samoan communities, as a collective entity, have shown an awareness of the dilemma and have attempted to address the problem. It is a sign that the Samoan language is valued by Samoan people who want to keep the language alive.[36] The irony is, despite the attempts of the migrants to preserve something dear to them, these sites cannot survive, or at least move forward as a thriving community, without engagement with society at large.

Although it may be too soon to make a judgment on a relatively recent initiative, there is a sense of hope that implementation of bi-lingual education and bi-culturalism can improve academic proficiency of young Pacific Islanders, drawing the Pacific community away from the unfavorable generalizations as an under-achieving and marginalized community. Looking at the overall scope of social living, the Pacific Islands people are generally known for low adult literacy levels, student literacy levels,[37]

34. Taumoefolau et al., "Linguists and Language Maintenance," 24.

35. Starks and Refell, "Reading TH," 383, citing Bell, Davis, and Starks, "Languages of the Manukau Region."

36. Taumoefolau et al., "Linguists and Language Maintenance," 24.

37. Toloa, McNaughton, and Lai, "Bi-literacy and language development in Samoan bilingual classrooms," 513.

under-achievement in schools, poor health, poverty, housing, unemployment, crime[38] and income levels on the lower spectrum of the socio-economic scale.[39]

The importance of maintaining the Samoan language for the church, particularly the Congregational Christian Church Samoa (CCCS), is clearly obvious, because it is a Samoan church. The authenticity of its Samoan-ness remains a living presence when all aspects of the church from worship and cultural traditions are carried out in the mother tongue.[40] What is interesting here and quite ironic is the fact that the established indigenous gospel, that characterizes the Samoan church, carries with it the baggage of colonialism.

According to Samoan belief, any diversion from these established ways is a travesty to the Samoan Christian heritage. It was the major reason why a group of Samoans in the early 1960's broke away from the Pacific Island Presbyterian Church and established the CCCS in New Zealand. Besides the distinction of being a religious congregation, the CCCS also serves as a transplanted replication of the Samoan village in New Zealand. In addition to the Samoan language practices are the extra community activities such as singing, dancing and sports targeting the younger people to participate in communal gatherings that promote cultural protocol and language enhancing activities.[41]

However, contrary to belief, the conventional idea of the CCCS as a guardian of the Samoan language is narrow minded and largely uncritical. Amituana'i-Toloa implies that the secure language domains, such as the church, are vulnerable to the language shift but she does not explicitly address the problem.[42] The deception, I believe, is masked by the ignorance of the CCCS to adapt its ministry to the New Zealand context, and the changing dynamics of the evolving world.

In the Samoan churches, it is evident that there is an increasing social differentiation within its congregations. Although many church members are bilingual and speak both Samoan and English, it is clear that the migrant community are fluent in Samoan while the New Zealand-born generations are generally comfortable with English and have a limited command of

---

38. "Pasifika: Identity or Illusion" (Herald article 4/8/2007). 7% make up the New Zealand population/ 11% prison population/ 13% convicted violent offenders (Ministry of Justice conference).

39. Tuafuti and McCaffery, "Family and Community Empowerment through Bilingual Education," 481.

40. Tiatia, *Caught between Cultures,* 113.

41. Mugler and Lynch, *Pacific Languages in Education,* 231.

42. Amituana'i-Toloa, "To Each a Language," 80.

the Samoan language.[43] There are dissimilarities in personalities, interests, worldviews and interpretations of the Christian faith. Sadly, essentialism is at the fore when the differences are overlooked by church leaders and the decision makers with the objective of maintaining the status quo. While the migrant community is geared to preserving elements defined by the Samoan Christian identity, the New Zealand-born generations have been influenced by ideas and perceptions of the diverse world and tend to be more open to an awareness of cultural overlap, hybridity and the need for change.

The challenge for the church is this: Should it continue to preserve the Samoan language or be open to bilingualism? Explicitly, the basis of my response to this challenge is linked to three key features. First, the motivation to preserve the Samoan language is not shared by all members of the Samoan churches. Despite the attempts of the traditionalists to enforce strict measures for the use of the Samoan language, the reality is, most of the New Zealand-born Samoans on a regular basis speak the language they feel comfortable with, which is English. Hybridity in the view of the migrant community can be contentious and disruptive in its experience.

Second, for many New Zealand-born Samoans, oratory and the cultural protocols associated with the language are imperceptible because they are physically, mentally and spiritually detached from the contiguous signs that animate, or bring to life the Samoan language.

Many of the proverbs come from a specific situation; the context may be fishing, the plantation fields, nature, relationships within the family, service, authority, or ethical conduct, and from these everyday experiences object lessons are formed for the immediate context. What is problematic here is that the context described in formal language is alien to many New Zealand-born Samoans. Without explicit explanation of oratory expressions, one will find little sense and meaning in language. Instead of fishing, planting taro or serving the chief, the everyday experiences of a New Zealand-born Samoan mostly likely evolve around Smart phones, video games, surfing through Facebook and playing sport. Hunkin preserves the significance of the traditionalist view by endorsing the relatedness of language to the indigenous, cosmological signs and expressions. He states:

> ... the fullness of that truth is mitigated by the fact that asserting "Samoan-ness" is ultimately rendered redundant if one is unable to articulate the nuances of that Samoan-ness, most of which are best captured and made apparent through the Samoan language- Samoan terms and expressions.[44]

43 Tiatia, *Caught between Cultures*, 8.

44. Hunkin, "To Let Die," 208.

Taking this view into consideration, the relevant question here is this: Can there be many shades of what is considered Samoan-ness? To the traditionalists, the original and authentic expressions reflect the fullness of truth. But in a continually evolving contemporary world where migration, transplanting, intercultural, cross-cultural, multi-cultural, multi-faceted, hybridity and many other forces are at play, the idea of relevance becomes increasingly significant. This leads us back to the question: What is the value of language? Is it the same for all members?

Last but not least, if the Samoan communities in diaspora (especially the CCCS) opt to preserve the Samoan language and culture, then the incompetent speakers of the Samoan language, mainly the New Zealand-born Samoans, will be marginalized as they do not meet the expectations of the community. Of more concern is the fact that community and church leaders are reluctant to use bilingualism in teachings and in worship. The Christian message is therefore delivered to competent speakers, while the New Zealand-born generations become victims of misunderstanding. The inherent belief of those who preserve the Samoan language is that it will survive. Like the tortoise, it may seem slow and ineffective but in the long run it can win! Really?

WORKS CITED

Amituana'i-Toloa, Meaola. "To Each a Language: Addressing the Challenges of Language and Cultural Loss for Samoans." *AlterNative*. Special Supplement Issue—Ngaahi Lea 'a e Kakai Pasifiki: Endangered Pacific Languages and Cultures 6.2 (2010) 79–85.

Bell, Allan, Karen Davis, and Donna Starks. "Languages of the Manukau Region: A Pilot Study of Use, Maintenance and Educational Dimensions of Languages in South Auckland." Report prepared for the Woolf Fisher Research Centre, University of Auckland, 2000.

Dickie, John. "Samoan Students Documenting Their out of School Literacies: An Insider View of Conflicting Values." *Australian Journal of Language and Literacy* 34.3 (2011) 247–59.

Fisher, Amanda. "Samoan Language under Threat in New Zealand Promoting Their Mother Tongue." *The Dominion Post*, 7 June 2010, A 14.

Giles, Howard. Donald, Taylor, and Richard, Bourhis. "Towards a Theory of Language in Ethnic Group Relations." In *Language, Ethnicity and Intergroup Relations,* edited by Howard Giles, 307–48. London: Academic.

Grace, George W. *An Essay on Language.* Columbia, SC: Hornbeam, 1981.

Howarth, Penny. "Globalising literacy: the challenge of ethnolinguistic diversity in New Zealand." *Literacy- Special Issue: Literacy and Politics* 45.3 (2011) 141–49.

Hunkin, Galumalemana A. "A Frequency Based Word List for Teaching the Samoan Language." *New Zealand Studies in Applied Linguistics* 17.1 (2011) 16–31.

————. "To Let Die: The State of the Samoan Language in New Zealand." *AlterNative: An International Journal of Indigenous Peoples* 8.2 (2012) 203–14.

Kroskrity, Paul V. *Regimes of Language: Ideologies, Polities and Identities*. Santa Fe: School of American Research, 2000.

Mooney, Annabelle, and Betsy Evans. *Globalization: The Key Concepts*. London: Taylor & Francis, 2007.

Mugler, France, and John Lynch. *Pacific Languages in Education*. Suva: University of the South Pacific, 1996.

Phillipson, R. "Realities and Myths of Linguistic Imperialism." *Journal of Multilingual and Multicultural Development* 18.3 (1997) 238–48.

Schieffelin, Bambi B, Kathryn A. Woolard, and Paul V. Kroskrity. *Language Ideologies: Practice and Theory*. Oxford: Oxford University Press, 1998.

Schreiter, Robert J. *The New Catholicity: Theology between the Global and the Local*. Faith and Cultures Series. Maryknoll, NY: Orbis, 1999.

Splosky, B. "The Samoan Language in New Zealand Educational Context." Unpublished report presented to the Department of Education, Wellington, 1988.

Starks, Donna and Hayley Refell. "Reading TH: Vernacular Variants in Pasifika Englishes in South Auckland." *Journal of Sociolinguistics* 10.3 (2006) 382–92.

Taumoefolau, Melenaite, Donna Starks, Karen Davis and Allan Bell. "Linguists and Language Maintenance: Pasifika Languages in Manukau, New Zealand." *Oceanic Linguistics* 41.1 (2002) 15–27.

Taumoefolau, Melenaite, Donna Starks, Allan Bell, and Karen Davis. "The Role of Second Language Acquisition Theory and Practice in Pasifika Language Maintenance in New Zealand." In *Language Acquisition Research: Papers Presented at a Ministry of Education Forum Held in 2003*. Wellington: Ministry of Education Research Division, 2004.

Tiatia, Jemaima. *Caught between Cultures: A New Zealand-born Pacific Island Perspective*. Auckland: Christian Research Association, 1998.

Toloa, Meaola. Stuart McNaughton and Mei Lai. "Bi-literacy and Language Development in Samoan Bilingual Classrooms." *International Journal of Bilingual Education and Bilingualism* 12.5 (2009) 513–31.

Tomlinson, Matt, and Miki Makihara. "New Paths in the Linguistic Anthropology of Oceania." *Annual Review of Anthropology* 18 (2009) 17–31.

Tuafuti, Patisepa, and John McCaffery. "Family and Community Empowerment through Bilingual Education." *International Journal of Bilingual Education and Bilingualism* 8.5 (2005) 480–503.

————. "Multiple Challenges in Research within the *fa'aSamoa* Context." *Pacific-Asian Education Journal* 23.2 (2011) 33–42.

Wenger, Etienne. *Communities of Practice: Learning, Meaning and Identity*. Cambridge: Cambridge University Press, 2006.

Witvliet, Theo. "Christian Identity in Cross-Cultural Perspective." In *Christian Identity in the Cross-Cultural Perspective*, edited by Brinkman E. Martien and Keulen V. Dirk. Zoetermeer: Meinema, 2003.

Woolard, Kathryn A., and Bambi B. Schieffelin. "Language Ideology." *Annual Review in Anthropology* 23 (1994) 55–82.

INDEX

www.ingramcontent.com/pod-product-compliance
Lightning Source LLC
Chambersburg PA
CBHW061734270326
41928CB00011B/2235